W9-ADN-107

Teaching Poetry
in High School

Teaching Poetry in High School

Albert B. Somers
Furman University

National Council of Teachers of English
1111 W. Kenyon Road, Urbana, Illinois 61801 1096

Staff Editor: Zarina M. Hock

Editorial Assistant: Jessica L. Creed

Interior Design: Doug Burnett

Cover Design: Pat Mayer

NCTE Stock Number: 52899-3050

It is the policy of NCTE in its journals and other publications to provide a forum for the open discussion of ideas concerning the content and the teaching of English and the language arts. Publicity accorded to any particular point of view does not imply endorsement by the Executive Committee, the Board of Directors, or the membership at large, except in announcements of policy, where such endorsement is clearly specified.

Library of Congress Cataloging-in-Publication Data

Somers, Albert B., 1939–
     Teaching poetry in high school/Albert B. Somers.
        p.   cm.
      ISBN 0-8141-5289-9 (pbk.)
       1. Poetry—Study and teaching (Secondary) I. Title.
     PN1101.S63 1999
     808.1'071'2—dc21   99-32205
                                                   CIP

This book is dedicated
to the memory of my parents,
Albert B. Somers Sr. and Margaret Pritchard Somers

Contents

A Note to the Reader

O ccasionally in a poem, a poet will imagine his audience, as Ted Kooser does in "Selecting a Reader" (p. 55) . For this book, my imagined reader is a high school teacher who is fond of poetry, and open to new approaches, new possibilities. She may be a little gun-shy from teaching it—fine—but she hasn't given up. She is a teacher of everyday, ordinary students, the kind who think they don't like poetry but often find, with someone's help, that they do.

This book has a single broad purpose: to encourage future readers of poetry. I think we need to teach poetry in such a way that more of our students will occasionally want to read it after they leave us.

You would expect me to be a reader of poems, and I am, but I don't pretend that liking poetry is easy. It takes a little work. As Chapter 3 explains, I reject far more poems than I embrace. Still, the ones I love burn brightly in my imagination. They are stuck on my walls, tucked away in folders and books, in boxes and cubbyholes. I often swap poems with friends and colleagues, and among the poems I've shared are "Spring" (p. 44) and "For the Ex-Wife on the Occasion of Her Birthday" by Thomas Lynch. I once sent a copy of "Flying at Night" (p. 55) to a former student serving in the Peace Corps, whose response led me to include it here.

This book assumes that anyone can like poetry, that a lot of poetry is approachable and fun. And poetry is fun to do things with—to talk about, write, write about, act out, and so on. As teachers, we can mine these veins no end.

A few parts of the book may need elaboration:

- Chapters 1 and 2: These chapters establish the context, offering my take on the American mind-set toward poetry and about the role schools have played in creating it.

- The poems in the book: I've included over forty. In some cases, though, I've cited or even described a poem, but not included it—for several reasons. For one thing, publishing a poem requires acquiring permission, a time-consuming process. Moreover, the famous ones (such as Langston Hughes's "Mother to Son") are easily found. And most important, if I ask you, in effect, to go looking for a poem, you may find others you like even more.

- The classroom scenarios included here and there: These vignettes are not transcribed recordings of classes. They are the synthe-sized—and sometimes imagined—gleanings of hundreds of high school classes I have taught or observed over the last thirty-five years. The names of teachers and students are fictitious.

For the most part, *Teaching Poetry in High School* is a practical book. I offer guidelines and ideas, but none of them is foolproof or totally new. Certainly many of my suggestions are not unique to me; I have borrowed and refashioned from so many sources that I've lost count. Where I can, I try to give credit.

Throughout the book, I cite numerous resources, some of which are out of print. Happily, many of these out-of-print books can still be found in public and college libraries.

The book voices strong opinions, which I hope will help to open many conversations about poetry's place in the classrooms of America. That can only be healthy for both the art and the audience. I would like to be a part of such a dialogue. If you have comments or questions about the book or the subject, if you'd like to share a poem, or even if you need a copy of a poem I've mentioned that you can't find—let me hear from you.

Permissions

We gratefully acknowledge the publishers who generously gave us permission to reproduce the following material:

"The Drunkard and the Pig" from *The Oxford Book of American Light Verse* published by the Oxford University Press, 1979.

"An Aeronaut To His Love." Reprinted by permission of Louisiana State University Press from PATTERNS OF POETRY: AN ENCYCLOPEDIA OF FORMS, by Miller Williams. Copyright © 1986 by Louisiana State University Press.

"On Reading Poems to a Senior Class at South High" by D. C. Berry. Reprinted by permission of the author.

"Shooting Rats at the Bibb County Dump" from *Armored Hearts: Selected & New Poems* © 1995 by David Bottoms. Reprinted by permission of Copper Canyon Press, Post Office Box 271, Port Townsend, Washington 98368.

LUCILLE CLIFTON: "reply" copyright © 1991 by Lucille Clifton. Reprinted from QUILTING: POEMS 1987–1990 with the permission of BOA Editions, Ltd., 260 East Ave., Rochester, NY 14604.

"November Night." From VERSE by Adelaide Crapsey. Copyright 1922 by Algernon S. Crapsey and renewed 1950 by The Adelaide Crapsey Foundation. Reprinted by permission of Alfred A. Knopf, Inc.

"who are you, little i," copyright © 1963, 1991 by the Trustees for the E. E. Cummings Trust, from COMPLETE POEMS: 1904–1962 by E. E. Cummings. Edited by George J. Firmage. Reprinted by permission of Liveright Publishing Corporation.

"Small Dark Song." Reprinted from Philip Dacey: *How I Escaped from the Labyrinth and Other Poems* by permission of Carnegie Mellon University Press © 1977 by Philip Dacey.

"Adolescence—I," from Rita Dove, *The Yellow House on the Corner*, Carnegie-Mellon University Press, copyright © 1980 by Rita Dove. Reprinted by permission of the author.

"The Sacred," from BETWEEN ANGELS by Stephen Dunn. Copyright © 1989 by Stephen Dunn. Reprinted by permission of W. W. Norton & Company, Inc.

Lines from "Keepsakes" copyright 1966 William Stafford from *The Rescued Year* (Harper & Row). Reprinted by permission of The Estate of William Stafford.

"Galatea" by Karen Tellefsen. Used by permission of the author.

"By Accident" by Jane O. Wayne. Reprinted by permission of the author.

Charles Wright "Nouns" from *Hard Freight* © 1973 by Charles Wright, Wesleyan University Press, by permission of University Press of New England.

James Wright "A Blessing" from *The Branch Will Not Break*. Copyright © 1963 by James Wright. Wesleyan University Press by permission of University Press of New England.

Lila Zeiger (L. L. Zeiger) "The Fish," THE WAY TO CASTLE GARDEN (Pittsford, N.Y.: State Street Press, 1982).

"Zimmer's Head Thudding Against the Blackboard," is from FAMILY REUNION: SELECTED AND NEW POEMS, by Paul Zimmer, © 1983 by Paul Zimmer. Reprinted by permission of the University of Pittsburgh Press.

I Background

1 Poetry in America

In America these days, poetry is news.

On April 1, 1998, both *The New York Times* and *USA Today* published major stories celebrating the current enthusiasm for poetry in American culture. *The Times* story cited figures and facts: an increase of poetry sales by 30 percent in 1996 and 25 percent in 1997 and the beginning of an ambitious project by Poet Laureate Robert Pinsky to record 1,000 ordinary Americans reading their favorite poems (Van Gelder 1998, E3). *USA Today* featured a cover article on the beginning of a month-long effort by a man named Andrew Carroll to give away 100,000 books of poems. A modern-day Johnny Appleseed, Carroll would drive a Ryder truck from New York to San Francisco, spreading books at a tollbooth near the Walt Whitman Bridge outside Philadelphia, at a 24-hour wedding chapel in Las Vegas, and at points in between (Wilson 1998, D1–D2). The two articles ushered in the third annual celebration of April as National Poetry Month.

In many such ways, the last few years have seen a remarkable turnaround in poetry's ever-struggling battle for cultural acceptance in America. Sales *are* up. David Unowsky, owner of the Hungry Mind Bookstore in Minneapolis, is exultant: "We've seen across-the-board growth. Poets who never sold poetry are selling it, poets who sold it are selling even more. And I mean all types of poetry, hardcover and paperback, new poets and old poets, Beat poets and slam poets. Sales during National Poetry Month were sensational" (Perilli 1997, 38, 40).[1]

Not just men in trucks are giving poetry away. Anthologies by the thousands have been placed in hotel rooms à la Gideon bibles. In some cases, people have actually run off with them (Scott 1994, B1). In New York, placards with poems have been posted in subways between the advertisements in a program called Poetry in Motion. Its creator, Alan F. Kiepper, the president of the Metropolitan Transit Authority (and also a poet), describes an experience he himself had in response to his own creation:

> It was on a Brooklyn-bound A train; I was reading the Emily Dickinson poem "'Hope' is the Thing with Feathers," which is mounted in the train. I'd read it dozens of times. It had become routine—like reading the back of a cereal box. But I read it again, and—bang—I got it. For a moment, everything was clear. Other things in my life, confusing things, also seemed to make sense." ("Poetry Underground," *The New Yorker,* 1992–93, 57–58)

A more energized sign of resurgence is the poetry slam. A variation of the poetry reading, the slam is an "event," often set in urban coffee-houses or bars, where participants read their poems over an open mike in competition with each other and receive, not unlike divers or figure skaters, ratings of 1.0 to 10.0 from judges holding up cards. Slams are rowdy, populist affairs, and one has to wonder if they genuinely support the cause of serious poetry. One critic has referred to them as "verse gong shows"; another, as metaphorical fistfights among poets. Marc Smith, the promoter of the Chicago slam and a traveling consultant for others, sees them as opportunities to lift poetry out of the snobbery of high culture and return it to the people. Whatever they are, slams have caught on. Scores of cities throughout the country and the world now have them, and an international poetry slam championship is held annually (Conniff 1992, 77–80).

The proliferation of poetry readings and poetry performances is perhaps the most hopeful sign of renewal. According to *Time*, poetry gatherings became so popular in the early 1990s that the New York City *Poetry Calendar* (itself a sign of activity) listed an average of fifteen a night (Simpson 1991, 76–77). Publishers and bookstores throughout the country have taken to sponsoring series of poetry readings in an effort to develop interest in the genre. One small publisher, Copper Canyon Press in Port Townsend, Washington, even launched a Poetry Appreciation Program sponsored by a grant from the Lila Wallace-Reader's Digest Fund (Parisi 1994, 20).

Colleges and universities, of course, have long been the most fertile ground for poetry activity. Any school worth its academic freedom has at least one (often several) published poets in its English department, and many have official poets in residence. Other opportunities for poets to flourish are plentiful. For example *1999 Poet's Market* catalogs over 1,800 outlets that publish poetry,[2] 150 contests and awards for poets, over 80 conferences and workshops where writers can hone their skills, and 78 organizations useful to poets—while admitting that these are incomplete lists. It has never been easier for a writer to earn a living as a poet.[3]

Often in recent years interest in poetry has been heightened by the media. In a graveside scene in the film *Four Weddings and a Funeral*, a 1994 Academy Award nominee, one of the characters recites the W. H. Auden poem "Funeral Blues" as a memorial to his friend. Audiences were so moved by the scene that Vintage Books later published the poem in a special edition called *Tell Me the Truth about Love*. The movie *Il Postino* stimulated interest in the poetry of Pablo Neruda by depicting a friendship between the Nobel laureate and his mailman.

Radio and television and even cyberspace have also created interest. National Public Radio often features commentaries on poets and occasionally readings, especially on its Weekend Edition. Garrison Keillor always ends his daily five-minute radio program, *The Writer's Almanac*, by reading a poem. MTV's *Unplugged* series has often featured performance poets. In early 1994, WNYC-FM and New York's Unterberg Poetry Center sponsored "The Poets' Voice," a series of readings that aired for thirteen weeks on public radio stations across the country (Schemo 1995, C11). During the 1980s and 1990s, television series such as *Voices & Visions*, *The Language of Life*, and *The United States of Poetry* have promoted poets to a wider audience. And as Chapter 12 points out, the Internet has created an enormous democratic outlet for aspiring poets anxious to have their work read and reacted to.

Scholars have also weighed in with opinions in support of poetry's revival. In an essay entitled "What's the Matter with Poetry?," F. D. Reeve answers his own question with, in effect, the word "Nothing." Poetry is alive and well, he claims, "in bookstore corners, upstairs cafes, reading rooms, clubs, schools, churches and public radio programs" (1993, 711). Besides the proliferation of poetry readings, he cites the tremendous boom in the publication of poems in recent years: "The country is jumping with . . . lots of little magazines like *Free Lunch* and *Waterways* and *Crazy Quilt* and *Mississippi Mud*" (709). The distinguished American poet Donald Hall published an essay in 1994 called "Death to the Death of Poetry," in which he argues that every generation wrings its hands about the disappearance of poetry from the cultural mainstream:

> As I grew up [Hall writes], from the 1930s to the 1950s, poets seldom read aloud and felt lucky to sell a thousand copies. In the 1990s the American climate for poetry is infinitely more generous. In the mail, in the rows of listeners, even in the store down the road, I find generous response. I find it in magazines and in rows of listeners in Pocatello and Akron, in Florence, South Carolina, and in Quartz Mountain, Oklahoma. I find it in books published and in extraordinary sales for many books (26).

So, it would appear at last that poetry is thriving in America. Or is it? In 1992, the poet and scholar Dana Gioia presented a much bleaker picture in his influential book, *Can Poetry Matter? Essays on Poetry and American Culture*. Gioia argues persuasively that poetry's place in American culture remains in the back row.

> Daily newspapers no longer review poetry. There is, in fact, little coverage of poetry or poets in the general press. From 1984 until this year [1991], the National Book Awards dropped poetry as a

category. Leading critics rarely review it. In fact, virtually no one reviews it except other poets. Almost no popular collections of contemporary poetry are available except those, like the *Norton Anthology*, targeting an academic audience. It seems, in short, as if the large audience that still exists for quality fiction hardly notices poetry. A reader familiar with the novels of Joyce Carol Oates, John Updike, or John Barth may not even recognize the names of Gwendolyn Brooks, Gary Snyder, or W. D. Snodgrass (3).

Even earlier, in *The Place of Poetry: Two Centuries of an Art in Crisis*, Christopher Clausen writes that "since the end of the eighteenth century, poetry in England (and subsequently in America) has been an art in continual crisis. . . . This crisis has faced every poet since Wordsworth, and it has never been resolved. The place of poetry in English and American civilization has become more and more peripheral . . . " (1).

For both the naysayers and the optimists, a particular publishing event in early 1995 sheds light on the issue. In January of that year, former President Jimmy Carter came out with a modest little volume of poetry called *Always a Reckoning*. The book contains forty-four poems mostly about Mr. Carter's rural upbringing, his life in small-town Georgia, and even some of his political experiences. Not surprisingly, it caught on with the public and managed to ride the bestseller list for several weeks, reaching as high as ninth on *The New York Times* chart.

As with many popular books, especially books of poetry, the critical reception was lukewarm. For example, Michiko Kakutani of *The New York Times* wrote that the book consists of "well-meaning, dutifully wrought poems that plod earnestly from point A to point B without ever making a leap into emotional hyperspace, poems that lack not only a distinctive authorial voice, but also anything resembling a psychological or historical subtext." They are, she contended, very personal poems with little depth and less imagination (1995, C17).

The public and critical reception to Mr. Carter's book reveals a lot about how we Americans feel about poetry. Some of us claim to like it. We laugh with our children at Shel Silverstein and Jack Prelutsky, and we chuckle among our friends over an amusing limerick. We write poems to mark special events (I wrote one to my first grandchild when she was born), or we select a greeting card because of its sentiment. Some people memorialize a deceased loved one with a poem they send to the local newspaper. Some buy a copy of *The Best-Loved Poems of the American People* for an end table that needs a special touch. We like Helen Steiner Rice, James Kavanaugh, Rod McKuen, and Susan Polis Schutz, and we think we like Robert Frost.

So we like poetry—sort of. It can often please us and sometimes even move us. But what exactly is this poetry that we like? For the great majority of Americans, it is verse—"light metrical composition seen as distinct from serious poetry" (*American Heritage Dictionary of the English Language*, s.v. "verse"). Verse is the Hallmark card, the lyrics to the country-and-western song, the patriotic tribute, the Valentine treat. Almost invariably it is simple, direct, accessible in a single reading, usually sentimental (often sad), and sometimes funny. It has a definite beat and most of it rhymes. Here is a good example by an anonymous poet:

A Tribute to Mothers

Hers is the hand that steadies the cradle.
Hers the support on the stairstep below.
Hers is the glance acknowledging effort.
Hers is the whisper that eases the blow.

Hers is the candle extinguishing darkness,
Strong affirmation repelling the gloom.
Hers is the faithful and untiring presence
Gracing the invalid's comfortless room.

A mother is always a voice of allegiance,
The nod of approval when doubt perseveres,
The one single image of hope and devotion
Echoing down through an absence of years.

The poetry that most of us like is not what scholars, critics, and teachers refer to as serious poetry. If we Americans like James Whitcomb Riley and the poems of celebrities like Jimmy Stewart, Ally Sheely, and the Hall-of-Fame baseball player Phil Rizzuto, we don't like James Merrill, Adrienne Rich, or Linda Pastan. With some justification, most Americans believe that serious poetry takes itself far too seriously. It is complex, subtle, unpleasant, pretentious, and virtually impenetrable. We agree with the columnist Russell Baker, who writes, "I gave up on new poetry myself thirty years ago, when most of it began to read like the coded messages passing between lonely aliens in a hostile world" (1986, 36). A few think it's even subversive. In contrast to the earlier verse, consider this far more provocative—and substantial—poem, which is also about motherhood:

The Fish

Lila Zeiger

I had about as much chance, Mother,
as the carp who thrashed
in your bathtub on Friday,

swimming helplessly back and forth
in the small hard pool you made for me,
unaware how soon you would
pull me from my element
sever my head just below the gills
scrape away the iridescence
chop me into bits and pieces and
reshape me with your strong hands
to simmer in your special broth.
You bustled about the house
confident in your design,
while I waited at the edge
imploring you with glossy eyes
to keep me and love me
just as I was.

Despite the encouraging figures mentioned earlier, serious poetry rarely sells. In *Teaching Literature to Adolescents: Poetry*, written over thirty years ago, Stephen Dunning quotes the poet Josephine Miles: "In a country of millions, a reputable poet does well to sell 500 copies of a book, and these mostly to libraries" (1966, 5). He also cites the almost pitiful annual showing of *Poetry*, the nation's most prestigious magazine devoted to the genre, which in 1997 celebrated its eighty-fifth year of publication. As of 1965, Dunning notes, *Poetry* had an all-time circulation high of 7,450 subscribers—again, one must suspect, mostly libraries (3). Since Dunning's book, the circulation of the magazine has remained steadily in the 6,000–8,000 range, with 7,851 subscribers on the rolls in 1998. (If it were not so sad, it would be laughable to compare these figures with those of *TV Guide*, *The New Yorker*, or perhaps even magazines devoted solely to fiction.)

Even English majors and many English teachers do not often read the work of serious contemporary poets.[4] We do not know who they are. If you will, take a little test. Look over the following list of names and identify those persons who are *comparatively* well-known practicing poets, i.e., well known in the poetry world (five names are fabricated):

1. John Riegel
2. Julia Lynn
3. Daniel Tierstein
4. Susanne Bavosa
5. Kenneth Leeds
6. Yusef Komunyakaa

7. Philip Levine
8. Jorie Graham
9. Lisel Mueller
10. Charles Wright

The five real people on the list are all winners of the Pulitzer Prize for poetry within the last ten years (they are the last five names), yet many people do not know them. As Gioia points out, we would do much better with a similar list of fiction writers.[5]

So what are we to make of all this? Is poetry currently enjoying a genuine rebirth that will endure? Or is all this activity like the famed River Platte—a mile wide and an inch deep? As with so many issues involving cultural standards, both views are valid. In many ways the country has indeed experienced an impressive renewal of interest in the genre spurred on by easier access to poets through readings, the media, the World Wide Web, and the growth of small presses. Despite these encouraging signs, however, the range of poetry's rise from cultural obscurity in the last decade has been extremely narrow. Its renewal has been funded more by foundations and universities than by a reading and buying public. Serious poetry—the work of people like William Stafford, Gary Soto, and Sharon Olds—remains largely the province of college seminar rooms and elite, independent publishers and bookstores who handle it largely at a loss. In Gioia's words, "most poetry is published in journals that address an insular audience of literary professionals, mainly teachers of creative writing and their students" (7). And as more than one observer of cultural affairs has noted, there are probably more writers of poetry in this country than readers.

Still, poetry lovers and teachers of poetry should take considerable comfort in the gains we have made, regardless of where and with whom, and look for opportunities to extend poetry's audience and influence even more. Without question, the most promising setting for making significant progress—for creating and nurturing future readers of poetry beyond the college campus—is in the public schools. There, where the audience of young adults is so deeply in touch with emotion and rhythm and with the sounds of language (all of which are essential qualities of poetry)—there, the untapped potential for strengthening the appeal of the genre seems limitless. The future of poetry rests, as it always has, in the classrooms of American schools.

Notes

1. Such optimism is not unanimous, however: Godine and Farrar, Straus and Giroux are two publishers that report little growth in poetry sales over the same period.

2. These outlets range from well-established magazines like *The Kenyon Review* and *Ploughshares* to hand-stapled newsletters.

3. But still not easy. A piece on National Public Radio's *All Things Considered* in the spring of 1996 indicates that many poets, perhaps most, still wait tables, sort mail, tend bar, pump gas, harvest mint, and even taste-test scotch for a living.

4. It is equally doubtful that we—I certainly include myself—spend huge amounts of time reading Keats, Shelley, and Emerson once we are liberated from college assignments.

5. The point here is not to embarrass the reader. I would probably fail a similar test of names of poets taken at random from those published last year in, say, *Poetry* magazine. The point is that most of us do not know as many names of contemporary poets as we would if we truly supported the genre.

2 Poetry in the Schools

Imagine a high school English classroom, someone presenting a few poems to the students for response and discussion. He is wary of indifference, but what he gets is something else—intelligent, lively, rapt participation. For an hour there is mutual immersion in poetry. Imagine talk, questions, laughter, engagement and affirmation, verbal high fives. When the bell rings and it is over, everyone leaves, none of them quite the same.

On Reading Poems to a Senior Class at South High

D. C. Berry

Before
I opened my mouth
I noticed them sitting there
as orderly as frozen fish
in a package.

Slowly water began to fill the room
though I did not notice it
till it reached
my ears

and then I heard the sounds
of fish in an aquarium
and I knew that though I had
tried to drown them
with my words
that they had only opened up
like gills for them
and let me in.

Together we swam around the room
like thirty tails whacking words
till the bell rang
puncturing
a hole in the door

where we all leaked out
They went to another class
I suppose and I home

where Queen Elizabeth
my cat met me
and licked my fins
till they were hands again.

Ah—the speaker is a poet. Easy for him. A visiting poet is just that—a visitor, an invited guest. As a poet, he has a certain measure of authenticity. He is a participant in a particular class on a particular day. (On another occasion, his worst suspicions confirmed, this one might go home and kick the cat off the couch.) Also, the poet is mostly reading, talking about the source of an idea or two, about problems he had with this poem or that.

A visiting poet is the genuine article. Visiting poets are practitioners, but they are not out to get the students to study their poems. They are not going to explain what the poems mean. They are not asking kids to take notes. They will not give a test. They have no curricular expectations or responsibilities (e.g., the students will be able to identify the rhyme scheme of "The Raven").

HIGHLIGHT 2.1

Poets-in-the-Schools

Few methods are as tried and true as the visiting poet. To quote one of them, Sandra McPherson, "It's good to bring poets in to talk informally with the class as well as have poets read to them. The more [students] can be exposed to the person, the human being, the better" (Cooke and Thompson 1980, 139).

For many years, one of the best opportunities for connecting classes with poets has been the Poets-in-the-Schools programs operated throughout the country. In most states, such programs are managed and funded by the state arts council and focus their efforts on getting students to write poetry (addresses of the various arts councils are available at the Internet Web site for the National Endowment for the Humanities: http://arts.endow.gov/). Three of the largest are the Teachers & Writers Collaborative, 5 Union Square W., Seventh Floor, New York, NY 10003; California Poets-in-the-Schools, 870 Market Street, Suite 1148, San Francisco, CA 94102; and Writers and Artists-in-the-Schools, COMPAS, 304 Landmark Center, 75 W. Fifth Street, St. Paul, MN 55102. In some places, local efforts are organized, like the International Poetry Forum in Pittsburgh, Pennsylvania, whose "Poets-in-Person" initiative brings local poets to work in area classrooms.

The League of Canadian Poets offers a resource guide for teachers, *Poets in the Classroom*, edited by Betsy Struthers and Sarah Klassen. The book features essays by twenty-one Canadian poets on the teaching of poetry. Topics include getting motivated, working with themes, structuring workshops for different ages, and developing ideas into finished poems. The League's address is 54 Wolseley St., Suite 204, Toronto, Ontario M5T 1A5.

For a teacher of poetry, it's very different. A teacher has a curricular agenda, a complex array of goals and expectations influenced on a daily basis by her textbook, her curriculum guide, her college courses, her degree of interest in poetry, and her ideas of what students need and can tolerate. With such a complex set of factors to consider, is it possible for teachers, themselves the most frequent readers of poetry in classrooms, to generate the same attention and enthusiasm as the speaker in the poem?

Of course it is. In fact, many teachers *do* enjoy this kind of response in their classes. They have a gift for infusing their students with not only a knowledge of poetry, but a love for it as well. Perhaps unknown to even themselves, they have a secret.

What is it? What do these exceptional teachers of poetry do? Whatever it is, scholars have been trying to identify it for almost a century. In *The Teaching of Poetry in the High School*, written over eighty years ago, Arthur Fairchild argued that the secret is elusive:

> [T]he primary qualification is a special talent which no artificial means can supply. That talent cannot be described, yet we know it when we find it. The secret of it seems to be imagination. He who possesses this talent instinctively puts himself in the pupil's place, catches his point of view, apprehends his difficulty, and uses the subject-matter in hand as the means of awakening and furthering his intellectual and emotional life (1914, 9).

Seventy years later, writing more specifically on the basis of research, Molly Travers is more explicit:

> [Good poetry teachers] like poetry and take it seriously and expect pupils to work at it; are enthusiastic; emphasize the pleasure of poetry; are flexible, experimental, and like novel teaching situations; provide more amusing and varied activities; consult pupils on choice of poems; allow conversational and informal discussion; interact with pupils in consultation and discussion; seek out pupils' views, listen to their interpretations, and treat them with respect and seriousness; do not make pupils afraid of saying the wrong thing, offering sympathy and encouragement when ideas are voiced; encourage exploration of pupils' personal experiences in relation to poems; [and] support the feeling that the emotional experience of poetry is real (1984, 380).

In a separate article, Travers more pointedly describes a specific teacher's secret:

> He taught a class of over thirty pupils, packed into a crowded classroom with solid wooden desks. His first degree had been in science, and he had spent a year working on the railways, another on a farm. He had a passion for poetry and read a good deal himself.

He believed utterly in its value, and that it could be made accessible to everyone. He found the hostility pupils often bring to poetry an "exciting challenge" and he would use anything to create interest, though he always emphasized the difference between light poetry and that which deals with the vital things of life. He worked furiously to counter the modern tendency to neglect poetry in the curriculum, but felt that often he was "piddling in the Pacific." He made colored sheets of all kinds of poetry for his class, read aloud with vigor, and allowed pupils to contribute their own anecdotes and comments; but at the same time poetry was taken very seriously. He was highly organized, dominating, but not a show-man, and very accepting of his pupils' contributions. The *secret* [my italics] appeared to be a deep personal conviction, a profound belief in the pupils, a wide knowledge of poems which appealed at all levels, an ability to read poetry aloud and talk about it at the pupils' level—but seriously, a wide variety of classroom activities, and an inspiring classroom manner (1987, 216–17).

Teachers like this—and there are many of them—have a clear commitment to poetry, a sense of its enduring value and importance. They personalize poetry. They go to great lengths to engage and involve their students. Good poetry teachers pay homage to two important shrines—pleasure and personal relevance—but they don't stop there. They use poetry to challenge their students to think, to read with patience and insight, to see connections and relationships, to write with imagination, precision, and depth.

Despite the undeniable presence of many such teachers in American schools, more than a few contemporary writers (including poets) have concluded that schools and teachers are, in general, a large part of the problem that poetry faces. The poet Judson Jerome recalls his own experience:

[B]efore I started school, I loved poetry. I had memorized many poems. My aunts and my grandmother read poetry aloud to me. My grandfather (who had less than five grades of schooling) wrote poetry. I knew that poetry was an important part of life, that writing poetry was something men and women do.

Then, in school, I learned that poetry was also something to be studied. Very gradually in elementary school, more quickly in high school, and very rapidly in college I learned that I had the wrong understanding of poetry altogether (1991, 299).

The Pulitzer Prize-winning poet Stanley Kunitz feels that "one of the areas in which [the American system of education] has most significantly failed is in teaching students how to cope with poetry." For Kunitz, a particular shortcoming has been the "injury done to the imagination of the child" (Packard 1987, 28).

The noted humorist Russell Baker contends that "poetry is vital to us until school spoils it" (1986, 34). Even more damning is John Ciardi's remark on the demise of the genre as children encounter it through the grades:

> The school system annually receives into its beginning classes an audience that overflows with the joy and immediacy of poetry. The same system annually graduates from its high schools a horde of adolescents who, with rare exceptions, are either wary of poetry or hostile to it. . . . Certainly the school system cannot be expected to accomplish by itself a kind of education society wants, yet some part of the decay of poetic pleasure between grade one and grade twelve must be chargeable to the schools. Poetry, in the high schools, is almost always badly taught (1989, 125).

Ciardi's final sentence is a blunt indictment—and surely overstated. Still, coming from a poet who wrote for children as well as adults, a critic, and the author of one of the most respected books about poetry ever written, *How Does a Poem Mean?*, the comment cannot be ignored. Even though we may reject its tarring of every teacher with the same brush, it suggests a need for us to rethink what we do.

Exactly what is it that we teachers do with poetry? How much time do we spend on it? How do we typically approach it? What materials do we use? If there is some truth to the criticisms of Jerome, Baker, and Ciardi (among others)—as well as to the assumptions reached in Chapter 1 about the status of poetry as an art form in America—in what ways are we teachers blamable? Answers to these questions are tentative: for one thing, the all-inclusive *we* always allows for numerous exceptions. Still, from an array of sources (articles and books, lesson plans on the Internet and elsewhere, personal observations of classes, surveys and studies, anecdotes, curriculum guides and especially textbooks) we can infer a reasonably accurate profile of how poetry is often taught in American schools. In grades 8–12, it is taught with a rather heavy emphasis on poetry as a genre (and on poetic devices), on historical periods and movements, and on great poets. Students are often encouraged to write poems, but in general the focus is on *study*. Perhaps the most discouraging fact is the time we seem to spend on poetry—or the lack of time. According to Applebee's important study, *Literature in the Secondary School*, public school teachers spend 14 percent of their literature-related classroom time on the teaching of poetry (as opposed to 51 percent on book-length works (novels and plays) and 23 percent on short stories (1993, 41). The nature of much of the poetry instruction that occurs in American classrooms can be illustrated, I believe, by the following hypothetical scenario of a ninth-grade poetry class:

Scenario: Teaching "I Wandered Lonely as a Cloud" by William Wordsworth

Burdened with bookbags, the students enter the room in dribs and drabs like adolescent hunchbacks. They greet the teacher, Mr. Novak, then shrug their loads to the floor, laughing and commiserating. One or two take quick seats, absorbed in themselves. Random snippets of talk ricochet around: "Cool beans! . . . "She was not." "Was!" . . . "Yeah, for a week, maybe two." "Bummer." Mr. Novak takes it all in, absorbing some, deflecting the rest. He stands near the door eyeballing the roll. Suddenly, to a girl he spots in the back— "You didn't see me last night, didja? But I was there! Oh, I was there! Section 6, row 10, seat, uh, 25, 26 . . . whatever. You were great." She slumps in her desk beaming. He sidles over to a boy for a quick nudge and a whisper. Finally, the bell rings and the hubbub abates. Mr. Novak steps quickly to the front.

Mr. Novak: OK, group, books! Page 628, "I Wandered Lonely as a Cloud." How many read it? Howmanyhowmanyhowmany? What? Three people! Jeez, what is it with you guys? It's twenty-four lines, for crying out loud! You coulda read it over your oatmeal. Awrighttt! I'll read it to you. It's a nice poem. . . . It's all right. *[He proceeds.]*

I Wandered Lonely as a Cloud

William Wordsworth

I wandered lonely as a cloud
That floats on high o'er vales and hills,
When all at once I saw a crowd,
A host of golden daffodils;
Beside the lake, beneath the trees,
Fluttering and dancing in the breeze.

Continuous as the stars that shine
And twinkle on the milky way,
They stretched in never-ending line
Along the margin of a bay:
Ten thousand saw I at a glance,
Tossing their heads in sprightly dance.

The waves beside them danced; but they
Out-did the sparkling waves in glee:
A poet could not but be gay,
In such a jocund company:
I gazed—and gazed—but little thought
What wealth the show to me had brought.

For oft, when on my couch I lie
In vacant or in pensive mood,
They flash upon that inward eye
Which is the bliss of solitude;
And then my heart with pleasure fills,
And dances with the daffodils.

What is wrong with this picture? Not the teacher entirely. He is much of what we want a teacher to be: alert, lively, funny, savvy, and totally committed to kids. Still, here at the very outset of his ninth-grade English class, he has a problem, and the problem is the poem. Mr. Novak is making a yeoman effort, but even he finds it hard to drum up much enthusiasm for the work ("It's all right"). Although Wordsworth was a major nineteenth-century poet, using his poems in the ninth grade—this one in particular— makes little sense. With its stilted language, fluttery sentiment, and silly images ("tossing their heads in sprightly dance"), the poem has almost nothing to offer. Why on earth would a teacher choose it? The answer is simple: because it is there—in his literature book—and because he is wedded to the sad, self-defeating notion that the dusty old standards are still worth teaching. He is unwilling or unable to acknowledge the fact that poems like "I Wandered Lonely as a Cloud" are all but dead on arrival.[1]

Mr. Novak: All right. It's a nice poem. It has a nice sentiment. Now, before we take a closer look at it, I want you to get out your notes and look up here at the screen. I want to give you some information on William Wordsworth, OK? Now, Wordsworth—and you'll study this guy more in the twelfth grade—was one of the most important English poets of the nineteenth century. OK? He was born in 1770 in what is called the Lake District of England—eyes up here, please, Jeremy . . . *Jeremy!*—and he became an important Romanticist, which means . . .

The lecture drones on for five or ten minutes, maybe longer. Mr. Novak may use a graphic organizer and a picture or two (of Wordsworth, the Lake District, etc.). He might even toss in a juicy tidbit about the poet's personal life—all in the name of "background information." The problem with all this for young adults is that (1) it is insufferably dull, most of it, (2) it is peripheral, (3) it places undue emphasis on the "study" of poetry, and (4) it makes no imaginative effort to engage the students.

Mr. Novak: Any questions? *[There are none.]* All right, let's take a closer look at "I Wandered Lonely as a Cloud." In this poem, Wordsworth is, of course, remembering a scene from his youth in the Lake District, OK? Now, what does he compare himself to? . . . A cloud, right? Felipe? Right. And what does he see? . . . Charisse?. . . Randy? . . . Hellllo. Anyone out there? Hey, it's right there in line 4—"a host of golden daffodils." It's a scene of great natural beauty: "They stretched in never-ending line/ Along the margin of a bay." So, here we have the poet lying in his den in later years, a couch potato—"in vacant or in pensive mood"—when he has this flashback, this "bliss of solitude." And what does this moment signify? Anyone? It signifies, group, what I was just mentioning in the background material. It signifies one of Wordsworth's most important literary concepts—now get this down; it's a biggie!—"emotion recollected in tranquility." What this means is. . . .

———————

Mr. Novak is working hard. He strides around the room, holding the book in one hand, exhorting with the other. He teases and cajoles, pleads and harangues. Although his love for Wordsworth is lukewarm, he is where he wants to be—onstage with a captive (if not captivated) audience. In a sense, though, despite his great natural enthusiasm for teaching and his genuine love for students, Mr. Novak is, at this moment at least, wringing the very life out of poetry. He represents us teachers of poetry at our worst (I too have "been there, done that"). We take a poem and pontificate. We wax, we exude, we explicate, we hold forth. We trot out our college notebooks and our histories of Romanticism. If we ask a question, it is too often barely worth asking or we answer it ourselves, or both. We take a poem that is questionable in the first place, and we talk it to death.

———————

Mr. Novak: OK, guys, enough about the poem. We've got, what, fifteen minutes left. I want you to have some fun. I'm gonna divide you into four or five teams, and I want you to look through the poem and find examples of all the devices we've been studying, you know, simile, metaphor, alliteration, assonance, consonance, all that stuff. The group that finds the most examples will get ten extra points on Friday's test, OK? Any questions? You have fifteen minutes, and then we'll go over them. Let's count off: Jack, one; Ramon, two; Silvie, three. . . .

———————

Here at last the class is involved, and there's an element of fun and competition and even application in it, but in a larger sense the involvement is frantic and mindless, like a "Where is Waldo" exercise or one of those puzzles where you find words hidden in a maze of letters. There is no effort on the teacher's part to have the students consider the purpose of the devices or their originality or their relationship to the poem as a whole. At worst, the activity is rote and pointless; at best, it is highly suspect in both purpose and direction.

In summary, the problems in this scenario with this well-intentioned teacher are multiple:

1. The choice of the poem is all wrong. This is not to say that Wordsworth (or Blake or Whittier or even Philip Freneau) is never an appropriate choice, but that he is (they are) more often than not a very poor fit in most American classrooms.

2. The poem presents little opportunity for interpretation and discussion, and what little there is is dominated by the teacher.

3. The focus is more on the context of the poem, its backdrop, than on the poem itself.

4. The emphasis on form and technique is misguided.

5. There is no imagination in the lesson, no creative effort to engage the students in response.

6. The whole focus on the study of poetry is misguided, guaranteed to fail with all but the most diligent and cooperative students (and even with many of them).

Like Mr. Novak, too many of us never really take a hard, honest look at how we teach poetry. *Unquestioningly, unthinkingly,* we teach the genre the way it was taught to us in high school and college or the way our textbooks suggest that we teach it. A metaphor comes quickly to mind: too often we see ourselves as Caretakers of Poetry in the Museum of Musty Old Standards. We have our students turn to page 543 where we dust off an old relic and deliver hosannahs on its greatness. Sometimes, with the relic out of its case, we turn it about to catch whatever light there is; sometimes we pick at it with a pointed instrument.

Another metaphor makes far more sense: teacher as Talent Scout in—if you will—a Field of Dreams. In the past, talent scouts (now, I suppose, they're called agents) used to canvass the countryside looking for exceptionality in any number of "fields" (music, baseball, comedy, etc.). When they found individuals who truly "had it" (an Elvis, a Mickey Mantle, a Tracy Chapman), they would spirit the innocents away, sign them up, and set about (with the help of coaches and teachers) to develop and refine. The best teachers of poetry do likewise: they *discover* and *develop*, except here the discoveries are raw and unknown poems, poems with potential, gems; and the development is the act of creating ways to make them work in the classroom. The many good poetry teachers in this country are always on the lookout for new poems, ever aware that a fresh supply is only a book or a magazine away; and always looking for ways to make sure the poems they find (like the singers or ballplayers) reach and work their magic on an audience. We should all be talent scouts for poetry.

For teachers who are dissatisfied with their teaching of poetry, teachers whose minds are open to the potential for change, the rest of this book explores ways to make it work. In very practical terms, the book offers guidelines, resources, ideas, possibilities for something better.

There are, of course, no panaceas, no clear and certain solutions. Even if someone offered them, I'm not sure I'd want to listen. Part of our problem in the past is the singular assumption that there was just one way, a way that for the most part hasn't worked. We've turned out students who could vaguely remember that Poe wrote a poem about a raven croaking "Nevermore!" but who haven't read a serious poem since graduation. For the future of poetry (not to mention our students), we have to do better. I think we can.

HIGHLIGHT 2.2

Poems about School

"After School: Room Three" by William Stafford

"Beating Up Billy Murphy in Fifth Grade" by Kathleen Aguero

"Commencement, Pingree School" by John Updike

"Country School" by Ted Kooser

"Cruel Boys" by Gary Soto

"The Desk" by David Bottoms

"An Elementary School Classroom in a Slum" by Stephen Spender

"First Practice" by Gary Gildner

"For Talking" by Denise Nico Leto

"The Geography of Children" by Jane Flanders

"Having the Wrong Name for Mr. Wright" by Helen Barolini

"The High School Band" by Reed Whittemore

"In an Urban School" by Toi Derricotte

"Janie Swecker and Me and Gone with the Wind" by David Huddle

"Junior High Dance" by Alison Joseph

"On Driving Behind a School Bus for Mentally Retarded Children" by Grace Butcher

"On Reading Poems to a Senior Class at South High" by D. C. Berry

"On the Death of a Student Hopelessly Failing My Course" by Gregory Cuomo

"The School Children" by Louise Glück

"To David, about His Education" by Howard Nemerov

"Yuba City School" by Chitra Banerjee Divakaruni

"Zimmer's Head Thudding Against the Blackboard" by Paul Zimmer

"Zimmer in Grade School" by Paul Zimmer

Two useful collections are *Gladly Learn and Gladly Teach: Poems of the School Experience,* edited by Helen Plotz (Greenwillow, 1981) and *Learning by Heart: Contemporary American Poetry about School,* edited by Maggie Anderson and David Hassler (University of Iowa Press, 1999).

Note

1. The "cultural literacists" will surely take issue with this, but people like Harold Bloom and William Bennett have probably spent less than ten authentic minutes in a public school classroom in the last twenty years. Two points: (1) I do not favor banishing the canonical poets outright, but I would limit them to the classes for which they are appropriate. And (2) I do not propose a watered-down curriculum in poetry. I propose one that is intellectually challenging and emotionally engaging at the same time.

II Selection

3 Selecting Poetry to Teach

Three Poems

One of the biggest barriers to the successful teaching of poetry in today's schools—especially to students' liking it—is our choice of what to teach. Consider, for example, the following poems about death:

Death, Be Not Proud

John Donne

Death, be not proud, though some have called thee
Mighty and dreadful, for thou art not so;
For, those whom thou think'st thou dost overthrow;
Die not, poor Death, nor yet canst thou kill me.
From rest and sleep, which but thy pictures be,
Much pleasure; then, from thee, much more must flow,
And soonest our best men with thee do go,
Rest of their bones, and soul's delivery.
Thou art slave to fate, chance, kings, and desperate men,
And dost with poison, war, and sickness dwell,
And poppy, or charms can make us sleep as well,
And better than thy stroke; why swell'st thou then?
One short sleep past, we wake eternally,
And death shall be no more; Death, thou shalt die.

Thanatopsis

William Cullen Bryant

　　To him who in the love of Nature holds
Communion with her visible forms, she speaks
A various language; for his gayer hours
She has a voice of gladness, and a smile
And eloquence of beauty, and she glides
Into his darker musings, with a mild
And healing sympathy, that steals away
Their sharpness, ere he is aware. When thoughts
Of the last bitter hour come like a blight
Over thy spirit, and sad images
Of the stern agony, and shroud, and pall,
And breathless darkness, and the narrow house,
Make thee to shudder, and grow sick at heart;—
Go forth, under the open sky, and list
To Nature's teachings, while from all around—

Earth and her waters, and the depths of air—
Comes a still voice—Yet a few days, and thee
The all-beholding sun shall see no more
In all his course; nor yet in the cold ground,
Where thy pale form was laid, with many tears,
Nor in the embrace of ocean, shall exist
Thy image. Earth, that nourished thee, shall claim
Thy growth, to be resolved to earth again,
And, lost each human trace, surrendering up
Thine individual being, shalt thou go
To mix for ever with the elements,
To be a brother to the insensible rock

Turns with his share, and treads upon. The oak
Shall send his roots abroad, and pierce thy mould.

    Yet not to thine eternal resting-place
Shalt thou retire alone, nor couldst thou wish
Couch more magnificent. Thou shalt lie down
With patriarchs of the infant world—with kings,
The powerful of the earth—the wise, the good,
Fair forms, and hoary seers of ages past,
All in one mighty sepulchre. The hills
Rock-ribbed and ancient as the sun, the vales
Stretching in pensive quietness between;
The venerable woods—rivers that move
In majesty, and the complaining brooks
That make the meadows green; and, poured round all,
Old Ocean's gray and melancholy waste,—
Are but the solemn decorations all
Of the great tomb of man. The golden sun,
The planets, all the infinite host of heaven,
Are shining on the sad abodes of death,
Through the still lapse of ages. All that tread
The globe are but a handful to the tribes
That slumber in its bosom.—Take the wings
Of morning, pierce the Barcan wilderness,
Or lose thyself in the continuous woods
Where rolls the Oregon, and hears no sound,
Save his own dashings—yet the dead are there:
And millions in those solitudes, since first
The flight of years began, have laid them down
In their last sleep—the dead reign there alone,
So shalt thou rest, and what if thou withdraw
In silence from the living, and no friend
Take note of thy departure? All that breathe
Will share thy destiny. The gay will laugh
When thou art gone, the solemn brood of care
Plod on, and each one as before will chase
His favorite phantom; yet all these shall leave

Their mirth and their employments, and shall come
And make their bed with thee. As the long train
Of ages glide away, the sons of men,
The youth in life's green spring, and he who goes
In the full strength of years, matron and maid,
The speechless babe, and gray-headed man—
Shall one by one be gathered to thy side,
By those, who in their turn shall follow them.

So live, that when thy summons comes to join
The innumerable caravan, which moves
To that mysterious realm, where each shall take
His chamber in the silent halls of death,
Thou go not, like the quarry-slave at night,
Scourged to his dungeon, but, sustained and soothed
By an unfaltering trust, approach thy grave,
Like one who wraps the drapery of his couch
About him, and lies down to pleasant dreams.

Will

Maxine Kumin

For love, for money, for reasons less than plain
one swims the Channel or the Hellespont,
masters mountains, in drought prays down the rain,
burns barns or bridges and hurries to the front.
God serves the choosey. They know what to want
And how to bear hope out to the edge of pain.
Nothing drops from them by accident.
But one, in a warm bath opening his vein
and leaning back to watch his act of will,
knows even the chestiest Leanders drown,
the Alps have avalanches they can spill,
nor does the front line always shoot to kill;
and also knows, as the watered pulse runs down,
—that would-be suicides are sometimes found.

Besides their subject, the first two poems are similar in several ways: They are old. They are familiar to many of us, having been written by poets who have long been famous. (John Donne lived from 1572 to 1631 and William Cullen Bryant from 1794 to 1878). The poems are classics in the genre. For decades, they have been included in anthologies as staples of the literature curriculum. In fact, as noted in Chapter 2, some of us tend to teach them because they are so easily available—in the book. On the other hand, it is likely that many teachers are reading the third poem for the first time and are unfamiliar with the poet.

Which poem do you like best? Obviously, if we polled a hundred English teachers, each poem would have its sponsors. Surely, quite a few readers—perhaps a majority—would prefer "Death, Be Not Proud":

- "I've always loved it, ever since I studied it in college."
- "I like what it says, the idea that death is ultimately defeated."
- "I like the fact that it's short and so condensed in its expression."
- "I admire the way Donne designed it, as an apostrophe. He diminishes death by talking to it as he would any person."
- "Well, it's a classic, one of the great poems in the English language."

Comparatively few would choose "Thanatopsis." Some readers who haven't seen this poem since high school or college probably didn't even finish reading it. Although I was once required to memorize the last nine lines, the experience was hardly uplifting: I now have to force myself through the whole thing. For generations, "Thanatopsis" was one of the best known of all American works (and still is widely taught), but the poem is long and stilted, and it no longer speaks to most of us. Finally, a large number of teachers would choose "Will" despite their unfamiliarity with it or perhaps with Maxine Kumin.

Now, which of the poems would be preferred by high school students, the most likely school audience for all three? If a class of tenth graders who had never read them were handed copies and asked to rank them in preference, how would the poems fall? There is simply no question about this: most of the students would like "Will" the most and "Thanatopsis" the least. A few would like the Donne poem (and many more could be taught to like it).

The huge majority of American students and quite a few English teachers would prefer "Will" for obvious reasons. For one thing, it is brief—like "Death, Be Not Proud," a sonnet. It is written in accessible language—"God serves the choosey," "shoots to kill," "would-be suicides." It uses rhyme and alliteration effectively—"and leaning back to watch his act of will." And of course it deals with a topic of intense interest to many teenagers. It is a very contemporary poem.

If we are truly interested in promoting the appreciation and understanding of poetry in American schools, we should seriously question teaching a work like "Thanatopsis"—except, perhaps, in the very limited context of historical significance. The poem continues to be included in high school textbooks for three reasons: it is old and, for textbook publishers (who are more conservative than Jesse Helms), therefore safe; publishers don't have to pay permission fees to use it since it was written over 175 years ago; and these same publishers think it is what we teachers want to teach. The truth is most teachers don't want to teach "Thanatopsis"— how could they?—but many of them have been led, under the guise of promoting our cultural heritage, to think that they should. It is far easier to build a case for teaching "Death, Be Not Proud" and easier still to justify the teaching of poems like "Will."

Guidelines for Selection

The first step good teachers of poetry take in approaching the genre is to throw away the textbook (or at least set it aside). Then they set about to create their own anthology. With poems (unlike short stories, novels, or plays), this is extremely easy—for two reasons: wonderfully teachable poems are easy to find and, because of their length, easy to use.

If the selection of poems to teach is so important—and I think it is crucial—there should be a few guidelines for teachers to have in mind as they make their choices. Here are five to consider:

GUIDELINE ONE

As Stephen Dunning so persuasively argued in *Teaching Literature to Adolescents: Poetry* over thirty years ago, teachers should make every effort to teach only poems that they like—*really* like. It would be torture—for me as well as my students—if I were forced at gunpoint to teach "Thanatopsis." The same would be true for countless other poems. There are many poems that I like (I have a file folder with hundreds) and quite a few I dearly love, but I am extremely selective. Every teacher should be.

Corollary: Occasionally we all have to teach works we don't embrace. If I were teaching a unit on Robert Frost, I would probably teach "Stopping by Woods on a Snowy Evening" even though it is not my favorite of his poems. Similarly I might also feel compelled in some settings to teach "The Love Song of J. Alfred Prufrock" by T. S. Eliot or perhaps even something by Keats or Shelley. But I would try to keep to a minimum the poems I am lukewarm about.

GUIDELINE TWO

Sometimes, teachers may not like poetry and therefore not enjoy teaching it because they genuinely prefer fiction or drama. (Some may even prefer essays.) And some teachers *think* they don't like poetry. I would contend, though, that any lover of literature in general—of the written word well used—can be led to a liking of poetry, *some* poetry. It is merely a matter of discovering it. Many teachers are unaware that hundreds of superb poems are out there waiting to be taught—in books, magazines, journals, even on the Internet most of them by fine contemporary poets we've never heard

of. Writing in the summer 1992 issue of *American Scholar,* the poet
Suzanne Rhodenbaugh comments on this in a memorable article entitled
"One Heart's Canon":

> I've learned . . . that the world of poetry is inexhaustible not just with
> respect to any one poem, which can be read and loved over and
> over, but also with respect to poetry's multifariousness, its bounty.
> I've learned that every conceivable subject or tone or theme or
> setting has, somewhere, been addressed by some poet, and that
> there are almost infinite options as to poetic strategy, and the sum
> called "style" (393).

One of the reasons we often think we don't like poetry is that we
don't understand a lot of it—or think we don't and, for that matter, think we
can't. We pick up a copy of *The New Yorker* in the dentist's office and read
a few poems, none of which makes a lot of sense to us, and we conclude
that all modern poetry is esoteric and unfathomable. If the truth be known,
a lot of modern poetry, like a lot of modern art, *is* hard to understand. But
much of it is wonderfully readable and teachable—like the following poem:

The Sacred

Stephen Dunn

After the teacher asked if anyone had
    a sacred place
and the students fidgeted and shrank

in their chairs, the most serious of them all
    said it was his car,
being in it alone, his tape deck playing

things he'd chosen, and others knew the truth
    had been spoken
and began speaking about their rooms,

their hiding places, but the car kept coming up,
    the car in motion,
music filling it, and sometimes one other person

who understood the bright altar of the dashboard
    and how far away
a car could take him from the need

to speak, or to answer, the key
    in having a key
and putting it in, and going.

I love this poem, and surely a lot of high school students would like
it as well.

Corollary: If by chance you are the rare teacher of literature who
truly dislikes poetry, who is unable to develop even the slightest fondness

for it, perhaps you shouldn't teach it. Far better to own up to it and teach fiction and drama with flair and excitement than to try to fake affection for poetry. Your students will be the first to see through you, and you will have driven another nail into the poetry coffin.

GUIDELINE THREE

Create your own portfolio of poems you like to teach, your own "heart's canon." There are lots of ways to do this and many of them can be fun. But finding poems can also be frustrating: for every fifty poems I read or *begin* to read (many I never finish), there may be two or three keepers. Here is a poem I found several years ago and kept, a poem I truly love:

A Blessing

James Wright

Just off the highway to Rochester, Minnesota,
Twilight bounds softly forth on the grass.
And the eyes of those two Indian ponies
Darken with kindness.
They have come gladly out of the willows
To welcome my friend and me.
We step over the barbed wire into the pasture
Where they have been grazing all day, alone.
They ripple tensely, they can hardly contain their happiness
That we have come.
They bow shyly as wet swans. They love each other.
There is no loneliness like theirs.
At home once more,
They begin munching the young tufts of spring in the darkness.
I would like to hold the slenderer one in my arms,
For she has walked over to me
And nuzzled my left hand.
She is black and white,
Her mane falls wild over her forehead,
And the light breeze moves me to caress her long ear
That is delicate as the skin over a girl's wrist.
Suddenly I realize
That if I stepped out of my body I would break
Into blossom.

Poems like these—poems you will embrace as warmly as a song—are numerous, but they don't typically appear in daily newspapers or in popular magazines like *Newsweek, People,* or *Esquire.* Over the years, I've had luck finding poems I like in three sources: the so-called "little magazines" like *Cimarron Review, Shenandoah,* and *The Hudson Review;* annual collections like *The Best American Poetry, 1999;* and the countless anthologies of various types available in bookstores and libraries.

Little Magazines

There are hundreds of small, obscure magazines devoted to poetry (or literature in general) that survive despite the genre's lack of a broad public audience. Most of them appear quarterly and operate in the red year after year, funded by either universities or foundations. They publish the works of competent, serious poets, the comparatively famous as well as talented newcomers.

Some of these magazines have been around for decades. Others sputter along for a few years before dying off for lack of support. Many have straightforward or scholarly titles (*The Beloit Poetry Journal, The Hudson Review, The Kenyon Review*), some more evocative names (*Ploughshares, Prairie Schooner, Midstream*).

Little magazines are not always easy to find. The most common sources—in ascending order of likelihood—are large bookstores (especially those in college towns and major cities), public libraries, and college libraries. Wherever one finds them, they are easy and quick to browse through. Often I've been known to hurriedly copy a poem from a magazine onto the back of a bank deposit slip while sitting at a table at Barnes & Noble.

HIGHLIGHT 3.1

A Little Magazine Sampler

The Antioch Review, Box 148, Yellow Springs, OH 45387

The Beloit Poetry Journal, RFD 2, Box 154, Ellsworth, ME 04605-9616

Blue Unicorn, 22 Avon Road, Kensington, CA 94707

The Carolina Quarterly, 501 Greenlaw Hall, CB #3520, University of North Carolina at Chapel Hill, Chapel Hill, NC 27599-3520

Cimarron Review, 205 Morrill Hall, Oklahoma State University, Stillwater, OK 74078-0135

The Hudson Review, 684 Park Avenue, New York, NY 10021

The Kenyon Review, Kenyon College, Gambier, OH 43022

Ploughshares, Emerson College, 100 Beacon Street, Boston MA 02116 ▶

Poet Lore, The Writer's Center, 4508 Walsh St., Bethesda, MD
20815

Poetry Northwest, University of Washington, 4045 Brooklyn,
NE, Seattle, WA 98105

Prairie Schooner, University of Nebraska, 201 Andrews Hall,
Lincoln, NE 68588-0334

Shenandoah, Troubadour Theatre, 2nd Floor, Box I-B, Washington and Lee University, Lexington, VA 24450-0303.

The Southern Review, 43 Allen Hall, Louisiana State University, Baton Rouge, LA 70803

The Threepenny Review, P. O. Box 9131, Berkeley, CA 94709

Annual Collections

The best-known annual collection of poems is *The Best American Poetry
19—.* Begun in 1988, the series is published by Scribner Poetry and edited
by David Lehman, with each annual edition separately edited by a poet,
e.g., John Hollander, Richard Howard, and Louise Glück. Another series
worth exploring is *The Anthology of Magazine Verse and Yearbook of
American Poetry,* which was published frequently during the 1980s and
may still be found in libraries. Each annual volume includes hundreds of
poems selected from the work of contemporary poets as well as a
bibliography of works of the featured authors, lists of books and magazines
that publish poetry, lists of biographies and commentaries on specific
poets, and awards and prizes for poetry. The most recent edition, for 1997,
was edited by Alan F. Pater and published by Monitor Book Company.

HIGHLIGHT 3.2

Poetry Magazine

Without question, the most prestigious magazine devoted solely to poetry in
America is called, aptly enough, *Poetry.* Founded in 1912 by Harriet Monroe,
Poetry has always devoted itself to the promotion of serious contemporary
poets. Within its pages over the years has appeared a pantheon of American
writers, including T. S. Eliot, Robert Frost, Carl Sandburg, Edwin Arlington
Robinson, Sara Teasdale, Wallace Stevens, William Carlos Williams, Langston
Hughes, Amy Lowell, and Edna St. Vincent Millay. More recently, the magazine

▶

has featured the works of poets like David Wagoner, Howard Nemerov, May Swenson, Rita Dove, A. R. Ammons, Li-Young Lee, and Sylvia Plath.

In 1978, *The "Poetry" Anthology: 1912–1977* was published to honor "sixty-five years of America's most distinguished verse magazine." The volume, edited by Daryl Hine and Joseph Parini and published by Houghton Mifflin, remains one of the best anthologies available to teachers. Despite its prestige, *Poetry* has never been a huge commercial success. As noted elsewhere in this book, its number of total annual subscriptions has never reached 10,000.

Poetry is a valuable resource. It is one of the few literary magazines that appear monthly, and a typical issue has several poems that could be used in a classroom. Every high school library should subscribe. The address is *Poetry*, 60 West Walton Street, Chicago, IL 60610.

Anthologies

The best sources of teachable poems are non-annual anthologies. Every year, it seems, more and more are published, all of them useful and many truly superb. Many contain a historically broad range of poems, but the most useful collections for teachers confine themselves largely to contemporary works. They can be organized into several categories, listed here with some of the best examples (and others provided in Appendix A):

1. Recent collections for a general audience

The Harvard Book of Contemporary American Poetry. 1985. Edited by Helen Vendler. Features several poems and mini-biographies of acclaimed poets such as Rita Dove, James Wright, A. R. Ammons, James Dickey, and Sylvia Plath.

The Norton Anthology of Modern Poetry. 1988. Edited by Richard Ellman and Robert O'Clair. 3rd ed.

The Norton Anthology of Poetry. 1997. Edited by Margaret Ferguson et al. Shorter 4th ed. Covers the entire historical sweep.

The Oxford Book of Comic Verse. 1994. Edited by John Gross. Includes everyone from Chaucer to Edward Lear and Dorothy Parker, even examples of the Burma-Shave roadside jingles.

The Pittsburgh Book of Contemporary American Poetry. 1993. Edited by Ed Ochester and Peter Oresick.

2. Well-established general collections for a young adult audience. Some of these books are out of print, but still available in libraries.

The Invisible Ladder: An Anthology of Contemporary American Poems for Young Readers. 1996. Edited by Liz Rosenberg. A fine collection featuring the poetry and commentaries (and even pictures) of thirty-eight poets.

Peeling the Onion: An Anthology of Poems. 1993. Edited by Ruth Gordon.

Reflections on a Gift of Watermelon Pickle and Other Modern Verse. 1966. Edited by Stephen Dunning et al. The most widely used anthology for young adults ever and still in print; intended for younger adolescents, but useful anywhere.

Reflections on a Gift of Watermelon Pickle and Other Modern Verse. 1995. Edited by Stephen Dunning et al. 2nd ed. This edition has a multicultural flavor.

Some Haystacks Don't Even Have Any Needle. 1969. Edited by Stephen Dunning et al. The high school version of *Reflections*; a superb collection; out of print, but can still be found in libraries.

Zero Makes Me Hungry: A Collection of Poems for Today. 1976. Edited by Edward Lueders and Primus St. John. A collection ahead of its time in recognizing poets of color.

3. Collections by Paul Janeczko—In the last fifteen years, Janeczko has become the most prolific and best compiler of poetry anthologies aimed specifically at young adults. Every high school library should have several of his books available for teachers and students. Most of them remain in print.

Dont Forget to Fly: A Cycle of Modern Poems. 1981.

I Feel a Little Jumpy around You: A Book of Her Poems & His Poems Collected in Pairs. 1996. Co-edited with Naomi Shihab Nye. Perhaps the best collection available in paperback.

Pocket Poems: Selected for a Journey. 1985.

Postcard Poems: A Collection of Poetry for Sharing. 1979.

Strings: A Gathering of Family Poems. 1984.

4. Thematic collections

American Sports Poems. 1988. Edited by R. R. Knutson and May Swenson.

Crazy to Be Alive in Such a Strange World: Poems about People. 1977. Edited by Nancy Larrick.

Drive, They Said: Poems about Americans and Their Cars. 1994. Edited by Kurt Brown.

Learning by Heart: Contemporary American Poetry about School. 1999. Edited by Maggie Anderson and David Hassler.

The Oxford Book of War Poetry. 1984. Edited by Jon Stallworthy.

Pierced by a Ray of Sun: Poems about the Times We Feel Alone. 1995. Edited by
   Ruth Gordon.

Tangled Vines: A Collection of Mother and Daughter Poems. 1992. Edited by
   Lyn Lifshin.

HIGHLIGHT 3.3

Shinder's List of Family Anthologies

Few collectors of poetry have specialized to the degree that Jason Shinder
has. Taking up where Lyn Lifshin's *Tangled Vines: A Collection of Mother
and Daughter Poems* leaves off, he has compiled the following anthologies,
each of which is useful to teachers looking for poems about family:

First Light: Mother and Son Poems

More Light: Father and Daughter Poems

Divided Light: Father and Son Poems

Eternal Light: Grandparent Poems

Like the Lifshin collection, all were first published by Harcourt Brace.

---

5. Collections with a multicultural emphasis:

Cool Salsa: Bilingual Poems on Growing Up Latino in the United States. 1994.
   Edited by Lori M. Carlson.

*Every Shut Eye Ain't Asleep: An Anthology of Poetry by African Americans since
   1945.* 1994. Edited by Michael S. Harper and Anthony Walton.

In Search of Color Everywhere: A Collection of African American Poetry. 1994.
   Edited by E. Ethelbert Miller. A work of art with illustrations by Terrance
   Cummings.

The Open Boat: Poems from Asian America. 1993. Edited by Garrett Hongo.

Unsettling America: An Anthology of Contemporary Multicultural Poetry. 1994.
   Edited by Maria Mazziotti Gillan and Jennifer Gillan. Organized by
   themes rather than ethnic groups.

6. Books of young adult poems—While all the anthologies listed above
are comprised of poetry written for adults, the following are books written
expressly for adolescents:

Buried Alive: The Elements of Love. 1996. Ralph J. Fletcher. New York: Atheneum.

Class Dismissed: High School Poems. 1982. Mel Glenn. New York: Clarion Books.

Class Dismissed II: More High School Poems. 1986. Mel Glenn. New York: Clarion Books. These two volumes by Glenn feature unrhymed poems written from the point of view of typical high school students, like "Candie Brewer," "Juan Pedro Carrera," and "Lance Perkins (Football Star)." The last is a concrete poem in the form of a football field (each line is "numbered" G, 5, 10, 15, etc.), the words showing a broken-field runback of a punt for a touchdown.

I Am Wings: Poems about Love. 1994. Ralph J. Fletcher. New York: Bradbury. Thirty-one poems in two groupings—Falling In and Falling Out [of love]. This book and Fletcher's *Buried Alive* (above) are also available in a combined paperback edition, *Room Enough for Love* from Aladdin (New York, 1998).

Jump Ball: A Basketball Season in Poems. 1997. Mel Glenn. New York: Lodestar.

Ordinary Things: Poems from a Walk in Early Spring. 1997. Ralph J. Fletcher. New York: Atheneum.

Stories I Ain't Told Nobody Yet. 1989. Jo Carson. New York: Orchard Books. Poems from a rural perspective.

Who Killed Mr. Chippendale?: A Mystery in Poems. 1996. Mel Glenn. New York: Lodestar. Poems about students, teachers, and townspeople provide the clues for solving a murder mystery.

HIGHLIGHT 3.4

Collections for a Deserted Island: Five Picks

With so many excellent anthologies available and budgets often stretched, here are five I would give to a young adult (or buy for a school) on a deserted island:

I Feel a Little Jumpy around You

The Norton Anthology of Poetry

The Oxford Book of Comic Verse

Reflections on a Gift of Watermelon Pickle

Unsettling America: An Anthology of Contemporary American Multicultural Poetry

And since the island is deserted . . . perhaps a sixth: *Pierced by a Ray of Sun: Poems about the Times We Feel Alone.*

GUIDELINE FOUR

For the classroom, select from your personal portfolio the poems that have "teachability," poems with at least a chance of being liked by many of your students. Which raises a question: what are the qualities of poems that many young adults will like?

In his book *Can Poetry Matter? Essays on Poetry and American Culture*, the poet Dana Gioia comments on this question of "popular poetry" in part by discussing the Iowan writer Ted Kooser as a popular poet:

> [U]nlike most of his peers he writes naturally for a nonliterary public. His style is accomplished but extremely simple—his diction drawn from common speech, his syntax conversational. His subjects are chosen from the everyday world. . . . [He] is uncommonly entertaining. His poems are usually short and perfectly paced, his subjects relevant and engaging. Finishing one poem, the reader instinctively wants to proceed to another. It has been Kooser's particular genius to develop a genuine poetic style that accommodates the average reader and portrays a vision that provides unexpected moments of illumination from the seemingly threadbare details of everyday life. . . . He has achieved the most difficult kind of originality. He has transformed the common idiom and experience into fresh and distinctive poetry (1992, 93–94).

Here is one of Kooser's poems:

Epitaph for a Sky Diver

for the memory of J. L.

The sun, like a new dime,
burned in the pocket of sky
while he fell like a penny
pitched with a wish down a well.

Many students would like this brief poem partly because it possesses some of the qualities in poetry they appreciate:

Contemporaneity: Most young people—most people in general—prefer the literature of the here and now. Comparatively few of us spend much time reading the fiction and poetry from any century other than our own. This is even truer of the young: if we can get them to read fiction at all, most of them will look for Grisham, Conroy, and Alice Walker. If they can be led to like poetry, it will be the poetry written in today's language about timeless topics that are cast in a new light.

Brevity: Young adults are no different from most of the rest of us. When I browse through a new anthology of poems I've found, I am unconsciously guided by three factors: titles, the first few lines, and length.

Especially length. Like most late twentieth-century Americans, I am often in a hurry, preconditioned by a world of fast food and channel changers to skim and scan, to review content impatiently in quick gulps. For this reason—however intellectually bereft it may be—I take more note of short lyric poems, twenty lines or less. I tend to bypass the poems that extend for more than a page.

Titles and first lines often override length, of course. I like David Wagoner's "Staying Alive," a poem of eighty-three lines, the first of which caught my eye: "Staying alive in the woods is a matter of calming down." I also like Elizabeth Bishop's "The Fish" (seventy-six lines) as well as many others that are longer than a sonnet. But length matters, especially to students.

Titles can be telling, like the following poems that grabbed my attention at first glance and might entice students as well:

"Do Not Dump Rubbish Here" by Rafael Alberti

"Hamlet Ought to Die in the First Act" by Werner Aspenstrom

"Preface to a Twenty-Volume Suicide Note" by Imamu Amiri Baraka

"Turning the Double Play" by David Bottoms

"Beating Up Billy Murphy in Fifth Grade" by Kathleen Aguero

"Coyote Skull: A Lesson for a Child" by Michael L. Johnson

"The Vagaries of Twelve Year Old Lust" by Bruce Logan

"Attila the Hen" by Robert Bess

"How I Went Truant from School to Visit a River" by Mary Oliver

"Boy, Fifteen, Killed by Hummingbird" by Linda Linssen

"The Rural Carrier Stops to Kill a Nine-Foot Cottonmouth" by T. R. Hummer

"Skinnydipping with William Wordsworth" by Maxine Kumin

Incident: Most of us—young adults in particular—like poems where there is an element of dramatic conflict or the semblance of a story, as in Gary Snyder's well-known "Hay for the Horses, " William Stafford's even better known "Traveling through the Dark," and the following poem by Robert Hayden:

The Whipping

The old woman across the way
   is whipping the boy again
and shouting to the neighborhood
   her goodness and his wrongs.

Wildly he crashes through elephant ears,
   pleads in dusty zinnias,

while she in spite of crippling fat
   pursues and corners him.

She strikes and strikes the shrilly circling
   boy till the stick breaks
in her hand. His tears are rainy weather
   to woundlike memories:

My head gripped in bony vise
   of knees, the writhing struggle
to wrench free, the blows, the fear
   worse than blows that hateful

Words could bring, the face that I
   no longer knew or loved. . . .
Well, it is over now, it is over,
   and the boy sobs in his room,

And the woman leans muttering against
   a tree, exhausted, purged—
avenged in part for lifelong hidings
   she has had to bear.

HIGHLIGHT 3.5

Narrative Poetry

Most of the poems recommended (and included) in this book are brief lyric poems of twenty lines or less. As noted in this chapter, many that students will especially like are based on happenings—a driver coming upon a car-struck deer in "Traveling through the Dark," someone observing an old woman chasing after a boy with a stick in "The Whipping." All of us like a story.

Which brings us to narrative poems. Most narrative poems are long, but many are so compelling that students will like them despite their length. Here are some favorites, both traditional and modern:

Traditional

"Casey at the Bat" by Ernest Thayer

"The Cremation of Sam Magee" by Robert W. Service

"The Highwayman" by Alfred Noyes

"Paul Revere's Ride" by Henry Wadsworth Longfellow

Modern

"David" by Earle Birney, *Some Haystacks Don't Even Have Any Needle*

"Driving Lesson" by Michael Pettit, *The Music of What Happens*

"Summer Killer" by T. Alan Broughton, *The Music of What Happens*

Concreteness of language: Adolescents also like vivid images like the ones in Hayden's poem: "shouting to the neighborhood," "dusty zinnias," "strikes and strikes the shrilly circling/ boy." Many would like the first few lines of "Her Sleep" by Jill Hoffman:

> Wasps or hornets rattle on the sills
> and fill the vestibule with danger;
> my daughter, rocked by lullabies
> of wind, naps inside mosquito netting
> like a bride before the veil is lifted
> for the rough world to injure with its kiss.

Accessible language: Students are attracted to poems written in the approachable language of contemporary America, like "Spring" by Linda McCarriston (p. 44), "Love in Brooklyn" by John Wakeman (p. 111) and "Conversation with a Fireman from Brooklyn" by Tess Gallagher, the first nine lines of which read,

> He offers, between planes,
> to buy me a drink. I've never talked
> to a fireman before, not one from Brooklyn
> anyway. Okay. Fine, I say. Somehow
> the subject is bound to come up, women
> firefighters, and since I'm
> a woman and he's a fireman, between
> the two of us, we know something
> about this subject. . . .

Humor: All of us like humor—anywhere—but especially in poetry. Most young adults would surely chuckle at the following anonymous poem that appears in *The Oxford Book of American Light Verse*:

The Drunkard and the Pig

> It was early last December,
> As near as I remember,
> I was walking down the street in tipsy pride;
> No one was I disturbing
> As I lay down by the curbing,
> And a pig came up and lay down by my side.
> As I lay there in the gutter
> Thinking thoughts I shall not utter,
> A lady passing by was heard to say:
> "You can tell a man who boozes
> By the company he chooses";
> And the pig got up and slowly walked away.

Middle-schoolers may still guffaw at Shel Silverstein and Jack Prelutsky (see Highlight 3.6), but their more sophisticated older brothers and sisters may prefer the more subtle poetic humor of Dorothy Parker and John Updike or the satire of a Tom Lehrer.

HIGHLIGHT 3.6

Prelutsky for Adults (and Young Adults)

Along with Shel Silverstein, Jack Prelutsky has long been the indisputable poet of choice among children, who love his outrageous humor in books like *The New Kid on the Block: Poems* and *Nightmares: Poems to Trouble Your Sleep.* By the time these same kids reached high school, though, Prelutsky was passé—until 1991, when he came out with *There'll Be a Slight Delay and Other Poems for Grown-ups.* The title itself may attract adolescents, but if it doesn't, some of the poems will, especially "The Dreaded Hemorrhoid," "Computer, Computer," "A Staunch Republocrat," and "I Watched a Televangelist." Be forewarned: all of the poems are fun, but a few, like "They Did It in the Shower," are rated R. The book is published by William Morrow and Company.

Strong emotion: As teachers, we have an obligation to lead students away from an insistence upon excessive sentimentality in poetry, but young adults are drawn to poems with an intensity of feeling, like "A Blessing" by James Wright (p. 31) and "On a Child Who Lived One Minute" by X. J. Kennedy.

Rhythm and rhyme: Immersed as most of them are in their own worlds of music, adolescents like almost anything with a strong beat, poetry included. They also like poems that rhyme, often resisting our best efforts to steer them away from a dependence upon it.

Few poems, if any, will reflect all these qualities. Many, however, include enough of them to ensure their popularity with many students, like (again) the well-known "Traveling through the Dark" and the following poems:

Zimmer's Head Thudding against the Blackboard

Paul Zimmer

At the blackboard I had missed
Five number problems in a row,
And was about to foul a sixth,
When the old, exasperated nun
Began to pound my head against
My six mistakes. When I cried,

She threw me back into my seat,
Where I hid my head and swore
That very day I'd be a poet,
And curse her yellow teeth with this.

By Accident

Jane O. Wayne

Because I brought him here
I hold his hand
while the surgeon cleans his leg,
a boy I hardly know, a child
my daughter's age. Years ago
a black nurse held
my white hand in a hospital and I
squeezed then just as he does now
a stranger never thanked
never forgotten.

I know how it happens,
how pain softens us as easily
as habit hardens, how
we meet now and if we meet again
we both avert our eyes.
The boy and I,
as from the gash itself,
the white seams gaping on the raw red,
we turn away. Often I think we can,
given half a chance, love anyone.

Shooting Baskets at Dusk

Michael McFee

He will never be happier than this,
lost in the perfectly thoughtless motion
of shot, rebound, dribble, shot,

his mind removed as the gossipy swallows
that pick and roll, that give and go
down the school chimney like smoke in reverse

as he shoots, rebounds, dribbles, shoots,
the brick wall giving the dribble back
to his body beginning another run

from foul line, corner, left of the key,
the jealous rim guarding its fickle net
as he shoots, rebounds, dribbles, shoots,

absorbed in the rhythm that seems to flow
from his fingertips to the winded sky
and back again to this lonely orbit

of shot, rebound, dribble, shot,
until he is just a shadow and a sound
though the ball still burns in his vanished hands.

Spring

Linda McCarriston

Down Route 2, the farmers
are hauling hen-dressing
in flat, open wagons.
The stink is terrific.

The fields on either side
fan out in long arcs
of mud and shiny stubble;
even the crows, laboring
from tree to tree,
seem fresh, and everything
is ready to start over.

So a tractor heaves off
over the shallow bank,
and the farmer hums
or whistles, thinking
of his cows, his taxes,
or his woman, while today
paints a first wash of red
over his face and forearms.

Saddled to his big John Deere,
he throws the spreader switch,
flinging the stuff
in every direction, then rides on
through the stench and roar
like a free man, like a man
on top of something other
than a half-ton
of chicken shit: like how
you imagine a rich man, maybe,
with his money.

Terrorist Poem

Frank Finale

*(There were 2,492 terrorist acts around the world last year,
claiming 6,166 lives and 3,607 injuries.)—Risks International
Inc., Alexandria, Virginia*

This poem is dangerous.
This poem wears a ski mask
& carries a banana clip full of clichés.
It is not afraid

to die for a cause. This poem
disguised itself & slipped past
your security. It
holds you hostage in your
own office & will not release you
till demands are met.
This poem is part of an underground
network of poems trained to infiltrate
& disrupt. You can not
escape it. If this poem can not get
what it wants, there are a thousand more to take its place.

Already   it has killed your time.

One other quality should be mentioned—*identification*. We all like to read about subjects we're interested in. Many of the poems I like, as you have perhaps inferred, are about animals and nature, baseball and other sports. Young adults are similarly drawn to subjects they know and like— cars, basketball, fashion, horses, music, food, relationships, motorcycles, cats and dogs, computers, school. And the amazing thing is this: there are wonderful poems out there about all of these subjects and more. For this reason . . .

GUIDELINE FIVE

Give students the opportunity to create their own personal portfolios. Begin a poetry unit by allowing them to look through a wide range of anthologies and other books of poetry you've gathered from the school library, the public library, your own personal collection, and other sources. Their assignment: find three (or five or ten) poems they really like. To plan for this, you need to collect not only poems, but books of poems. Visit flea markets, yard sales and Friends of the Library book sales in your community. Scavenge old textbooks and magazines. Let fellow teachers and parents know that you are constantly in the market for used poetry books. For this to work, you'll need twenty-five or thirty books or folders with dozens of poems, but the effort will pay off: for perhaps the first time, your students will find poems that they like and, with luck, some they will treasure, as did the student who once pasted the following poem by e. e. cummings in the door of her school locker:

who are you, little i

(five or six years old)
peering from some high

window; at the gold

of november sunset

(and feeling: that if day
has to become night

this is a beautiful way)

HIGHLIGHT 3.7

Cowboy Poets

Teachers looking for poems often find them in the most unlikely places—in this case, on the range. One of the most engaging personas on the poetry frontier in the last ten years has been the cowboy poet. The roots of cowboy poetry can be found in the poems of Robert Service and the songs of Roy Rogers and Gene Autry. The genre has shown up on *The Tonight Show* and public radio's *Morning Edition*. Its best-known advocate is Baxter Black, whose work is clever, funny, and satiric. Cowboy poetry portrays the life of the cattle drive, rodeo, and bunkhouse. For the most part it is amusing and sentimental, and almost all of it rhymes. Teachers can draw from a number of books, including these:

Coyote Cowboy Poetry. 1987. Baxter Black. Coyote Cowboy Company.

Cowboy Curmudgeon. 1992. Wallace McRae. Gibbs Smith Publishers.

Cowboy Poetry: A Gathering. 1985. Edited by Hal Cannon. Gibbs Smith.

Croutons on a Cow Pie. 1992. Volumes One and Two. Baxter Black. Stockman & Coyote.

Graining the Mare: The Poetry of Ranch Women. 1994. Edited by Teresa Jordan. Gibbs Smith.

Home on the Range. 1997. Selected by Paul Janeczko. Illustrated by Bernie Fuchs. Dial.

Maverick Western Verse. 1994. Edited by John Dofflemyer. Gibbs Smith.

New Cowboy Poetry: A Contemporary Gathering. 1990. Edited by Hal Cannon. Gibbs Smith.

4 Contemporary Poets in the Classroom

In her collection of poems *Heroes in Disguise*, Linda Pastan writes about what it is like to discover a new poetic voice:

> Finding a new poet
> is like finding a new wildflower
> out in the woods. You don't see
>
> its name in the flower books, and
> nobody you tell believes
> in its odd color or the way
>
> its leaves grow in splayed rows
> down the whole length of the page. . . .

This is the way it is with contemporary poets. They are wonderfully fresh and inviting. But there is a problem: they are so numerous that a searcher for poems—a teacher—can often feel overwhelmed. Where to begin?

As the previous chapter suggests, little magazines and anthologies are among the best sources. Another is the hundreds of books of poetry featuring the work of individual poets and published, in many cases, by major publishing houses or university presses or, more often, small independent publishers whose names are as obscure as the poets themselves (Thunder City Press, Best Cellar Press, Bonewhistle Press, Alice James Books, etc.). Many of these poets are mentioned in Chapter 3, but teachers in search of writers and works with potential appeal to their students need a better way—a system of sorts—for making distinctions and choices.

An approach I've used and recommend begins with a reference series called *American Poets since World War II*, which is part of the many-volumed *Dictionary of Literary Biography*. Published by Gale Research, *American Poets since World War II* consists of five editions, each of which presents a lengthy biographical and critical discussion of the works of selected American poets who have dominated the field in this country in the last fifty years. The initial series (Volume 5 of the *DLB*) considers 132 poets; the second series (Volume 105), thirty; the third series (Volume 120), sixty-six; and the fourth and fifth series (Volumes 165 and 169), eleven new poets each. The total of 250 poets is a roll call of the best in modern

American poetry—and a worthy starting point for any teacher looking for new poets to teach.

Still, many of these poets remain unknown to most of us, and certainly more than a few of them write poetry that, for whatever reasons, is often inappropriate for high schools. (A primary reason is inaccessibility.) So the question remains: how to glean from a list of 250 poets the names of those whose work is particularly "teachable."

A sensible method would be to identify those poets among the 250 whose work most often appears in acclaimed anthologies compiled with young adult audiences in mind—especially the works cited in Chapter 3 by Dunning and Janeczko. If a poet appears in, say, half of the identified collections, one could infer a comparatively high degree of potential appeal for adolescents.

With this hypothesis in mind, my winnowing out began with a baseline list of fifteen acclaimed anthologies published between 1966 and 1996 (for full bibliographic information, see Appendix A):

- *Crazy to Be Alive in Such a Strange World* (Larrick)
- *Don't Forget to Fly* (Janeczko)
- *Going Over to Your Place* (Janeczko)
- *A Green Place* (Smith)
- *I Feel a Little Jumpy around You* (Nye and Janeczko)
- *Looking for Your Name* (Janeczko)
- *Mindscapes* (Peck)
- *Pictures That Storm Inside My Head* (Peck)
- *Pocket Poems* (Janeczko)
- *Postcard Poems* (Janeczko)
- *Reflections on a Gift of Watermelon Pickle* (Dunning), 1st or 2nd edition
- *Some Haystacks Don't Even Have Any Needle* (Dunning)
- *Sounds and Silences* (Peck)
- *Strings* (Janeczko)
- *Zero Makes Me Hungry* (Lueders and St. John)

Again, each of these collections consists of the work of poets who write for an adult audience but *whose work is considered of high potential interest to young adults.* Once more the question: of the 250 acclaimed poets featured in the Gale series, which ones appear in at least half of the fifteen anthologies?

Five poets meet this standard:

1. *William Stafford*—13 appearances (23 different poems)
      Comment: Stafford, who died in 1993, often wrote thoughtful poems about nature and human relationships that are excellent for discussion, for example, "A Ritual to Be Read to Each Other," and "Traveling through the Dark," the title poem in the book of the same name which won the National Book Award for poetry in 1962. Here is one of his shorter works:

> **Vacation**
>
> One scene as I bow to pour her coffee:—
>
> > Three Indians in the scouring drouth
> > huddle at a grave scooped in the gravel,
> > lean to the wind as our train goes by.
> > Someone is gone.
> > There is dust on everything in Nevada.
>
> I pour the cream.

2. *John Updike*—11 appearances (15 poems)
      Comment: More famous for his fiction, Updike writes poetry noted for its humor, clever use of language, and wry observations of affluent suburban life. Among his anthologized poems are "Commencement, Pingree School" and the popular "Ex-Basketball Player."

3. *Galway Kinnell*—11 appearances (8 poems)
      Comment: Kinnell's poem "First Song" appears in four of the fifteen anthologies. Two of his many other poems worth teaching are "Two Set Out on Their Journey" and "Blackberry Eating."

4. *John Ciardi*—8 appearances (12 poems)
      Comment: Unlike most of these poets, Ciardi often wrote expressly for young people. His poems are not unlike Updike's—often witty, observant, self-perceptive. Among his most promising titles for the high school classroom are "In Place of a Curse," "Counting on Flowers," "The Size of Song," "On a Photo of Sgt. Ciardi a Year Later," and "On Being Much Better Than Most and Yet Not Quite Good Enough."

5. *May Swenson*—8 appearances (9 poems)
      Comment: An observant, engaging poet. One of her best-liked poems is the puzzler "Southbound on the Freeway" with its surprising, almost philosophical twist at the end. Others include "Cat & the Weather,"

"After the Dentist," "Cardinal Ideograms," "The Centaur," and "Analysis of Baseball." Two of her most imaginative books are *Poems to Solve* and *More Poems to Solve*.

Significantly, one other poet—Donald Hall—appears seven times with eight poems. Hall is one of America's most prolific and respected poets. He writes of a seemingly inexhaustible range of subjects that interest him—baseball, chain saws, love, history, farming, death, nature, weddings, photographs of China, and many more. In the words of one admirer, Hall would be the best person he could think of to ask the question, "How should I lead my life?" Among Hall's most popular poems for teaching are "The Man in the Dead Machine" (p. 97), "The Stump," "Valentine," and "Names of Horses."

Ten poets appear six times: Ted Kooser (with 15 poems), Theodore Roethke (with 12), David Wagoner (11), Denise Levertov (8), Nikki Giovanni (8), Edward Field (8), David Ignatow (7), Linda Pastan (7), Peter Meinke (7) and Lucille Clifton (7). Kooser, Pastan, and Clifton are featured later in the chapter.

Roethke is comparatively well known; two of his poems—"My Papa's Waltz" and "Elegy for Jane"—are often anthologized in high school textbooks and taught in the schools. Wagoner, who has particular appeal to older students, often writes about outdoor subjects, as in "Staying Alive" and "Snake Hunt." Levertov is an uncommonly observant poet of everyday life—a garden, a dead squirrel in the driveway, an old man walking dogs in the rain.

Giovanni is an African American poet whose poems are also frequently taught, especially "Kidnap Poem," "Knoxville, Tennessee," and "The World Is Not a Pleasant Place to Be." Field has written that his poetry "speaks for the unloved and unwanted, because of the rejection I felt, growing up, from teachers and other kids. . . ." (Nye and Janeczko, 226). This feeling is clearly expressed in his poem "Nightmare." Ignatow is often a poet of urban settings and situations ("Bowery," "The City") and of our opportunities and failures to communicate, as in his popular "With the Door Open" and "Two Friends." Meinke is among the least known of these ten, but several of his poems have begun to appear in classrooms, such as "Advice to My Son," "The Poet, Trying to Surprise God," "Dear Reader," and "This Is a Poem to My Son Peter."

Four other writers show up five times: Howard Nemerov, one of my favorites—with eleven poems; A. R. Ammons (6 poems), the beat poet Lawrence Ferlinghetti (6), and Robert Hayden (4 poems, including "The

Whipping" and "Those Winter Sundays," an extremely popular poem that appears in four of the fifteen anthologies).[1]

So while these twenty American poets (and their 201 poems) are not sure bets in the classroom, they do offer a useful jumping-off place for teachers looking for promising modern work. And there are many other fine poets who show up fewer times in the count but whose poems often shine with potential: James Wright ("A Blessing," "Mutterings over the Crib of a Deaf Child," "Autumn Begins in Martins Ferry, Ohio," and "Lying in a Hammock on William Duffy's Farm in Pine Island, Minnesota"), Richard Wilbur ("The Writer," "Boy at the Window," and "Piazza di Spagna, Early Morning"), Ronald Koertge ("Modifications" and "Letter to Superman"), James Dickey, Gary Snyder, and Paul Zimmer.

Finally, there are many fine American poets whose names are not among the 250 in the five-volume Gale series—because their stars have ascended more recently, because as members of underrepresented groups their work has been insufficiently promoted, and in at least four instances (Eve Merriam, Robert Francis, Phyllis McGinley, and Donald Justice) for other reasons.

Merriam is missing perhaps because she is considered mostly a children's poet. Wry and playful, she often writes poems about poetry ("How to Eat a Poem," "Some Uses for Poetry," "Inside a Poem") and about language ("Metaphor" and "Onomatopoeia"). Francis and McGinley were omitted, it seems, because they had published much of their poetry prior to World War II—the cutoff for the Gale series. Francis published a great many poems that appeal to young adults because of their accessibility and their subjects—like family, animals, and sports. Three are included later in the text. McGinley wrote mostly in the 1940s, 1950s, and 1960s. Many of her poems, especially "Advice to Fathers," "A Certain Age," "Fourteenth Birthday," and "Portrait of a Girl with a Comic Book," offer perceptive observations of the tumultuous, sensitive lives of adolescent girls.

The absence of Justice from the Gale series is puzzling. A winner of the Pulitzer Prize for poetry, he is generally considered one of America's finest poets, and some of his poems are often anthologized and taught, especially "Crossing Kansas by Train," "Poem to Be Read at 3 A.M.," "Sonnet to My Father," and "Counting the Mad."

Additional volumes in the Gale poetry series and more anthologies published in the future for young adults will surely include more poems by writers whose work has gained particular attention in the last decade or two. Among many more, these might include Jim Hall, Judith Hemschemeyer, David Huddle, Vern Rutsala, Keith Wilson, Ronald Wallace, Michael

McFee, Maurya Simon, Billy Collins, Mary Jo Salter, and Sandra McPherson.

Even more significantly, these books will also extend the long-delayed recent efforts to recognize more poets from a variety of cultural backgrounds, writers like Reuben Jackson, Sonia Sanchez, Sandra Cisneros, Jimmy Santiago Baca, Li-Young Lee, Yusef Komunyakaa, Cathy Song, Quincy Troupe, and Toi Derricotte. The work of these poets will continue to help teachers, schools, and society at large to broaden their vision and their conception of America as a nation of inclusion.

Among all these modern poets, a few seem particularly appropriate for young adults because of the simplicity of their language and forms, the relevance of their subject matter, and the genuineness of their voices. Here are ten who deserve a closer look.

HIGHLIGHT 4.1

American Poet Laureates

Many of us may associate the term "poet laureate" with the comparative ancients: surely Longfellow and Whittier were among our first. Actually, the office of poet laureate was created by Congress in 1985. The first was Robert Penn Warren, who served a one-year term in 1986–87. Since then, in order, we've had Richard Wilbur, Howard Nemerov, Mark Strand, Joseph Brodsky, Mona Van Duyn, Rita Dove, Robert Hass, and Robert Pinsky. Poet laureates don't really have to do much—work with the Library of Congress as poetry consultant, present a public poetry reading and lecture—but they serve as important symbols and spokespersons for the genre. Many of them (Brodsky and Pinsky come especially to mind) have worked long and hard as advocates.

Several states also have poet laureates. For a click-on map that identifies them, check this Internet address: http://www.sunnyday.com/poetlaureate/map.html

Sandra Cisneros

Sandra Cisneros writes of the barrio in both poetry and fiction. A book of her short stories, *Woman Hollering Creek and Other Stories*, won the Lannan Foundation 1991 Literary Award for Fiction and PEN Center West Award for best fiction of 1991; and her poetic coming-of-age novel, *The House on Mango Street,* won the American Book Award from the Before

Columbus Foundation. Much of her poetry has been collected in *My Wicked Wicked Ways* (Turtle Bay Books, 1992). A native of Chicago, Cisneros now lives in San Antonio.

Cisneros often writes of family, of disappointment, anger, and regret. Her style is spare and passionate with the emotion carried by precise nouns and vigorous verbs. The women who speak in her autobiographical poems are strong, independent, and defiant. They convey a sauciness, a sense of rebellion that girls especially will like.

X. J. Kennedy

X. J. Kennedy is one of those few poets who are just as comfortable writing for young people as they are for adults. Among his poems for the latter which are also appropriate for older adolescents are the poignant "On a Child Who Lived One Minute" and the following:

> **At the Last Rites for Two Hotrodders**
>
> Sheeted in steel, embedded face to face,
> They idle now in feelingless embrace,
> The only ones at last who had the nerve
> To meet head-on, not chicken out and swerve.
>
> Inseparable, in one closed car they roll
> Down the stoned aisle and on out to a hole,
> Wheeled by the losers: six of fledgling beard,
> Black-jacketed and glum, who also steered
> Toward absolute success with total pride,
> But, inches from it, felt, and turned aside.

Kennedy has written several volumes of light verse for mostly young adolescents, including *Brats*, *Fresh Brats*, and *One Winter Night in August*. The last title also includes several poems for special calendar occasions, like "Martin Luther King Day." More often than not, Kennedy uses rhyme and traditional patterns. His interest in poetry for young people led him and his wife Dorothy to write one of the most useful books for introducing the topic—*Knock at a Star: A Child's Introduction to Poetry*. Kennedy is a native of New Jersey and has spent most of his recent years in Massachusetts. Useful representative editions of his poetry are *Cross Ties: Selected Poems* and *Dark Horses: New Poems*.

Rita Dove

Rita Dove is a poet who speaks to African Americans and everyone else who is interested in enslavement as a human evil and in the universal subjects of love, courage, hope, and despair. A native of Ohio, she is the author of a novel, *Through the Ivory Gate*, a collection of short stories, and six volumes of poetry. Among the latter, *Thomas and Beulah* is perhaps the most acclaimed, having received the Pulitzer Prize in 1987, and *Selective Poems* (1993) is the most representative. Dove was the youngest person and the first African American to be named, in 1993, Poet Laureate of the United States.

In *The Yellow House on the Corner, Thomas and Beulah,* and other books, Dove is especially concerned with the heritage of slavery in America, with its condition and its long and lingering shadow. Many of her poems are combinations of what she calls the historical and the lyrical, like the prose poem "Kentucky 1833." Dove's Thomas and Beulah poems trace the lives of her grandparents through the twentieth century as they migrate north from the rural South, meet and marry in Akron, raise four daughters, endure the Depression and war, and consistently prevail. The poems are meant to be read in sequence.

Kirkland C. Jones has written that "[Rita Dove] is not the stereotypical woman writer, nor is she simply the traditional African-American author. She appreciates the aesthetics of race and gender but does not feel the need to raise the color problem for mere color's sake" (1992, 51). Many of her poems concern the universal human condition, like this one:

Adolescence—I

In water-heavy nights behind grandmother's porch
We knelt in the tickling grasses and whispered:
Linda's face hung before us, pale as a pecan,
And it grew wise as she said:
  "A boy's lips are soft,
    As soft as baby's skin."
The air closed over her words.
A firefly whirred near my ear, and in the distance
I could hear streetlamps ping
Into miniature suns
Against a feathery sky.

Ted Kooser

Ted Kooser lives and writes in Nebraska and has been called a regional poet, but his poetry is not provincial. His work is highly personal and reflective, observing and commenting on the speaker's (and surely the poet's) experience with the events of ordinary life. The language is simple and direct, the poems easy to read. In many of them, there is dry and subtle humor; in all of them, a clear lack of pretension.

Selecting a Reader

First, I would have her be beautiful,
and walking carefully up on my poetry
at the loneliest moment of an afternoon,
her hair still damp at the neck
from washing it. She should be wearing
a raincoat, an old one, dirty
from not having money enough for the cleaners.
She will take out her glasses, and there
in the bookstore, she will thumb
over my poems, then put the book back
up on its shelf. She will say to herself,
"For that kind of money, I can get
my raincoat cleaned." And she will.

In the words of the poet and critic Dana Gioia, Kooser's work "is on a decidedly human scale. He offers no blinding flashes of inspiration, no mystic moments of transcendence. He creates no private mythologies of fantasy worlds. Instead he provides small but genuine insights into the world of everyday experience" (1992, 94). His "Epitaph for a Sky Diver" (p. 38) is one example of his unique perception, the following poem another:

Flying at Night

Above us, stars. Beneath us, constellations.
Five billion miles away, a galaxy dies
like a snowflake falling on water. Below us,
some farmer, feeling the chill of that distant death,
snaps on his yard light, drawing his sheds and barn
back into the little system of his care.
All night, the cities, like shimmering novas,
tug with bright streets at lonely lights like his.

Although his poems have appeared in several anthologies, including many aimed at adults (he is featured, for example, in *The Pittsburgh Book of Contemporary American Poetry*), Kooser remains comparatively unknown. Many of his most appropriate poems for the classroom can be found in *Sure Signs: New and Selected Poems* and *Weather Central*.

Paul Zimmer

In Paul Zimmer's poetry, his own persona is often the central, compelling force: "Zimmer in Grade School," "How Zimmer Lost Religion," "What Zimmer Would Be," "Zimmer and His Turtle Sink the House," "Zimmer Imagines Heaven," and "Zimmer's Head Thudding against the Blackboard," perhaps his best-known poem, which we read in the previous chapter (p. 42). In these and others, the speaker, in the words of Thomas Goldstein, "emerges as a confused, uncoordinated misser of trains, a dangerous hunter, an incompetent mechanic, and an indefatigable schlemeil" (1980, 421). The poems are autobiographical, highly personal, self-conscious, and often wickedly funny. Some poke fun at authority or pretention; others pay homage to life's small pleasures and wonders.

Zimmer is a native of Canton, Ohio. By trade, he has managed university presses and bookstores at UCLA, the University of Pittsburgh, the University of Georgia, and the University of Iowa. Zimmer is the recipient of three Pushcart Prizes and two National Endowment for the Arts Poetry Fellowships. His work is featured in *The Pittsburgh Book of Contemporary American Poetry* and in his own collections, which include *The Zimmer Poems, The Republic of Many Voices, Family Reunion: Selected and New Poems* and *Crossing to Sunlight: Selected Poems, 1965–1995.* Besides the titles mentioned above, many students will like "Yellow Sonnet," "How Birds Should Die," and "A Final Affection."

Naomi Shihab Nye

Hoping to broaden the appeal of poetry among young adults, Naomi Shihab Nye has recently edited two volumes, *This Same Sky: A Collection of Poems from Around the World* and *The Space between Our Footsteps: Poems and Paintings of the Middle East.* She has co-edited two others, the second edition of *Reflections on a Gift of Watermelon Pickle* and *I Feel a Little Jumpy around You.* Still, she is primarily a poet. Her work is characterized by her interest in the simplicity and beauty of everyday life, the many places where she has lived, the family of humankind, and her own dual cultural background (Palestinian American). Her poems are often quiet, personal, observant, and introspective, like "Grandfather's Heaven" and the following:

Daily

These shriveled seeds we plant,
corn kernel, dried bean,
poke into loosened soil,
cover over with measured fingertips

These T-shirts we fold into
perfect white squares

These tortillas we slice and fry to crisp strips
This rich egg scrambled in a gray clay bowl

This bed whose covers I straighten
smoothing edges till blue quilt fits brown blanket
and nothing hangs out

This envelope I address
so the name balances like a cloud
in the center of the sky

This page I type and retype
This table I dust till the scarred wood shines
This bundle of clothes I wash and hang and wash again
like flags we share, a country so close
no one needs to name it

The days are nouns: touch them
The hands are churches that worship the world

In the book *The Place My Words Are Looking For*, Nye has written, "For me poetry has always been a way of paying attention to the world. We hear so many voices every day, swirling around us, and a poem makes us slow down and listen carefully to a few things we have really heard, deep inside" (Janeczko 1990, 7). Many of Nye's poems will fit the classroom nicely, especially "Famous," "The Trashpickers, Madison Street," "The Passport Photo," and "Making a Fist." Her books of poetry include *Different Ways to Pray* and *Hugging the Jukebox*.

HIGHLIGHT 4.2

Poets from Other Countries

Of the many contemporary American poets who offer so much to the high school classroom, a large number represent our country's great cultural diversity, like Cisneros, Dove, and Nye. On a much larger scale, other countries around the world provide an even wider choice of poets, among them the well-known Nobelists Wislawa Szymborska (Poland), Seamus Heaney (Ireland), Derek Walcott (St. Lucia), Octavio Paz (Mexico), and Pablo Neruda (Chile).

Numerous anthologies of the work of these poets and many others are readily available. Three of the best are *Ain't I a Woman! A Book of Women's Poetry from around the World* by Illona Linthwaite, *99 Poems in Translation: An Anthology* by Harold Pinter et al., and *This Same Sky: A Collection of Poems from around the World* by Naomi Shihab Nye.

Linda Pastan

Linda Pastan has a gift for expressing the daily events and details of life in language that is spare and clear, unpretentious, and understated. A native of New York and longtime resident of Maryland, Pastan has published eight volumes of poetry, among them *Aspects of Love, The Five Stages of Grief, An Early Afterlife,* and *Carnival Evening: New & Selected Poems, 1968–1998.* One of Pastan's most notable qualities is her use of comparisons to convey an unusually perceptive view of experience, as in "Grammar Lesson" and the following poem:

To the Field Goal Kicker in a Slump

It must be something
like writer's block,
when nothing will go
between the margins,
when language won't soar
high enough,
when you wake
in the morning and know
you've chosen
the wrong game.

Often her subjects and her mood are somber. She writes of the complexities of marriage and family, of aging and loss, and especially mortality, as in "Cousins," "1932–," and "Writing while My Father Dies." Many of Pastan's poems will be admired by adolescent girls especially:

Lullabye for 17

You are so young
you heal as you weep,
and your tears
instead of scalding
your face like mine
absolve
simply as rain.

I tried to teach you
what I knew: how men
in their sudden beauty
are more dangerous,
how love refracting light
can burn the hand, how memory
is a scorpion

and stings with its tail.
You knew my catechism
but never believed. Now
you look upon pain
as a discovery all your own,
marveling at the way it invades
the bloodstream, ambushes sleep.

Still you forgive
so easily. I'd like
to take your young man
by his curls and tear
them out,
who like a dark planet circles
your bright universe

still furnished with curtains
you embroidered yourself,
an underbrush
of books and scarves,
a door at which
you'll soon be poised
to leave.

Gary Soto

Gary Soto is a native of Fresno, California. His first book of poems, *The Elements of San Joaquin*, won the 1976 United States Award of the International Poetry Forum. Since then he has published other volumes of poetry for adults (*The Tale of Sunlight, Black Hair, Who Will Know Us?, Home Course in Religion*) as well as poems in prestigious magazines like *Nation, Ontario Review, Harper's*, and *Poetry*. Soto also writes for young readers, both fiction (*Baseball in April and Other Stories* and *Jesse*) and poetry (*Neighborhood Odes*). Soto's poems for adults often portray the regrets of lost childhood and the indelible effects of the past upon the present. Some depict the dehumanized lives of factory workers and the dusty, deprived world of poor Chicano farm laborers in the great central valley of California where he grew up.

Field Poem

When the foreman whistled
My brother and I
Shouldered our hoes,
Leaving the field.
We returned to the bus
Speaking
In broken English, in broken Spanish
The restaurant food,
The tickets to a dance
We wouldn't buy with our pay.

From the smashed bus window,
I saw the leaves of cotton plants
Like small hands waving good-bye.

Soto's poems are often appropriate for young adults. In Part One of *Black Hair*, poems like "Cruel Boys" and "Being Human" would work well with high school students as would the poem "Oranges," in which the speaker, a boy of twelve, expresses the quiet joy of walking down the street with a girl for the first time:

> . . . Outside,
> A few cars hissing past,
> Fog hanging like old
> Coats between the trees.
> I took my girl's hand
> In mine for two blocks,
> Then released it to let
> Her unwrap the chocolate.
> I peeled my orange
> That was so bright against
> The gray of December
> That, from some distance,
> Someone might have thought
> I was making a fire in my hands.

Many of Soto's poems are "skeletonic," long and narrow on the page. They portray familiar subjects in simple words and vivid imagery. The poems are often reminiscent and joyful, celebrating the pleasures of childhood—tortillas, fireworks, a water sprinkler, a day in the country, a snow cone truck, a favorite cat.

Lucille Clifton

Lucille Clifton is a poet who expresses great pride in being black and in being a woman. She often celebrates African American men and women in her poetry, presenting them as unheralded monuments to courage and endurance. Like Pastan, Clifton was born in New York but now lives in Maryland, where she has served as poet laureate. Her collections include *Good Times: Poems*; *Good News about the Earth*; *An Ordinary Woman*; *The Book of Light*; *Quilting: Poems, 1987–1990*; and *The Terrible Stories*. She has also written an autobiography, *Generations: A Memoir*.

> **Reply**
>
> *[from a letter written to Dr. W. E. B. Dubois by Alvin Borgquest of Clark University in Massachusetts and dated April 3, 1905:*
>
> *"We are pursuing an investigation here on the subject of crying as an expression of the emotions, and should like very much to learn about its peculiarities among the colored people. We have been referred to you as a person competent to give us information*

on the subject. We desire especially to know about the following
salient aspects: 1. Whether the Negro shed tears. . . ."]

reply

he do
she do
they live
they love
they try
they tire
they flee
they fight
they bleed
they break
they moan
they mourn
they weep
they die
they do
they do
they do

David Bottoms

A sample of titles of poems by David Bottoms speaks volumes: "The Drunk
Hunter," "A Trucker Breaks Down," "Faith Healer Come to Rabun County,"
"Watching Gators at Ray Boone's Reptile Farm," and "Cockfight in a
Loxahatchkee Grove." Bottoms is a realist who writes vividly of darkness
and death in the world of stock-car races and county fairs, junkyards,
cemeteries, baptismal rites in Southern rivers, and country music in VFW
dance halls. A native of Georgia, he won the Walt Whitman Award for
young unpublished poets in 1979, a competition for which Robert Penn
Warren was the judge. Perhaps his most useful collection for teachers is
Armored Hearts: Selected and New Poems. The following is the title poem
for a collection published by Morrow in 1980.

Shooting Rats at the Bibb County Dump

Loaded on beer and whiskey, we ride
to the dump in carloads
to turn our headlights across the wasted field,
freeze the startled eyes of rats against mounds of rubbish.

Shot in the head, they jump only once, lie still
like dead beer cans.
Shot in the gut or rump, they writhe and try to burrow
into garbage, hide in old truck tires,
rusty oil drums, cardboard boxes scattered across the mounds,

or else drag themselves on forelegs across our beams of light
toward the darkness at the edge of the dump.

It's the light they believe kills.
We drink and load again, let them crawl
for all they're worth into the darkness we're headed for.

In summary, these ten poets and the many other voices of contemporary poetry provide teachers with a tremendous resource. Besides
appearing in the small magazines and various anthologies mentioned in
Chapter 3, their poems are also available in chapbooks and other
individual collections, books like Kooser's *Weather Central* and Nye's
Hugging the Jukebox. Much of their work is appealing and even
compelling to young adults, who see it as funny and sad, poignant and
tough, thoughtful, provocative, engaging, sometimes almost incandescent.
As in Linda Pastan's metaphor in the excerpt that opens this chapter, these
are poems and poets to be picked like flowers and used to bring color,
pattern, and light into a classroom.

HIGHLIGHT 4.3

Getting in Touch with Poets

Often students and teachers will become so enamored with a poet they'll
want to get in touch. Addresses are easy to find; here are two sources—the
first a book available in many libraries; the second, a Web site:

Who's Who in Writers, Editors, and Poets: United States and Canada.
     Edited by Curt Johnson. December Press. Check the most recent
     edition.

A Directory of American Poets and Fiction Writers. A directory search
     <http://www.pw.org/directry.htm> offered by *Poets & Writers
     Magazine.*

Suggestion: If you write a poet, send him or her a stamped, self-addressed
     envelope. This says, in effect, I value your response so much I'm
     going to make it as easy as possible for you to reply.

Note

  1. The comparative absence of poets of color from this list (sixteen of the
nineteen are white, all but three of them male) may reflect a bias in the selections
made by early compilers. More recent collections, such as the second edition of
Reflections on a Gift of Watermelon Pickle, seem to be redressing this wrong.

III Approaches and Methods

5 Approaching Poetry

magine everything in place—the poems in hand, most of them anyway, chosen by a teacher with an eye for what pleases her and what she hopes will please her students. She likes the poems—*really* likes some of them —but she is still on the lookout. A new collection sits waiting on her desk.

Her collection includes a sonnet by Shakespeare, a poem by Donne, three by Emily Dickinson, one each by Edna St. Vincent Millay and Langston Hughes. For the most part, though, the poems are contemporary, by poets known and unknown who speak to adults and adolescents in a clear, natural, authoritative voice. In all, she has gathered twenty or thirty poems she would like to teach. Still, questions remain.

When? And how? And for the moment, where?

The Ideal Poetry Classroom

The "where" refers of course to the setting. Obviously no classroom can be organized totally around the teaching of poetry, but it might be fun to think of how to design the room if it were. What would be the components of such a setting?

Besides movable desks, what I'd really want is a *poetry center or station* perhaps in a corner of the classroom or against a back wall on a table. Either way, I'd want the center near a bulletin board.

In the ideal center, I'd try to have (roughly in descending order of preference) the following:

- folders of hundreds of photocopied poems (Note: This is really all you need; make sure you've got permission to photocopy)
- collections galore, mostly single copies of the kinds of books mentioned in Chapter 3
- a tape player/recorder and blank tapes
- miscellaneous items for creating poetry and poetry books: pens, glue, colored paper, scissors, etc.
- a few standard dictionaries
- a rhyming dictionary
- a variety of magazines that publish poetry written by young adults, e.g., *Merlyn's Pen*
- copies of one or two "little magazines," like *Poetry* or *Shenandoah*
- a computer with word processing, Internet access, and CD-ROM (we're "blue sky" thinking here)

- a variety of regular magazines (*Time, Seventeen, Sports Illustrated, The New Yorker*, etc.)

The bulletin board would be an obvious site for

- poems students like (maybe a Poem of the Week)
- poems written by students
- news articles about poems and poetry (e.g., the announcement of the newest U.S. poet laureate, a calendar notice on a local poetry slam, the obituary of a famous poet, etc.)
- announcements of contests and competitions
- pictures of poets

HIGHLIGHT 5.1

Teaching Poetry on a Shoestring

Given the direst of economic circumstances, is it possible to teach poetry well on a limited budget? Yes, if a teacher is creative and resourceful. Here are some ways:

- Have the English department make a one-time purchase of a single class set of a modern poetry anthology to be used by multiple teachers in multiple classes year after year. At current prices, thirty copies of, say, the paperback version of *I Feel a Little Jumpy around You* would run about $270, or $27 a year over a decade's use.

- Limit the number of poems you teach to the entire class. If you fully discuss, say, five poems in a unit, you could probably squeeze all of them onto one or two transparencies for use with an overhead projector for a very small cost—in today's costs, under a dollar. Try to add five *new* poems each year to your collection.

- Work to make the school library an essential player in the school's poetry program. Ask the media specialist to order four or five new collections every year. When poetry units are taught, the library can send portable bookshelves of anthologies around to the teachers' classrooms.

The center would become an integral part of any poetry instruction. In the more conventional poetry classroom (with the Teacher as Orchestrator), the center would serve as library, listening station, news and information kiosk, and occasional refuge. In a more student-directed unit on poetry (with a more peripheral Teacher as Facilitator), the center would be the metaphorical (if not geographical) hub around which everything revolved. It would truly be a "center" from which materials and instructions were procured and used in a variety of ways.

The When and How—A Likely Starting Place

However a teacher sees herself—as tending toward Orchestrator or Facilitator (or maybe even Agitator)—the question of exactly what to do is often an anxious consideration. Clearly there are many things to do in a classroom with poetry—find it, share it, read it, write it, scan it, hear it, shape it, group it, perform it, dissect it, collage it (even, I suppose, deconstruct it). What poetry most needs, however, what it most deserves, is talking about. In a class getting started with poetry, the starting place is almost always a poem and the starting activity, talk. I would begin with a poem I really liked—"The Two-Headed Calf" by Laura Gilpin would be fine—and we would talk. Here is a possible classroom conversation with the teacher as a maestro of sorts.

Scenario One: Teacher as Orchestrator

Ms. Cato: I'm going to give you a word you've all heard and I want you to tell me your gut-level reactions to it. Free association, OK? The word is *freak.*

As teachers know, brainstorming is a kind of Preliminary Activity designed to prepare the students to read a poem with understanding. An activity like this can be extremely helpful and often even fun.

Jake: Weirdo.
Wendy: Skater.
Karl: Nose ring . . . baggy pants . . . Marilyn Manson.
Abitha: Someone gross . . . deformed.
Jeanie: An addict.
James: What d'ya mean "addict"?

Jeanie: You know, like a drug addict . . . a speed freak.

Tom: A freak of nature, like a guy with a club foot.

Ms. Cato: So it's an unpleasant word?

Wendy: Yeah, sorta. Like, people who try to be different, wear dark lipstick. Guys wiggin' out.

Tom: The Lion-faced Man.

Alex: Yeah. Ever see the movie *The Elephant Man?* He was a real freak.

Ms. Cato: So how would you define the word?

Jake: A weirdo.

Ms. Cato: Please, let's be a little more precise.

Wendy: A freak is a person who has to be different. Wants to be different, unique.

Tom: Or a person with a . . . deformity of some kind, a physical deformity.

Ms. Cato: Always a person?

Sybil: No. Could be an animal. I saw a picture of a five-legged sheep one time in the paper.

Ms. Cato: Do you remember how you felt when you saw the picture?

Sybil: Mostly curious, I guess . . . maybe a little disgusted. I don't know.

Ms. Cato: Why do you think we're sometimes disgusted by physical freaks?

Jeanie: They make us squirm.

Ms. Cato: I know, but why?

Jeanie: I guess because they're so . . . different.

Mason: We're not used to them.

Ms. Cato: All right. Would you agree that we're both intrigued and offended by them?

Students: [*A blend of nods, "sort ofs," and grunts*]

Ms. Cato: OK, let's look at a poem now about a freak, a physical freak.

———

Ms. Cato hands out copies of the poem "The Two-Headed Calf" (or shows it on a screen) and asks the class to read it. Then she reads the poem aloud. This repetition gives the students two looks (well, a look and a listen), which is important. We want comfort and familiarity. A longer, more involved poem might deserve three takes.

———

The Two-Headed Calf

Laura Gilpin

Tomorrow when the farm boys find this
freak of nature, they will wrap his body
in newspaper and carry him to the museum.

But tonight he is alive and in the north
field with his mother. It is a perfect
summer evening: the moon rising over
the orchard, the wind in the grass. And
as he stares into the sky, there are
twice as many stars as usual.

Mark: Yuck.

Ms. Cato: Obviously this is a poem about an animal, like the one Sybil mentioned. The poem's so short not much happens. What does happen?

Kim: Well, they find it and wrap it in paper and take it to a museum.

Tom: Yeah, sounds like it's dead.

Ms. Cato: And why do you think they take it to the museum?

Jeanie: I guess because it's a curiosity.

Abitha: But they wouldn't make a display of it, would they? That's gross.

Ms. Cato: Well, I don't know. I guess they could, but maybe they'd just put it in storage, maybe, you know, in formaldehyde or something. Anyway, in the first stanza, is it dead? What seems to suggest that it is?

Jeanie: Well, the word "body" . . .

Paul: I think they killed it.

Ms. Cato: What makes you think they killed it, Paul?

Paul: They didn't like it.

Alex: Most people don't like freaks.

Jeanie: Or maybe they thought it wouldn't live anyway, or maybe it just died that next morning.

Ms. Cato: Is there anything in the poem, in the first stanza, that indicates they did kill it for sure?

Jeanie: Not really.

The question is a brief foray in the direction of close reading, trying to get students to base their opinions on what the poem says. It's a way of reading poetry that has its origins in the New Criticism of the 1930s and '40s, but it still has value.

———————

Ms. Cato: So all we really know is that the farm boys found the body—or will find it—and wrap it in newspaper and take it to the museum. And again, why might they do this?

Kim: I guess they think the museum might be interested in it.

Ms. Cato: What do you think the farm boys themselves thought of it?

Jeanie: Well, they must have thought it was . . . interesting.

Susan: Maybe important?

Andrea: Hey, they're boys. They're into this kind of thing, maybe not freaks, but—

Sybil: Well, not just boys!

Paul: Oh, Lord. Here we go.

Sybil: I just think there's plenty of girls who'd've lugged that thing over to the museum as quick as any boy would.

Jeanie: I think it's interesting that we're all referring to it as "it," but the poet refers to it as "he."

Ms. Cato: Ah, that *is* interesting. What do you think that suggests?

Jeanie: That we see it as a thing.

———————

In discussions like this, students often pick up on things that we as teachers—overlook (or sometimes pretend to overlook).

———————

Ms. Cato: Seems that way, doesn't it? But would you agree that the farm boys are at least not offended by the calf?

Students: [Nodding]

Ms. Cato: OK. Now the second stanza is different. How? What does it do for us?

Jeanie: It takes us back . . . like a little flashback . . . to the night before.

Karen: The present—"tonight, he is alive. . . ."

Ms. Cato: Why, do you think?

[Silence at first]

James: 'Cause that's where the action is.

Ms. Cato: Meaning?

James: That's where it's at. He's *aliiive.*

Tom: I agree. I think he—or she, the poet—wants us to see him alive.

Ms. Cato: Why?

Karen: Because she wants to show that he's, I don't know, a living thing even if he is a freak of nature. He's alive.

Ms. Cato: What if the poem ended with the first sentence in the second stanza?

————————

In this discussion, is Ms. Cato winging it? Probably not. Most of her questions have been carefully considered. This is not to say, of course, that spontaneous questions won't occur to her, but in this particular role as an orchestrator, the teacher has planned many, perhaps most, of the questions ahead of time.

————————

Jeanie: It wouldn't be enough.

Ms. Cato: Why?

Jeanie: Because the next couple of lines talks about how nice it is with the moon and the orchard. The wind in the grass.

Ms. Cato: And why is that important?

Sallie: So the calf . . . can appreciate it.

Paul: Oh, come on! The calf can't appreciate anything. It's a calf, for crying out loud. Even if it does have two freaking heads.

Ms. Cato: OK. Nice pun, Paul, even if it was accidental. So if the calf can't appreciate it—and some might argue that it can't—what's Sallie getting at here?

Kim: [*Silence at first*] More that *we* appreciate it.

Ms. Cato: Say a little more about that. Appreciate the calf?

Kim: No. The evening, the—

Sallie: I think it means the calf too.

Kim: I guess that even though the calf is . . . a freak of nature, it can . . . or we can still . . . oh, I don't know.

Jeanie: We can still appreciate it as a living creature even though it's strange, grotesque.

Ms. Cato: And is there anything to the idea of the calf appreciating, despite Paul's objection?

Kim: Well, it *is* a newborn and *it* doesn't know it has two heads.

Susan: Yeah, you know, it's like a puppy. It can play and—what's the word?—frolic.

Paul: Yeah, but that business of it appreciating the moon and stuff. I still don't buy that.

Ms. Cato: So we agree that the calf might in a sense appreciate, I guess you could say, the newness of being alive—at least? Is that the important thing here?

Kim: No. I mean I think it's important, but not as important as what *we* appreciate. Look. It's a "perfect summer evening." But it isn't perfect. In a way it's a freakish summer evening, but it's still beautiful. That's what I like about this poem.

Mark: Yuck.

Jeanie: Yeah, it is kinda neat. The idea that even a freakish event like this can . . .I'm not sure how to say it.

Ms. Cato: Well, I think we've said it. Kim said it just then.

Tom: And really, who's to say what's a freak. To some people, maybe the moon shining in the orchard is freakish. You know, weird, ghoulish. Like Halloween.

Ms. Cato: Good point. OK, what do you make of the last couple of lines: "And/ as he stares into the sky, there are/ twice as many stars as usual"?

Ron: Well, obviously it means he's got two heads so he sees twice as many stars.

Sybil: Pleasssse, Ron.

Ron: Well, why not?

Andrea: Yeah!

Sybil: It doesn't say "he sees twice as many stars." It says "there are."

Again, advocates of close reading would applaud this distinction.

Andrea: So?

Sybil: So there's a big difference.

Ron: Like what, Miss Interpre-ta-tor?

Sybil: Like it means he doesn't see them. I mean he doesn't see them double. Help me, somebody.

Ms. Cato: Seems to me you don't need any help.

Kim: I think it means the sky is twice as bright.

Jeanie: Twice as beautiful.

Tom: Yeah.

Ms. Cato: Why would the poet want to say that? What's beautiful about it?

Karen: Just the idea maybe that this isn't a freak but something special. Maybe a sign.

Ron: Oh, Jeez.

Karen: No, really. Not a sign . . . a symbol. Only don't ask me a symbol of what.

Ms. Cato: Any more ideas about the last two lines?

———————

Notice how over the last minute or so of the discussion, the teacher almost disappears—or at least recedes. When students take over a discussion and begin talking to each other as much as to the teacher, there is real progress. As long as it's productive.

———————

Jeanie: Well, I like the idea that the calf might be special. Maybe in God's eyes it is special.

Kim: Oh, I just thought of something. Remember that *Life* magazine article a couple of years ago about those twin girls that were born with two trunks and heads but one body. I remember thinking how awful and I almost hated to look at them, but when I read the article I learned more about them . . . and then the more I looked at them and learned about them, the more . . . natural they seemed. And then I thought, they're *beautiful.* It was weird.

Karen: Oh, I remember that. It *was* weird, but yeah, I know what you mean.

Tom: I like "special" too, but I really think the important thing, like Susan said, is not what the calf sees, but what we see. The poet wants us to see the beauty of the night and the beauty of the calf too. Even though at first we see it as ugly. Again, like those twins.

Ms. Cato: We wondered earlier if the poet could have ended the poem at line 5. What about line 7? Could she have ended it there?

Jared: I don't think so.

Jeanie. No, it needs that last sentence, even though on first reading it almost seems silly.

Mark: I still think it's a gross poem.

Kim: You just miss the point.

Karen: He wants to miss the point.

Jeanie: I like the way the poet begins in the future, sort of, but it's almost like an afterthought. I guess it's a *before* thought. Anyway, she just mentions "tomorrow" offhand and then gets us back to what's important—"But tonight he is alive. . . ." I just think that's kinda neat.

Ms. Cato: Well, it's like any poem. Some of us like a poem, some of us don't. I really like this one because, as we've seen, it makes us think—or *re*think. One more question: How do you think the poet—or maybe more accurately, the speaker—feels about the calf?

James: He likes it.

Kim: She loves it.

Ms. Cato: Is this a sad poem?

Sybil: Yes.

Tom: In a way.

Karen: No. Not the way we've looked at it.

Kim: I think it's a hopeful poem.

Mark: I think it's a yucky poem.

So, this is one approach to poetry—Teacher as Orchestrator, preparing and executing the talking about a poem. In this discussion of "The Two-Headed Calf," Ms. Cato plans and nudges and responds, but hardly dominates. Of the 103 exchanges, almost three-fourths are by students. The teacher sets the agenda by choosing the poem and asking the questions, but she does not urge the discussion in any particular direction and she does not explicate. Mostly she asks questions—over twenty-five of them. Only twice does she offer an interpretation, and even then the remark reinforces a conclusion already reached by the class. The emphasis is clearly on student response, student interpretation.

In recent years, another approach to the teaching of poetry (really, to teaching in general) has seen increasing numbers of teachers adjusting their role in the classroom by removing themselves from the spotlight and giving students greater voice and choice in what they read and how they respond. In some cases, the best response is no response at all. We need to listen to what the poet Galway Kinnell says about the individual's right to remain silent: "the thing about poetry is that if you're moved by a poem you might not wish to say anything at all. You might wish to live with that poem in silence for a while" (Packard 1987, 72). As teachers, we need to keep this in mind. We also need to give students more freedom in the way they talk about poetry. In this kind of poetry class, Teacher as Facilitator suggests a different kind of scenario:

Scenario Two: Teacher as Facilitator

Mr. Jackson: OK, class. Remember now, for two days we've been spending time in here looking for poems on the theme you selected, poems about cars and driving and the like, and I asked you to be ready today to meet in groups. So we're going to do that. By now each of you should have one poem you're ready to present, OK? You seemed ready at the end of class yesterday, anyway. Anybody have any questions?

This day of reckoning was identified three days earlier when the class chose the theme, one of five offered by Mr. Jackson as possibilities (the others were people with disabilities, man versus nature, the elderly, and war). On that day, Mr. Jackson asked each student to find one poem about the topic that he or she liked and to prepare to have a group of four or five students talk about the poem. Thus, besides liking the poem, the student had to make sure the poem was to some degree "discussable," and had to write five questions about it designed to generate response. On the previous two days of class, Mr. Jackson had provided a copy of Drive, They Said: Poems about Americans and Their Cars, *a collection or two of poems by Stephen Dunn (who occasionally writes about cars), several general collections, and folders of dozens of other poems about the topic. He had also modeled the leading of a small-group discussion of a poem.*

Sherry: Do we have to write down the answers we get?
Mr. Jackson: No, but remember you're going to vote for the one poem of the five the group likes best and present it to the class as a whole. And that one we will want to pay more attention to. More on that when we meet back together as a class . . . Now, a couple of other things. Remember what

we said about "wait time." Just because no one jumps in with an answer doesn't mean they won't come up with one if you give them a few moments.

Group One (first poem). Just before the groups begin, the teacher gives one other instruction: "I asked you to come prepared today with five questions, but I want you to spend a moment right now choosing what you think are your three best ones. And just ask those."

Trevor: OK, the poem I chose is "The Sacred" by Stephen Dunn (see p. 30) *[He distributes copies of the poem to each person in the group and has students read it silently. Then he reads the poem aloud once.]* The reason I like this poem is because I think it captures the way I feel about cars. Like when I got my pickup last year, even though, you know, it wasn't new, it was still real special. I could get in it and pick up Karla and drive out to the quarry and we'd sit there and talk and listen to Rock 90. . . . I like the way the poem talks about "music filling it" and about "one other person who understood." I just think it's a cool poem. . . . OK, my first question is "Why do you think the students fidgeted when the teacher asked about sacred places?"

Alicia: [After a few seconds of silence] Maybe they thought it was too personal.

James: Or maybe some people don't have a "sacred place." I don't know, if you asked me that, I'm not sure what I'd say. Maybe my room.

Trevor: Yeah, I know. *Sacred*'s pretty heavy.

Carla: Some people might say "church," but, yeah, it is pretty personal.

Trevor: Do you think a teacher shouldn't ask a question like that?

Carla: No, I'm not saying that, but . . . I guess it depends on the situation. Maybe if the class had been talking about a story where a guy, like James said, considered his room sacred, you know, private, then the question might be obvious. I just think it's not easy for everyone to say.

Si: Well, she does sort of make it optional—"asked if anyone had a sacred place." Doesn't sound like she's forcing them to talk.

Trevor: Anybody else? . . . I'm kinda like you guys. I thought maybe some kids wouldn't want to talk about places they feel deeply about . . . OK, my second question is about the third stanza when everybody started talking about their rooms and hiding places. I guess we were just talking about this, but can you think of other places that guys might mention . . . besides their rooms or church?

Si: For some people it might be somewhere outdoors. I went to a wedding one time up in this place in the mountains that's like an outdoor theater. I could see a place like that being sacred to somebody.

Carla: Yeah, you're talking about Pretty Place, aren't you? Up at Caesar's Head?

Si: Yeah, that's it.

Carla: Or maybe even a bigger place. Like Cades Cove up in the Smokies. Have you guys ever been there? It is so beautiful.

An obvious risk with student-run discussions like this is tangents. Intentionally or otherwise, a group may stray off the topic. Here it hasn't happened—yet—but the teacher-facilitator has to circulate and maintain periscopic alertness to make sure it doesn't. Another thing: productive group work like this doesn't just happen. Most classes have to be taught to use the approach effectively.

Trevor: Alicia?

Alicia: What if someone said a place in their imagination?

James: Like what?

Alicia: Oh, I don't know. I guess I could see someone saying maybe that their special place is just the few moments before they drop off to sleep when everything is quiet and peaceful.

Carla: Yeah, I don't know why it *has* to be real.

Trevor: [*After waiting a moment*] OK, my third question—I guess my last question—is what do you think the poet means by the last two stanzas? Especially about "how far away a car could take him from the need to speak or to answer"?

James: Well, I don't have my own car yet, but I guess he's saying a car can take you so far away you don't have to answer to anybody.

Si: Yeah, a car can separate you from your . . . well, from almost anything. Your parents. Your job.

Carla: I know, but in a false sense, don't you think? It's temporary.

Si: Not necessarily. Remember last year when that kid from over in Gaffney just took off one night and drove all the way to, where was it? Colorado?

Carla: Yeah, but even then they caught up with him and brought him back.

Trevor: And besides, that wasn't his car. It was his dad's.

James: But still a car can get you . . . like, removed. Outta here.

Alicia: To me, it means psychologically removed.

Si: Freedom.

Alicia: Right. That's what it is. The freedom to go off somewhere, maybe even Colorado, but also the freedom to just be off in your own world, you know, with the music on. Just kind of drifting. Sometimes not even moving.

Carla: Yeah, just sitting there in a cocoon. I'm like Alicia. I think music's a big part of it. I can't imagine a car without a radio.

Trevor: But do you think "to answer" means anything different?

James: I think it means when you're in a car, your car especially, you're apart, you know. It's like that kid who had that disease and had to be totally isolated in that tent-like thing. Nobody can touch you, and you don't have to answer to anybody.

Si: Yeah.

Trevor: [After looking around the group] Anybody else? . . . OK, I guess I'm done. Don't you guys think this is a neat poem?

Si: Yeah, it's cool.

Alicia: I like it.

Carla: I think guys'll like it more than girls.

Si: You done good, Trev.

Carla: OK, I'll go next. . . . The name of my poem is "Driving Lesson" by Michael Pettit . . .

———

Group One proceeds on to read and discuss Carla's poem and then the poems of James, Alicia, and Si. The differences between this kind of approach and the earlier one are obvious: here the teacher establishes a format, provides students with several choices (theme, poem, questions), and then circulates and observes. He is, again, a facilitator. At the end of the discussions, he plans to ask each group to choose the poem they like the best (or perhaps the poem they think best portrays our affection for or our disillusionment with machines in general) for a more focused total class discussion. And he might assign a writing activity.

Whichever role a teacher sees herself playing in the poetry classroom, or whichever blend of roles (the more likely approach), she must also consider the question of organization: how to structure her teaching of poetry. There are several formats to consider.

Occasional Poetry

Some of the best teaching of poetry is unorganized—not chaotic, but occasional, spontaneous, and intuitive. Instead of teaching the standard unit on poetry, some teachers make a practice of reading a poem a day or making, say, every Monday poetry day. At the beginning of class, they read a poem they like—or ask a student to choose one—and invite discussion or assign a brief writing activity. Here's an example:

Small Dark Song

Philip Dacey

The cherry tree is down, and dead, that was so high,
And Wind, that did this thing, roams careless while you cry,
For Wind's been everywhere today, and has an alibi.

Questions: Who is the "you" in the poem? How is Wind characterized? As a total villain, or as partly admirable? Why do you think the poet chose to have the lines rhyme?

Activity: Change "down" to "charred" in line 1 and "Wind" to "Fire" in lines 2 and 3. Then rewrite the poem with other changes caused by the ones already made.

Or, having read the poem, the teacher leaves it alone. There are many poems that are best left undiscussed. "A Blessing" (p. 31) by James Wright may be one of these, a poem that describes the simple emotions conveyed by the speaker's seeing two horses in a field.

Occasional poems can be selected at random, or sometimes chosen to fit the circumstances, as with the following:

During or after a snowfall: "Snow" by Nan Fry, "Driving to Town Late to Mail a Letter" by Robert Bly, or "When It Is Snowing" by Siv Cedering.

Before Halloween: any of Jack Prelutsky's poems from *Nightmares: Poems to Trouble Your Sleep* or X. J. Kennedy's poem "Father and Mother."

Before the big Friday night football game: "Football" by Walt Mason, "Ties" by Dabney Stuart, or "Watching Football on TV (III)" by Howard Nemerov.

On the opening day of hunting season: "Deer Hunt" by Judson Jerome.

The first day of spring: "i thank you god for this most amazing" by e. e. cummings.

When a storm approaches: "Storm Warnings" by Adrienne Rich.

The day before the prom: "The Best Slow Dancer" by David Wagoner.

Martin Luther King's birthday: "Martin Luther King Jr." by Gwendolyn Brooks and "Martin Luther King Day" by X. J. Kennedy.

The opening of the World Series: "The Base Stealer" by Robert Francis (p. 93).

The day before Christmas break: "Under the Mistletoe" by Countee Cullen or "A Christmas Hymn" by Richard Wilbur.

A student's birthday: the appropriate poem from *A Year in Poetry: A Treasury of Classic and Modern Verses for Every Date on the Calendar.*

Another important occasion to celebrate with classes is National Poetry Day, which is observed every fall. In 1997, National Poetry Day fell on September 10; in 1998, September 16, the forty-fourth annual celebration. How do you find out the date? Usually it's publicized in a late summer issue of *Poetry* magazine, but other journals may refer to it as well. Not only that: in 1996, April was first designated as National Poetry Month. (To borrow an Eliot-inspired phrase from National Public Radio, for poetry lovers April is now the coolest month.)

HIGHLIGHT 5.2

Celebrating National Poetry Month

The advent in 1996 of April as National Poetry Month has created a cause and opportunity for lyrical celebration in classrooms and schools throughout the country. In the March 1996 issue of *American Libraries*, Lee Briccetti offers many creative ways for teachers and librarians to do this (p. 63):

- Host a reception for local poets.

- Display new poetry books in a library window. Display poetry posters available from organizations like Streetfare (POB 880274, San Francisco, CA 94188-0274) and Poetry in Motion (Transit Museum Gift Shop, Grand Central Terminal, Main Concourse, New York, NY 10017).

- Program electronic message boards to broadcast brief lines of poetry.

- Read a poem every day over the school intercom.

- Make and give away poems on laminated library bookmarks.

- Sponsor a school-wide poetry slam.

The Poetry Unit

Although some offer poetry through daily readings and special occasions, most teachers still teach the annual poetry unit. In the upper high school grades they often follow the pattern in the textbook and teach poetry (as well as fiction, drama, and nonfiction) according to identified historical periods—the Literature of Colonial America, English Romanticism, the Harlem Renaissance, etc. This approach offers the advantage of giving students a sense of the evolution of their literary heritage (typically the heritage of Western literature). Heavy devotion to it, though, runs the risk of overwhelming students with history and biography and of boring or alienating those whose ethnic background is something other than Anglo-European.

For most teachers, especially in grades 8–10, two or three weeks are reserved with anticipation (and sometimes not a little dread) for the genre-based unit heavy on poetic devices like simile and metaphor, meter, and personification. Or—some teachers organize a unit around a poet or an idea. This chapter provides brief overviews of all three approaches—*poetry as genre, the selected poems of a particular poet*, and *poetry centered around a specific theme*. A teacher's choice among them would depend on several factors:

1. her confidence in poetry as a genre (including poetic devices)
2. her priorities—what students should know about poetry and her views about the purposes of poetry in the English language arts curriculum
3. her personal interests and preferences
4. her feelings about what her students will best respond to

A Genre-Based Unit: An Introduction to Poetry

With any introduction to poetry, *I would begin Day One by showing students my own portfolio of poems I like.* I would begin to share some of them, but I would especially sell the idea that poems are highly personal. "What I like you may not—and vice versa—but I still want to show you some, and I want you to share yours as well." Then I would have them begin to compile their own portfolios.

At some point we would talk about what poetry is and isn't. This would be our avenue into poetry as genre. I would show a variety of poems (greeting cards, haiku, free verse, sonnets, etc.) and quasi-poems (Burma Shave jingles, concrete poems, found poems, raps, etc.), and as a class we would write our own definition of poetry.

Scenario

Mr. Shapiro: Group One, let's have your definition, please. Who's reading? Pete?

Pete: OK, here's our definition. "Poetry is usually words about feelings written down a page and rhyming or not rhyming, but always having rhythm."

This definition has been written with a marking pen onto a transparency and shown on a screen. Each new one is added so that all of the definitions can be seen simultaneously and compared.

Mr. Shapiro: Thank you. Group Two.

Shannon: Our group wrote, "Poetry is writing that is written in lines that are short or long and that have rhythm and sometimes rhyme."

Mr. Shapiro: Thanks, Shannon. Now Group Three?

Maya: Ours is kinda long. "Poetry is the writing of a person's deepest feelings about a subject, using a very condensed structure, lines that vary on the page, rhyme sometimes, rhythm always, and vivid images."

Pete: Ooooh—"condensed structure." I'm impressed.

Mr. Shapiro: Yes, and well you should be, Peter. That's important.

Maya: We didn't really think that some of the concrete poems we saw are poetry exactly.

Mr. Shapiro: That's fine. No problem. And finally, Group Four.

Julius [reading with a flourish and obvious anticipation]: Our group decided to write our definition as a poem:

> "Poetry is rap and sap and all that crap,
> Rhyme in time and feeling fine,
> Beat and heat and words too deep—"

that's all we could think of.

[Applause and laughter]

Mr. Shapiro: Well, I must say that was . . . unique. You guys deserve special recognition for creativity. Now, all of these certainly have merit. We need to look at all of them and see what they have in common, and decide as a class if we need to omit parts or change some of the things you mentioned or even add something. Someone help us get started. Remember now what we said last term about how a definition needs to begin.

Lisa: It needs to begin by telling its group or class, like "poetry is a kind of writing."

Mr. Shapiro: Right. *[He writes Lisa's beginning on the board.]* Now what? What is something that all four definitions mention, including Group Four's?

    The effort proceeds to synthesize a working definition from the raw material the groups have provided.

    We would have fun with poetry with a day or two on poems that are funny, recalling Prelutsky and Silverstein from earlier grades, but extending to Ogden Nash, Dorothy Parker, Paul Zimmer, John Updike, and others. We would perform poetry, singing, chanting, acting out. We might have our own classroom version of a poetry slam (see Chapter 7).

    I would use music. Early on, I'd bring in a song by Mary Chapin Carpenter or Sting or Jewel (who has published a collection of her poetry entitled *A Night without Armor*) and examine the lyrics. I'd play a rap or two. We would explore all these for the kinds of poetic devices all poets and lyricists use. And I'd have the students bring in their own examples of lyrics they like and find poetic (see Chapter 11).

    I would teach concepts and generalizations. I would begin with the broadest generalization of all: poets use a bag of tricks we call poetic devices for their effects; they make purposeful choices having to do with rhythm, rhyme, words, and sounds. We would examine simile and metaphor, onomatopoeia and oxymoron, irony, symbol, meter, and tone. And we would often talk about *why*—why did Laura Gilpin use a flashback in "The Two-Headed Calf"? Why did Richard Wilbur choose a starling and not a robin as a metaphor in "The Writer"? In "The Sacred," why did Stephen Dunn use the word "altar"? More on all of this in Chapter 9.

    We would write poems—and practice the concepts we have learned (Chapter 8).

A Unit Based on a Poet (Example: Emily Dickinson)

I would choose a poet I liked and could help students like. I couldn't do much with William Cullen Bryant or Robert Lowell, but a class and I could have a lot of productive fun with the likes of Poe, Lucille Clifton, and Naomi Shihab Nye. If a teacher likes her, Emily Dickinson is a strong choice because her poems are so brief and approachable. For the most part, though, I'd pick a contemporary poet.

I would teach only biographical information that influenced the poetry of "my" poet. I would try to sell the poet as a rebel, or at least an individual, and as someone who tried to tell the truth. With modern poets this is easy: almost all of them are unique and some are outcasts of sorts. Ezra Pound was labeled a madman. Gregory Corso spent time in jail as a young man. Gary Snyder is a Zen Buddhist and a staunch environmentalist. And even "ancient" poets stood out as different in their settings: Emily Dickinson was a recluse, a strange little study in white who never left her house.

I would occasionally choose a poet just for his or her topics. Again, perhaps Stephen Dunn because of his fondness for cars; Paul Zimmer because he often wrote about school; maybe Sharon Olds, who often portrays difficult relationship with parents and has written that "poets are like steam valves, where the ordinary feelings of ordinary people can escape and be shown" (Moyers, 1995, 216). Emily Dickinson wrote with intensity and perception about nature, loss, love, and death, all subjects of interest to young adults.

HIGHLIGHT 5.3

What to Do with a Poem

Whether the teaching of poetry is occasional or frequent, some teachers feel that poems offer few opportunities for activities. As if in response to this, Fox and Merrick (1981) once listed "thirty-six things to do with a poem," including these:

1. Have students make taped versions of poems for elementary school children to listen to.

2. Have students make poem posters individually or in pairs—Sell-a-Poem.

3. Ask them to listen to two different recorded readings of the same poem and discuss their preference.

4. Assign the writing of a parody of a poem or of certain poetic techniques (e.g., Donne's conceits or Paul Zimmer's autobiographical spoofs).

▶

5. Students can invent the story behind the poem: What happened before? What might happen next?

6. Let students project slides or transparencies during the reading of a poem.

For the other thirty, check the article, which is probably on microfilm at a local public or university library (Fox and Merrick, 33–34).

I would use media, especially video and the Internet. Videos often show the poet as a real flesh-and-blood person. Bill Moyers's excellent television series *The Language of Life* would be extremely useful here as would the lively CD-ROM *Poetry in Motion.* For Dickinson, I'd use the Annenberg/CPB production *Emily Dickinson* and maybe *Emily Dickinson: An Interpretation with Music* (Films for the Humanities & Sciences). Internet homepages are now available on numerous poets, including Dickinson, Frost, Whitman, and many contemporary poets. The media possibilities for bringing poets to life are almost countless.

I might occasionally pair poets. I'd try to match old and new (Ralph Waldo Emerson and Gary Snyder, Walt Whitman and Allen Ginsberg), man and woman (Donald Hall and Jane Kenyon, who were husband and wife), political poets (Robert Bly and Carolyn Forché), war poets from different eras (Siegfried Sassoon and Yusef Komunyakaa), and so on.

Depending on the poet and the class, *I might have students try their hand at parody.* Whitman with his barbaric yawp and Dickinson with her tight, idiosyncratic nuggets of insight offer great possibilities, but so do many moderns (cummings, Frost, Sandburg, Williams, etc.) and a few contemporaries such as Coleman Barks, who often writes little thumbnail poems. (See Chapter 8 for more on parodies.)

I would teach my poet for a week at the most. Then I'd have students present their own chosen poets, each in a snapshot.

Scenario

Claire: Cossandra and I chose Lucille Clifton. Here's a picture of her and oh, we found a *video* of her reading one of her poems too.

Claire and Cossandra are beginning their portrait of their poet. They have been briefed to present the slimmest of biographical data and a picture, and to read a representative poem they like and to entertain any questions about the poet and the poem. All of the class members are strongly encouraged to ask questions. The two girls show the video, and begin their brief report.

Cossandra: As you could see, Lucille Clifton is an African American poet. She is from Maryland and she writes poems mostly about black people and women, and about slavery. She was nominated for the Pulitzer Prize two times and she has six children. A lot of her poems are serious and sad, but some of the ones about women are funny.

Claire: The poem we chose by Lucille Clifton is "At the Cemetery, Walnut Grove Plantation, South Carolina, 1989." [*She shares the poem.*] We like this poem because it's about South Carolina and it tries to say something about what it was like to be a slave and unknown—anonymous, I guess you could say.

Cossandra: Yeah, I especially like the way the poem is addressed to the slaves and asks them to tell their name.

Claire: And that they did "honored work." We like that.

Cossandra: And we like the ending, the way Lucille Clifton says "here lies" four times like it has two meanings, you know, "here rests" and "here *lies*," untruths. And then the word "hear"—*h, e, a, r*—at the very end. Like she's saying, "Listen, these people have something worth hearing."

Claire: Anybody have any questions?

Michael: What do you think the untruths are?

Cossandra: Well, the untruths about slavery, you know, the fact that slaves did a lot of work and didn't get credit for it, and how people have lied about slaves being happy and all. Things like that.

Sharon: And just the whole idea in the poem—the way the poet says "I will testify" because she knows these slaves never had their story told. They had lies told about them.

A Unit Based on a Theme or Topic (Example: Poems about Photographs)

I would go to great lengths to pick a subject the students could identify with. Photographs would work because everyone has them and takes them, and because there are so many poems about them (e.g., "The Car in the Picture" by Patricia Hampl, "Looking in the Album" by Vern Rutsala, "Family Portrait, 1933" by Peter Oresick, and "Old Photograph Album" by Linda Pastan). Among the many other themes that would surely work at different grade levels are growing up, love, war, death, heroes, animals, sports, diversity, decisions, family, friendship, and poetry itself.

I'd get personal. With a theme like death, I would be careful, aware. But with war, we would invite a student's father or uncle to talk about Vietnam before reading a poem like "A Break from the Bush" by Yusef Komunyakaa. In a unit on decisions, we'd look at "Traveling through the Dark" by William Stafford and vote on what we'd do with the dead deer. And with photographs, students could bring cameras and take each other's pictures, or bring their parents' wedding album before we read "Portrait of My Mother on Her Wedding Day" by Celia Gilbert.

I would make the unit interdisciplinary, especially with music and art. In a unit on the poetry of war, we would play and sing some of the great patriotic anthems as well as anti-war songs that emerged from the 1960s (e.g., "Wooden Ships" by Crosby, Stills, and Nash and "Last Night I Had the Strangest Dream" by Ed McCurdy). For the theme of family, we would look at the classic *The Family of Man* by Edward Steichen. That book could also be used in the unit on photographs, as well as Ann Atwood's *Haiku-vision in Poetry and Photography*, a beautiful blend of color photographs and the haiku written about them. In a unit on love, we would draw up a tongue-in-cheek homepage called *The Cyrano Server* (http://www.nandotimes. com/toys/cyrano/), which writes personalized love letters in a variety of styles (steamy, intellectual, indecisive, surreal, desperate, poetic, and regretful) as well as "Dear Johns."

I might also blend poetry with fiction, drama, and nonfiction. Thematic units often work better with as much thrown into the mix as possible. A unit on growing up, for example, could use an initiation novel like *A Day No Pigs Would Die* or *A Separate Peace* as a planetary center with stories and poems spinning around it like so many moons. The poetry could include "Fifteen" by William Stafford, "Accomplishments" by Cynthia McDonald, "The Fish" by Lila Zeiger (p. 7), and "A Certain Age" by Phyllis McGinley. The unit on photographs could take advantage of a book like *Let Us Now Praise Famous Men* by James Agee and Walker Evans.

I would have students write frequently, not only poems, but other kinds of writing related to the theme. I might schedule a unit on animal poetry for the spring, when we would read, among others, "A Blessing" by James Wright (p. 31) and "Names of Horses" by Donald Hall. After the latter, I would assign everyone to watch the Kentucky Derby, then write a list poem the following Monday with names of horses the students consider poetic.

Scenario

Ms. Taylor: I want each group to take the ten names each person came up with over the weekend—so, forty or fifty names in all—and choose seven to ten that you think are especially poetic—evocative—for your list poem, OK?

For thirty minutes each of five groups works to complete its poem. Earlier, the teacher modeled a sample stem ("In a great gallop of muscle and grit, they tumble down the homestretch: . . ."), but now she asks them to write and shape one of their own. After the groups finish, they share their results. Here is one finished poem:

Wide of the turn
                                        wide and free

        the whips of the jockeys flash
            as the horses strain down the stretch
            in a blur of browns and greys:

                    Aspen
                    Gunrunner
                    Time in a Bottle
                    Gallant Fox
                    Turquoise Lady
                    Hailstone

        and in a rush,
                    Maximum Thunder

                winner by a nose.

In a unit on sports we would use poems like "400-Meter Freestyle" by Maxine Kumin and "Foul Shot" by Edwin A. Hoey as springboards for the writing of concrete poems. For poetry and photography, the students could write imaginary stories (or narrative poems) based on nineteenth century family portraits in books such as *An American Album* (American Heritage).

Almost any approach will work; I would use them all. Neither Orchestrator nor Facilitator would I be—not purely anyway. I'd be the Great Compromiser. I'd give my students a lot of say in what they read and write, but I would also teach poems and teach about poetry. In the early grades of high school, there is something about an Introduction to Poetry unit that appeals to me. I like the prospect of being perhaps the first teacher to show students that poetry can be both fun and intellectually *interesting*. Later (grades 10, 11) I'd almost surely teach thematic units and maybe a unit on someone like Frost or William Stafford or Lucille Clifton (all of whom I much admire). But I'd also pop in with poems here and there throughout the year.

What matters most is imagination and enthusiasm. Almost anything will work anywhere as long as the teacher has a serious ongoing love affair with poetry. Or at least an annual fling.

6 Responding to Poetry by Talking

P oems are perfect for talking about. They are tight little nuggets of
meaning—sights and sounds, happenings, points of view, reactions,
observations, exhortations, sighs, musings, meditations, teases, ex-
pressions of joy and disappointment, anger and delight.

Some are so brief the discussion may last only a minute or two:

Keepsakes

William Stafford

. . . .
Kids:
They dance before they learn
there is anything that isn't music.

Questions: Why do children dance? What is meant by "dance"? What
are some things that are "music"? That aren't? What makes you dance—
besides music?

That Dark Other Mountain

Robert Francis

My father could go down a mountain faster than I
Though I was first one up.
Legs braced or with quick steps he slid the gravel slopes
Where I picked cautious footholds.

Black, Iron, Eagle, Doublehead, Chocorua,
Wildcat and Carter Dome—
He beat me down them all. And that last other mountain.
And that dark other mountain.

Questions: What activity is the first stanza about? What are the
capitalized words at the beginning of stanza two? What is "that last other
mountain"? Why is it dark?

These are the kinds of poems that are good for tossing in at the
beginning of a class to get kids' brains in gear. "Hey, here's a poem I like.
Let's look at it and talk about it for a minute." Paul Janeczko's books,
especially *Postcard Poems* and *Pocket Poems*, are full of little gems like
these, quick, unassuming, fun to teach and chew over briefly with a class
before going on to something else. Sometimes they can lead to a lesson in
language (or some other topic in the curriculum):

Nouns

Charles Wright

Nouns are precise, they wear
the boots of authority;

Nouns are not easily pleased.
Nouns are assured, they know

Whom to precede and whom to follow,
They know what dependence means,

That touchstone of happiness;
They need no apologist.

When nouns fall to disuse, and die,
Their bones do not coalesce.

Such absences implicate
No person, place, or thing.

All these poems seem approachable enough. Still, part of the reason we may be reluctant to teach contemporary poetry is our feeling that somehow we just aren't up to it. These modern poets and poems are too difficult, we sometimes think. "I'd have to sit with the *OED* beside me to figure out what they mean." Or—"I'd have to spend hours in the library looking for critiques." As we pointed out in Chapter 3, the discomfort and anxiety are largely unfounded. Of course there are difficult contemporary poems, but there are just as many that are easily accessible. More important is the realization that teachers cannot be expected to answer all the questions raised by a poem. They must, says the poet Lois Harrod, allow their students "to enrich their own reading of the poem. . . . Teachers should not be afraid to ask questions about the poem that they do not know the answer to; they will be surprised how students will open the poem for them" (Lockward 1994, 68).

Another poet, Jane Cooper Todd, adds reinforcement: teachers must help students realize that "poems begin in questions, doubts, wonderings, speculations, unexplained emotions. A poem comes from what you don't know" (Lockward 1994, 68).

HIGHLIGHT 6.1

What Poets Have to Say about Their Own Poems

Sometimes it's interesting to read what poets have to say about their own work. Often in classes or workshops, poets will comment on the origin of an

▶

idea or the revision of a line or two. These kinds of remarks are also available to teachers and students in two books edited by Paul Janeczko. In *Poetspeak: In Their Work, about Their Work,* John Updike, Linda Pastan, Ted Kooser, Paul Zimmer, Joyce Carol Oates, Nikki Giovanni, Howard Nemerov, and fifty-five others give us insights into their work.

Here is what William Stafford says about his poem "Vacation," which we saw earlier (p. 49):

> When our train went by a windy, dry place in Nevada, I saw some people standing by a grave. Just a glimpse, I had—a piece of life given me and then snatched away. They were so still, and the wind buffeted them so, and the world stretched out around them, so lonely—and gone . . . And we on the train were elegant—warm, easy, ready to dine. The *form* it all took was just as it came to be in my poem: a glance out, a crash of dissonant life, and a calm (an apparently calm) return to our elegance.
>
> But it wasn't the same. But I let the reader or hearer decide that—with the help of the form (1983, 225).

Janeczko's companion book of poems and commentaries is *The Place My Words Are Looking For: What Poets Say about and through Their Work.* Two useful resources are *Speaking of Poets: Interviews with Poets Who Write for Children and Young Adults,* by Jeffrey S. Copeland, which includes writers like Gary Soto, X. J. Kennedy, Jimmy Santiago Baca, Eve Merriam, and Mel Glenn; and a follow-up volume, *Speaking of Poets 2* by the same author.

Just as there are no definitive interpretations of a poem, there are no sacred approaches to involving students in talking about a poem or questions to ask about a poem. There are, however, a few general guidelines that I have found helpful. The first six of them apply in particular to the Teacher as Orchestrator portrayed at length in Chapter 5.

GUIDELINE ONE

This is easily the most important of the seven: Do not tell students what a poem means. Help them discover what it *may* mean. One of the great advantages of contemporary poems—although we often see it as a threat—is their freshness. They have not been contaminated (*encrusted* might be a better word) by decades or even centuries of accumulated critical commentary. There are no Cliffs Notes for "Traveling through the

Dark" or "Ex-Basketball Player" or "Will." As teachers, we are therefore dependent upon ourselves and our students for interpretation.

GUIDELINE TWO

For discussion, choose poems that have some meat on them, poems with something to say. They can be very brief, of course, as we've seen, but they must depend on the kernel of an idea. A poem like "A Tribute to Mothers" (p. 7) is far too shallow and transparent to offer any possibilities for interpretation and discussion, especially in comparison with the much more interesting poem "The Fish" (p. 7). Here are two appealing poems by Robert Francis about baseball—one with much more potential for discussion than the other:

Pitcher

His art is eccentricity, his aim
How not to hit the mark he seems to aim at,
His passion how to avoid the obvious,
His technique how to vary the avoidance.

The others throw to be comprehended. He
Throws to be a moment misunderstood.

Yet not too much. Not errant, arrant, wild,
But every seeming aberration willed.

Not to, yet still, still to communicate
Making the batter understand too late.

The Base Stealer

Poised between going on and back, pulled
Both ways taut like a tightrope-walker,
Fingertips pointing the opposites,
Now bouncing tiptoe like a dropped ball
Or a kid skipping rope, come on, come on,
Running a scattering of steps sidewise,
How he teeters, skitters, tingles, teases,
Taunts them, hovers like an ecstatic bird,
He's only flirting, crowd him, crowd him,
Delicate, delicate, delicate, delicate—now!

I love both poems and both can be talked about, but "Pitcher" offers more possibilities: How is a pitcher eccentric? What is meant by line two? How do pitchers "avoid the obvious . . . [and then] vary the avoid-ance"? How is "every seeming aberration willed"? Etc., etc.

Corollary: Don't choose poems that preach; students justifiably hate them.

GUIDELINE THREE

Early on in a discussion, ask who the speaker is. This doesn't have to be the
very first question and for some poems (the two baseball poems, for
example) it doesn't need to be asked at all (or the answer is blatantly
obvious). Often, though, knowing who is doing the talking and knowing it
early can be critical. Of some of the poems we've seen before, identifying
the speaker is important in "The Fish" (p. 7), "On Reading Poems to a Class
at South High" (p. 11), and "Lullabye for 17" (p. 58). It is less important in
"Will" (p. 27) and in "Flying at Night" (p. 55). In the following poem by
Robert Hayden that we read earlier in Chapter 3, it is crucial:

The Whipping

The old woman across the way
    is whipping the boy again
and shouting to the neighborhood
    her goodness and his wrongs.

Wildly he crashes through elephant ears,   5
    pleads in dusty zinnias,
while she in spite of crippling fat
    pursues and corners him.

She strikes and strikes the shrilly circling
    boy till the stick breaks   10
in her hand. His tears are rainy weather
    to woundlike memories:

My head gripped in bony vise
    of knees, the writhing struggle
to wrench free, the blows, the fear   15
    worse than blows that hateful

Words could bring, the face that I
    no longer knew or loved. . . .
Well, it is over now, it is over,
    and the boy sobs in his room,   20

And the woman leans muttering against
    a tree, exhausted, purged—
avenged in part for lifelong hidings
    she has had to bear.

In this poem, the speaker is easy to identify—an observer, perhaps a
neighbor. However, the speaker's less noticeable shift in perspective in
stanza four is essential to understanding the poem. It would also be
important in this poem to discuss the speaker's attitude toward what he or
she sees.

Corollary One: Almost as important as identifying the speaker is
helping students understand the situation by asking, "What's going on

here?" In "The Whipping," it seems a neighbor is watching an old woman chase and beat a boy, perhaps a son or grandson. For teachers, this may seem so apparent as to not warrant a question, but for some students it may not be clear.

Corollary Two: For some poems, some kind of preliminary question or perhaps even a brief activity will help pave the way for students into the poem—or anticipate possible problems. This may not be necessary for "The Whipping," but some teachers might want to talk briefly about spankings—without getting personal—or they may want to explain what elephant ears are or define the word *purge.*

Corollary Three: Some teachers may disagree with this suggestion, but there are two questions I would refrain from asking at the beginning of a discussion. One of them is "Did you like this poem?" This question places the teacher in a no-win situation: if students say they hate the poem, the teacher who loves it may be deflated; if they say they love it, the teacher (at least one with a fair measure of cynicism) may not trust their response. An opening question I have even more reservations about is "What does it mean?" Too broad and *much too early.*

GUIDELINE FOUR

Carefully sequence the questions to follow the progression of the poem, more or less, from beginning to end—*and from the specific to the general.* This approach requires the teacher to build the way toward interpretation, to pave the way to meaning. It establishes the facts at first, clarifies the speaker and the context, and then, not unlike a detective with a magnifying glass, examines words and phrases line by line and stanza by stanza until, very gradually and finally, the class is indeed ready for a question like "What does it mean?" Here is a possible sequence of questions for "The Whipping":

1. Who is the speaker and what is he or she doing? (Can we tell whether the speaker is a man or woman? A child or adult? Is it the poet?)

2. What is happening?

3. How does the speaker react to the scene, especially in lines 1–11? Is he emotional or objective?

4. What do lines 1–11 mean? What might the colon at the end of line 12 suggest?

5. What does stanza four refer to? How do you know?

6. How does the speaker feel about the incident he remembers from his past?

7. What might he mean by "the face I no longer knew or loved"? As he looks back over the years at this incident, do you think his feelings toward the person who whipped him have changed? Why or why not?

8. What does "purged" mean? How is the old woman purged?

9. Why did she whip the boy?

10. Why do you think the poet used a dash at the end of line 22?

11. Why does the speaker (and through him the poet) repeat "it is over" in line 19? Is it over? In what way may it not be over? How is this ironic? (See Highlight 6.2.)

12. Do you think the poet is against whippings? Are you? Discuss.

Notice how the questions begin at the beginning—with what is happening at first (lines 1–11)—and then proceed through the poem (lines 11–12, stanza four, lines 17–18, and so on). They also move from the specific (Who is the speaker? What is happening?) to the general (Why did she whip the boy? Do you think the poet is against whippings?). There are other progressions at work here as well: the questions proceed from the relatively easy to the relatively difficult and from recall, more or less, to interpretative, personal (in question 12, "Are you?"), and even technical questions (question 10).

Is it difficult to design questions like these, questions that shape but do not limit discussion? No. What's even better, it's fun. The teacher as orchestrator wants involvement and thoughtful consideration and she welcomes productive diversion, but *she* selects the poem for discussion, *she* decides the initial focus and the direction of the talk, and *she* orchestrates the interplay. In carrying this activity through, she is engaging in perhaps the two most rewarding aspects of teaching English language arts —purposefully planning a creative, meaningful lesson around a piece of literature and then taking that lesson into the classroom and making it fly.

GUIDELINE FIVE

Allow for some diversion and divergence. Give students some rope while discussing a poem. Keep ever in mind that each reader, however young and unsophisticated, brings to a given poem his own background, her own experiences that illuminate a text. The poet Richard Wilbur describes his experience as a teacher: "I try to be uncertain even where I feel pretty strongly, not to impose any one way of reading, and to entertain seriously every decent suggestion which comes from the floor" (Packard 1987, 147). Another poet, Robert Kendall, advises against rigidly imposing "a single interpretation on [a] poem, since most poems can be read in a variety of ways" (Lockward 1994, 65). And listen to Stanley Kunitz: "A poem does not tell what it means, even to its maker. A prime source of its power is that it has its roots in the secrecy of a life and that it means more than it says. And a poem demands of its readers that they must come out to meet it, at least as far as it comes out to meet them, so that *their* meaning may be added to its" (Janeczko 1983, 74).

Be especially aware that poems often generate the most original insights from students whose backgrounds may be quite different from those of most teachers. It may be superfluous to suggest that "The Whipping" is such a poem.

Corollary: While allowing for diverse points of view and original insights, try to teach students to keep their eyes and their interpretations on the text. This is an important principle to teach: all views and interpretations of a poem are worth our consideration; they should be listened to and valued. Given this important principle, here is another: some insights are more valid than others, and the best opinions are those that are grounded in what the poem says.

This is a very delicate distinction, one that many adolescents may have difficulty with. To promote its understanding, I might try an exercise with the following poem:

The Man in the Dead Machine

Donald Hall

High on a slope in New Guinea
the Grumman Hellcat
lodges among bright vines
as thick as arms. In 1943,
the clenched hand of a pilot
glided it here
where no one has ever been.

In the cockpit, the helmeted
skeleton sits
upright, held
by dry sinews at neck
and shoulder, and webbing
that straps the pelvic cross
to the cracked
leather of the seat, and the breastbone
to the canvas cover
of the parachute.

Or say the shrapnel
missed him, he flew
back to the carrier, and every
morning takes the train, his pale

hands on his black case, and sits
upright, held
by the firm webbing.

Exercise: Have each student read "The Man in the Dead Machine" and the three brief interpretations that follow. They should then rank the interpretations, best to worst, in terms of their validity—how well they rely upon what the poem says as opposed to pure conjecture. Direct the students to meet in pairs (or trios) to compare their rankings and try to reach consensus. Then discuss the three interpretations as a whole class.

Interpretation One: The poem above shows an incident in the Vietnam War, where a plane crashes in an uninhabited jungle. The pilot finds another plane in the same area that contains a skeleton that remains strapped in the cockpit. This is a symbol of death to the surviving pilot, who then escapes back to his ship and later dedicates his life to working as a lawyer in the city, to which he rides the train every day from the suburbs.

Interpretation Two: This is a poem about a man who piloted a plane during World War II into a jungle. The poem gives us two possible results: (1) the pilot died in the crash landing and was never found, but his skeleton remains strapped to the seat; and (2) the pilot managed to escape and return from the war, but—and here is irony—he later suffers another kind of death, strapped to the boredom, repetition, and deadliness that comes with commuting to a meaningless job.

Interpretation Three: This is a poem about a man in a dead machine. The machine in the poem is the world of computers that we now live in and that the man flew from the war to work in. In the second stanza, the man is actually sitting at a computer. The machine is "dead" because men and women who work in front of computers are like computers themselves. They sit and gaze all day at a screen and for the most part type in information like robots.

In the class discussion that follows the small group work, the teacher would point out (or, even better, let the students point out) how only Interpretation Two resists the temptation to stray from the text of the poem. While both are worthy of respectful consideration, Interpretations One and Three make invalid factual inferences (e.g., ignoring the date) or move off into the kind of pure guesswork that is so often grounded in the misguided search for symbols.

GUIDELINE SIX

This is simple: before you initiate a discussion (again, here we're talking mostly about the teacher as orchestrator), always read the poem aloud to the class. Here is a sensible sequence: first have the class read the poem silently, explain any words that may be unfamiliar, and then read the poem aloud. It is important for us as teachers to remember that poetry is essentially an oral medium, and that much can be conveyed by a competent reader. (See Chapter 7 for more on oral interpretation.)

GUIDELINE SEVEN

Give students many opportunities to gain ownership of poems by allowing them not only to choose poems for discussion, but to control the discussion themselves. In many schools these days, teachers as facilitators (see Chapter 5 for a brief review) are involving students in *literature circles*, groups in which students talk about works, often on the basis of their own "think-aloud" jottings in journals. A blend of cooperative learning and independent reading, literature circles are defined by Daniels as

> small, temporary discussion groups who have chosen to read the same story, poem, article, or book. While reading each group-determined portion of the text (either in or outside of class), each member prepares to take specific responsibilities in the upcoming discussion, and everyone comes to the group with the notes needed to help perform that job. The circles have regular meetings, with discussion roles rotating each session (1994, 13).

In a poetry class, five groups might be given the same five poems to read, perhaps on a similar theme. Each group quickly decides which one of the five they would like to discuss. Then each group member rereads the chosen poem and writes down line-by-line, spur-of-the-moment reactions. Members of the five groups then meet to pool their responses. In some cases, group members are assigned roles. The following list of possible roles (with some modifications) is also from Daniels:

1. Discussion Director, whose job is to write down a few questions the group might want to consider

2. Literary Luminary, who should try at some point to direct the group's attention to a technical aspect of the poem

3. Connector, who should try to relate the poem in some way to the "real" world

4. Wordsmith, who should be prepared to define any potentially challenging vocabulary in the poem

5. Summarizer, whose responsibility is to sum up the discussion for the class as a whole when the groups have finished (A1–A8).

Other systems might have additional (or replacement) roles—for example, an Encourager, someone who tries to get people involved; a Poem Reader, whose job is to read it aloud; and perhaps a Co-Director so that the orchestration and question-asking are not dependent upon a single student.

Again, throughout the process the teacher serves as a facilitator. More often than not, she selects the poems for consideration (although students can do this too), determines group make-up, and monitors the discussions, jumping in only when necessary. The whole procedure is an exercise in freedom and responsibility for the students. Here is another example of how it might work (we saw an earlier one in Chapter 5):

Scenario

On Monday, students in Ms. Price's eleventh-grade class spent the period looking through collections like Strings: A Gathering of Family Poems *and* I Feel a Little Jumpy around You *and through folders of poems about families created by the teacher. Each student's goal: to find one poem about mothers and fathers that he likes and that he thinks will be interesting to talk about.*

On Tuesday, the class met in five or six groups, each group comprised of four or five students. In each group, each student presented his or her poem. After listening to the presentations, each group decided on one poem to lead the discussion of the next day. Each group also assigned the roles described above (Director, Connector, etc.). Today the class meets in a huge circle. Since Group One will go first, its five members—Miguel, Sherrie, Lori, Billy, and Ali—are scattered around the circle.

Ms. Price: Yesterday Group One, like the others, looked at the poems about mothers and fathers and decided on one to lead the rest of us in talking about. So—Miguel, what's your group's poem?

Miguel: Well, we liked a couple of them as a group, but we chose "Lullabye for 17" by Linda Pastan. It wasn't *my* favorite, but I go with the flow.

Ms. Price: All right, group, the floor is yours.

Miguel: Like I said, our poem is "Lullabye for 17." Lori's gonna read it, but before she does Billy's got a few words we thought we needed to go over.

Billy: Yeah, I'm the Wordsmith. Anybody know what *absolve* means? *[With no answer forthcoming, Billy reads from a sheet of paper.]* OK, *absolve* means to pronounce clear of blame or guilt; to relieve of a requirement or obligation.

Ms. Price: Everyone clear on that? If you absolve something, you free it from any kind of blame. It's sort of like a pardon. Like "I absolved Randy for his misbehaving in class."

Billy: Another word is *refracting.* Anybody know that one?

Ralph: Yeah, I remember that from science, I think. When light is refracted, doesn't it bend?

Billy: Yeah, or condenses. And the last one is *catechism.*

Mary: Oh, I know that from church. A catechism is a book about the religion. It's got questions and answers.

Billy: Right. OK, any questions about any of these?

[Lori then shows a transparency of the poem on the screen, asks the class to read it silently, and then reads it aloud.]

Lullabye for 17

You are so young
you heal as you weep,
and your tears
instead of scalding
your face like mine   5
absolve
simply as rain.

I tried to teach you
what I knew: how men
in their sudden beauty   10
are more dangerous,
how love refracting light
can burn the hand, how memory
is a scorpion

and stings with its tail.   15
You knew my catechism
but never believed. Now
you look upon pain
as a discovery all your own,
marveling at the way it invades   20
the bloodstream, ambushes sleep.

Still you forgive
so easily. I'd like
to take your young man
by his curls and tear   25
them out,

who like a dark planet circles
your bright universe

still furnished with curtains
you embroidered yourself,   30
an underbrush
of books and scarves,
a door at which
you'll soon be poised
to leave.   35

Miguel: OK, beginning with Ms. Price's standard first question: who's the speaker?

James: A mom.

Mary: A parent.

James: A *mom*.

Mary: Yeah, probably a mom.

Ali: Why a mom? Why not a dad?

Mary: Well, I don't think a dad would talk about men this way, you know, saying they're dangerous and stuff. It's a mom warning her daughter about the evil lurking in the hearts of all men.

Robin: As well she should.

Miguel: OK, OK. Who's she talking to?

James: Her daughter.

Miguel: And what's she saying to her?

James: Well, like Mary said, she's trying to tell her about men.

Ali: How does she feel about men?

Gail: She doesn't like them.

James: She doesn't like this one.

Shana: I want to go back to who she's talking to. I don't think she's talking to the daughter. I think she's just . . . well, sort of thinking about her. Thinking to herself.

Benny: Yeah, me too.

Miguel: What does she mean by "you heal as you weep"?

Mary: It just means she's tough . . . and forgiving.

Janie: I like that part about the rain and that word Billy mentioned—*absolve*. It's like the rain—the tears—wash away blame.

Miguel: OK . . . um, in the second part, the second stanza, why does she say that "men in their sudden beauty are more dangerous"? We planned this question just for you, Jerry.

Jerry: Cause, man, that's it! She's right on! We men, we have *sudden* beauty. We sneak up on chicks.

Robin: Let me tell you one thing, Jay-bo. You ain't sneaking up on me no time. *[Laughter]*

Ali: Maybe somebody else ought to take this one. Sondra?

Sondra: Well, seriously, I think it means *she*—the daughter—might think they're suddenly beautiful. You know, one day there's a guy you've never noticed right in your class, and then suddenly you notice him.

Mary: I think she means that *men* suddenly think they're beautiful. When that happens, watch out.

A student-run discussion like this can go on for several minutes if the poem, like this one, is provocative, the group well prepared, and the class willing and able. Here is how this one ends.

Sherrie: So our last sort-of summary question is, "What is the speaker most upset by?"

Benny: She's upset by the fact that her daughter lets men run over her.

Terri: I don't think that's it. I think she's upset by the fact that her daughter doesn't pay any attention to her.

Mary: I agree. I think she's bothered by her daughter coming to her own conclusions—

Sonia: And her daughter getting ready to leave. She feels like she's losing touch, losing her influence.

Sherrie: Anybody else? . . . OK, Lori, your turn.

Lori: Ta-daahhhh!—I have our technical question. Why do you think the poet chose the word *underbrush* in line 31 to describe her room? It's a— metaphor?

Ms. Price: That's right, Lori. Good.

Sonia: Because her room is so messy.

Benita: And the mess is on the floor.

Rob: This is kind of far-out, but maybe because she's leaving a secure place and heading out into a wilderness, the unknown.

Mary: But the underbrush of books and things is her room now.

Rob: Yeah, that's true. I don't know.

Miguel: Mrs. Price, what do you think?

Ms. Price: Well, I'm not sure. Maybe it is just the messiness. Maybe it's Pastan's way of trying to make her seem more human, more vulnerable, or the idea that as we grow up we often seem to be struggling through thickets of resistance. I don't know. All I know for sure is that you all did a very good job with this discussion. I'm proud of you. Have we finished? Anyone have any further questions or comments? . . . All right! Great! Now, Group Two.

———————

As with some of the previous scenarios, I am sure there are readers out there who are saying, "Only in your wildest dreams would this ever happen." And in some ways they are right. This kind of productive student-driven discussion won't just *happen. But it can happen in many, perhaps most, high school classrooms if teachers pave their way into it. I would begin in August or September with very approachable poems and short discussions. I would model the process with hand-picked groups, then gradually include everyone. It can happen. It does happen. But it does require a lot of preparation.*

As noted earlier, the engagement of students in the open, respectful, intelligent discussion of poems can be one of the truly rewarding aspects of teaching. It stimulates everyone—no one more than the teacher himself. Finding poems to talk about and designing the questions that will drive the discussion—this is exhilarating. It is so much more meaningful than assigning students the questions for "Ode to a Nightingale" or Amy Lowell's "Patterns" from the teacher's guide. It does take work, but more teachers need to drop their dependence on textbook questions and activities and realize that no one can write better questions for *their* students than they themselves. With this said, it may be presumptuous to include here at the end of the chapter a few more sets of questions for poems we've already seen. Keep this in mind: *these questions are merely samples,* starting points as easily ignored altogether as used. In fact, don't use them. Think of them as Ted Kooser sees his "selected reader" (p. 55). Give the questions a look and some thought; then reject them for something better—your own.

I. "The Fish" (p. 7).

    1. Who is the speaker?

    2. Is she speaking as a young person or from a greater distance?

How do you know?

3. Why do you think the mother would have had a fish swimming in her bathtub on a Friday? What might this imply about the speaker's background?

4. Why does the speaker compare herself to the fish?

5. Examine the comparison carefully. In what ways are the fish and the young girl alike? What does the word *iridescence* suggest? In your opinion, is the comparison a good one? Why or why not?

6. What does the speaker mean by "in your special broth"?

7. Ultimately, how does the speaker feel about her mother? Does she feel sadness? Regret? Does she hate her mother? Is she in any way complimentary toward her?

8. What is the speaker's primary regret? What did she wish for?

II. "On Reading Poems to a Senior Class at South High" (p. 11).

1. Who is the speaker and what is the situation?

2. How does the speaker view his audience?

3. With what does he compare the setting, the experience? What does he sense is happening? Why do you think he feels this way? Is he afraid?

4. What does he mean by "I had/ tried to drown them/ with my words"?

5. What does he mean by "they had only opened up . . . and let me in"?

6. How does he feel about the experience he has with the class?

7. What might be meant by the last two lines: what effect does the cat have on the speaker?

8. Do you think the controlling metaphor in the poem is effective? Why or why not?

III. "Will" (p. 27).

1. How are the various feats that people perform in lines 1–4 different?

2. Why do they do them? Are they heroic?

3. What does "hurries to the front" mean?

4. What is meant by "God serves the choosey"?

5. What does line 6 mean? Line 7?

6. Is the "one" of line 8 different from those in lines 1–4? How? Is he similar? What does he know? What does he hope for?

7. Why do some would-be suicides want to be found? What does this say about some acts of suicide?

8. Is suicide heroic or cowardly? Neither? Discuss.

HIGHLIGHT 6.2

Ciardi's Fulcrum

In his useful book (1960) on reading poetry intelligently, *How Does a Poem Mean?*, the poet and critic John Ciardi discusses a concept in Chapter 8 (p. 994 ff.) he calls the *fulcrum* of a poem, which may be helpful to teachers. Ciardi felt that poems "exist in countermotion," i.e., they contain elements that work against each other. Often there is, in effect, a change of pace whereby the poet's attitude toward the subject—and usually his technical handling of the poem as well—shifts. At the point (or points) where this occurs—the fulcrum—there is often a movement toward the revelation of possible meaning. In fact, the poem might be said to reach two "points"—a balance point (like the use of the word *fulcrum* in physics) and the point, or meaning, the poet intends for the reader to consider.

An obvious fulcrum can be found in the short poem "That Dark Other Mountain" by Robert Francis (p. 90). In the first seven lines, the speaker objectively describes his father's skill at descending mountains. In lines 5 and 6, he names some of the peaks "he beat me down." In the middle of line 7, however, the tone shifts noticeably with the word *And*, and the poem is not the same thereafter. The last two lines present a darker, more subdued tone suggested by the beginning of each sentence and the words *other* and *dark*.

Should teachers teach the fulcrum as a poetic concept? Not if they expect students to go on fulcrum hunts. As a way of getting older students to read more carefully, though, the concept could be useful.

(Quiz: It could be argued that "The Whipping" on p. 39 has two fulcrums. Where do you think they occur?)

HIGHLIGHT 6.3

Poems for Discussion: A Very Few among Many

"Accomplishments" by Cynthia McDonald

"Anti-Father" by Rita Dove

"The Aura" by James Dickey

"Barbie Doll" by Marge Piercy

"By Accident" by Jane O. Wayne

"Conversation with a Fireman from Brooklyn" by Tess Gallagher

▶

"Corner" by Ralph Pomeroy

"Cousins" by Linda Pastan

"Famous" by Naomi Shihab Nye

"final note to clark" by Lucille Clifton

"For My Daughter" by Weldon Kees

"The Heroes" by Louis Simpson

"How Things Work" by Gary Soto

"I Go Back to May 1937" by Sharon Olds

"Learning by Doing" by Howard Nemerov

"Looking in the Album" by Vern Rutsala

"Lying in a Hammock at William Duffy's Farm in Pine Island, Minnesota" by James Wright

"A Martian Sends a Postcard Home" by Craig Raine

"Mutterings over the Crib of a Deaf Child" by James Wright

"My Dim-Wit Cousin" by Theodore Roethke

"Speaking: The Hero" by Felix Pollak

"Standing between Two Ideas" by Maurya Simon

"Storm Warnings" by Adrienne Rich

"To a Blind Student Who Taught Me to See" by Samuel Hazo

"Two Set Out on Their Journey" by Galway Kinnell

"The Writer" by Richard Wilbur

7 Responding to Poetry by Performing

In May Swenson's poem "Southbound on the Freeway," the speaker is an alien hovering in a spaceship over a freeway. He is confused by what he sees below, unsure about the nature of the creatures on the beltway rushing hither and yon. Imagine an extension of the visit: among the curious crew there is a Minister of Culture, a kind of emissary of the arts. Appropriately disguised, she leaves the ship and happens upon a high school English class considering a poem. She is intrigued. She takes notes and later writes the obligatory report for her commander. The alien's main conclusion: in this world, poetry is strictly an intellectual pursuit. Poems are taken out, examined, picked over, talked and written about. Except for these cerebral considerations, nothing much is ever done with them.

If the report were intercepted by the FBI or CIA (or *The National Enquirer*) and passed on to the public, would we teachers be surprised? Not at all. We would be pleased: isn't this what we're supposed to do with poetry?

Well, maybe not entirely. For some time now poets themselves have written of other possibilities suggested by poetry's primitive origins. According to Stanley Kunitz (winner of both the National Book Award and the Pulitzer Prize for poetry), the genre "has its roots in magic—in the spell over things delivered by the priest or shaman of the tribe. The words of a poem go back to the beginning of the human adventure when the first syllables were not spoken but sung or chanted or danced. So it is that poetry always seems about to burst into song, to break into dance. . . ." (Janeczko 1990, 74).

Even a scholar like Dana Gioia (who is not only a poet but a translator of Italian poetry) argues for training the classroom spotlight on performance (1992, 23). Gioia realizes that performance has always been a major drawing card for younger children. Open any book on the teaching of poetry in elementary school and the pages are filled with suggestions for tying poetry to dance and chants, jump-rope jingles, mime and other movement, choral reading and readers theater, skits, role play and improvisation. In *The Teachers and Writers Handbook of Poetic Forms*, Ron Padgett defines the performance poem as one "written to be read or enacted in front of an audience." In recent years, he goes on to explain, the form has often been associated with social or political causes, where "the poet is speaking on behalf of a larger, often outraged community and, like the tribal shaman, envisions a better world" (1987, 143–44).

HIGHLIGHT 7.1

Poetry Alive!

Anyone who doubts the potential appeal of performance to high school students should attend a presentation by Poetry Alive!, a thriving theater company from Asheville, North Carolina, that travels to schools throughout the country putting on poetry shows. Since its founding in 1984, Poetry Alive! has performed in forty-six states and in several foreign countries. It annually conducts over 1,900 performances and some 200 teacher workshops involving 550,000 students—bringing "poetry from the page to the stage." Poetry Alive! does exactly what it says: it *enlivens* the genre by engaging students' imaginations and often drawing them out of the audience to read and mime and dance. Students of all ages love it.

Poetry Alive! can be contacted by mail at P. O. Box 9643, Asheville, NC 28815, by phone at 1-800-476-8172, or by e-mail at poetry@poetry alive.com. Or check out the troupe's Internet Web site at http://www.poetryalive.com.

Despite this growing acceptance of the idea, many teachers in high schools have been reluctant to move poetry from the podium to the stage, leery perhaps of losing control. (I know the feeling: there's a part of me that shies away from the demonstrative.) Still, there is a movement afoot. Whether motivated by the likes of Gioia, offbeat innovations like the poetry slam, or their own sense of desperation, many high school teachers throughout the country are edging their teaching over into performance. Typical among them is Mary Ellen R. McArthur, who asks her juniors each May to choose a poem studied during the year as the basis for an end-of-year oral presentation. Their poem has to be read or recited and "may incorporate visual, dramatic, technical, musical, and/or any other combination of the arts desired." The results are often memorable:

> Annie, Chinese-American and reserved, knocked us dead with Langston Hughes's "Dream Deferred," delivered dramatically in slouch hat and trench coat, to the sounds of a classic jazz recording. David, a recent immigrant from Sri Lanka, serious beyond his years, strode in, wearing traditional walking clothes and, leaning on a handsome carved staff, delivered a thought-provoking rendition of

Crane's "The Wayfarer" . . . Laura, a lovely black girl, arranged five unsuspecting classmates in a hand-holding, outward-facing circle around her and then, kneeling in the middle, softly, strongly pronounced Paul Laurence Dunbar's familiar words from "Sympathy": "I know what the caged bird feels, alas . . ." (1989, 69–71).

Occasions like these in Mary Ellen McArthur's class encourage the rest of us. With the crook of a finger or the gesture of an arm, they beckon us to try something new. If we respond, here are some of the many ways we might go about it:

Oral Interpretation

Listen to what poets themselves have to say:

- Donald Hall: "Poetry begins in the mouth" (Janeczko 1990, 102).
- Nancy Willard: "I think the best way to enjoy poetry is to read it out loud" (Janeczko 1990, 32).
- Eve Merriam: "What I'd like to stress above everything else is the joy of the sounds of language. I have only one rule for reading it: please read a poem OUT LOUD" (Janeczko 1990, 66).
- Tess Gallagher, in response to the question "Where would you start [to get students involved with poetry]?": "I've often started with sound. Getting them to enjoy the voice and word" (Cooke and Thompson 1980, 134).
- Stanley Kunitz: "Above all, poetry is intended for the ear. It must be felt to be understood, and before it can be felt it must be heard. Poets listen for their poems, and we, as readers, must listen in turn. If we listen hard enough, who knows?—we too may break into dance, perhaps for grief, perhaps for joy" (Janeczko 1983, 74).

In *The Uses of Poetry*, Denys Thompson contends that "the first language was poetic rather than prosaic in character" (1978, 19). Long before scribes and Gutenberg moved poetry to the page, an oral tradition was born and carried forth on the tongues of countless civilizations— through their bards, shamans, priests, and medicine men. Despite this long and enduring tradition, many teachers may have forgotten how moving a well-read poem can be. I will never forget hearing a Scottish colleague read Matthew Arnold's "Dover Beach," a poem I had never counted among my favorites. This man's oral interpretation lifted the poem off the page and made it fly around the room. Since then, "Dover Beach" has never been the same for me.

Many teachers may be uncomfortable reading poetry aloud, but as with any other skill, we can all improve. Books have been written on this topic,[1] and the general guidelines offered by several of them make a lot of sense:

1. Read the poem carefully to yourself several times for understanding.

2. Read with an eye for figurative language, especially for metaphors and similes that may dominate the poem, as in "The Fish" (p. 7).

3. Read with an eye for structure and organization and how they may dictate pace and rhythm. Notice divisions and balance, especially the possible presence of a fulcrum (see Highlight 6.2).

4. Write notes or mark the poem, e.g., indicating words that require the slightest "elevation" or emphasis.

5. Be alert to enjambment—the natural flow of one line over into the next.

6. Read slowly and naturally. Especially don't read sing-song.

7. Pause ever so slightly at the end of each line and somewhere within each line (at the *caesura*).

8. Have fun; be concerned with reading effectively, but not with perfection.

We need to involve students in oral reading as well and find ways to help them improve. One of the best approaches is to practice oral interpretation early in the fall, building and refining students' skills that can be drawn upon the rest of the year. Any mini-unit of this type taught in September would include, more or less, the guidelines given above. We would certainly talk about interpretation of tone and meaning as well as pronunciation, volume, pace, and intonation. As always, we would begin by looking at a poem. Some of the best ones for this kind of modeling are poems designed around dialogue. Among them is the following poem by John Wakeman:

Love in Brooklyn

"I love you, Horowitz," he said, and blew his nose.
She splashed her drink. "The hell you say," she said.
Then, thinking hard, she lit a cigarette:
"Not *love*. You don't *love* me. You like my legs,
and how I make your letters nice and all.   5
You drunk your drink too fast. You don't love *me*."

"You wanna bet?" he asked. "You wanna bet?
I loved you from the day they moved you up
from Payroll, last July. I watched you, right?
You sat there on that typing chair you have   10
and swung round like a kid. It made me shake.
Like once, in World War II, I saw a tank

slide through some trees at dawn like it was god.
That's how you make me feel. I don't know why."

She turned towards him, then sat back and grinned,   15
and on the bar stool swung full circle round.
"You think I'm like a tank, you mean?" she asked.
"Some fellers tell me nicer things than that."
But then she saw his face and touched his arm
and softly said, "I'm only kidding you."   20

He ordered drinks, the same again, and paid.
A fat man, wordless, staring at the floor.
She took his hand in hers and pressed it hard.
And his plump fingers trembled in her lap.

This is a sweet, amusing look at two people on the edge of falling in love, bantering fondly toward a kind of confirmation. It is rich with potential for reading aloud. In a class, we'd talk about what is going on, who and where the man and woman are and how they feel about each other. We'd discuss the all-important matter of tone, conveyed by his use of her last name (line 1) and phrases like "blew his nose" and "splashed her drink." How, I'd ask, would she say, "The hell you say" in line 2? (teasingly forceful). And we'd discuss the importance of getting just right the insistence of his retort in line 7—his vulnerability and earnestness in the whole second stanza. Lines 8–9 would offer a great look at enjambment, the continuation of one line into the next. We'd talk about the implications of italics ("You don't love *me*") and punctuation ("I watched you, right?"). In lines 17–18, I'd ask how a reader could best convey her gentle teasing. And how to best express, in line 19, the all-important change in tone (the *fulcrum*—p. 106), the subtle shifting down of pace and pitch over the last six lines toward understanding.

HIGHLIGHT 7.2

To Memorize or Not

Blessings on thee, little man,
Barefoot boy, with cheeks of tan!
With thy turned-up pantaloons,
And thy merry whistled tunes. . . .

From "The Barefoot Boy"

After more years, more decades, than I care to remember, I can still recall the beginning of John Greenleaf Whittier's mossy old nineteenth century classic

▶

"The Barefoot Boy," the first eighteen lines of which my wonderful sixth-grade teacher, Miss Eloise Starr, made us learn by heart. Should we have students memorize poems? The question is one of the most common asked by teachers in classes and workshops.

The answer—from not only me, but many poets and scholars as well—is "Yes." For me it's a qualified yes. I think memorization is fine as long as we give students some choice in the matter and we keep the required length to a reasonable limit, no more than twenty lines in most cases. Some teachers see memorization as outmoded, but it actually has a lot of virtues: it demands discipline from students, it requires them to practice oral interpretation, and it leads to a certain pride of accomplishment. Let's face it: all of us are secretly impressed when someone is able to reel off a few lines of poetry. In the words of Nancy Willard, "[a memorized poem] is a gift from someone who feels the way you do, it doesn't wear out, and you can enjoy it over and over again" (Janeczko 1990, 32–33).

Although its selections are mostly ancient classics, a useful book for teachers is *Committed to Memory: 100 Best Poems to Memorize* by John Hollander.

Many other poems could be used for this kind of groundwork in oral reading, among them these:

- "Dog Bone Blues" by Keith Gunderson
- "It All Started Yesterday Evening" by Roger McGough
- "Preface to a Twenty Volume Suicide Note" by Imamu Amiri Baraka
- "Mutterings over the Crib of a Deaf Child" by James Wright
- "The Rebel" by Mari Evans
- Many of the poems by Maya Angelou and many by Robert Frost

HIGHLIGHT 7.3

Poetry Out Loud

In this collection of over 100 poems, the stress is on stressed and unstressed—the fun of reading aloud. *Poetry Out Loud* mixes the old ("Casey at the Bat," "Jabberwocky," "Dover Beach," "My Heart Leaps Up") and the new (poems by the likes of Nikki Giovanni, Amy Clampitt, Adrienne Rich, Fred Chappell). Sections feature poems on Love and Wreckage; Light Verse

▶

and Poems That Tell Stories; Poems of Animals and the Natural World; Poems of Contradiction and Opposition; Poems of Vision; Poems of Alienation; and Art, Poetry, and the Making Thereof. Marginal notes by the editor, Robert Alden Rubin, provide details on the poems and hints on how to read them. For example, for Giovanni's "Master Charge Blues," Rubin suggests reading "lines 1 and 2 as one line, lines 3 and 4 as one line, and [pausing] between lines 5 and 6" to convey the traditional blues rhythm (21).

Poetry Slams in the Classroom

The ultimate—some might say the nadir—of oral interpretation is the poetry slam (see Chapter 1). A phenonemon that has swept the country since its origins in Chicago in the late 1980s, the poetry slam is a raucous, populist competition, usually held in a bar or cafe, where entrants read their poems over an open mike and submit to immediate ratings by judges who hold up numbered cards. Strict rules are enforced, like the following used for the 1996 National Poetry Slam held in Portland, Oregon (an event that drew teams from twenty-seven cities):

1. Poems can be on any subject, in any style.
2. Each poem must be original to its performer(s).
3. No performance should last longer than three minutes.
4. Performances will be timed by an official time-keeper.
5. Timing will begin when the performance begins, usually with the first utterance of the performer.
6. Scoring is on a scale of 0–10, with judges encouraged to give decimal places to the tenth (e.g., 7.3).
7. There will be four judges drawn from the audience and one assigned "guest" judge. The highest and lowest scores will be dropped from the total, leaving the performer with the middle three scores (between 0 and 30 points).
8. No props, costumes, prerecorded music or musical instruments are allowed.
9. Duos, trios, and quartets are allowed as long as the performed poem is written by one of the performers. (Machine 1 Web sites, 1997)

In the classroom (as in the cafe or bar), the poetry slam combines the dual appeals of performance and competition. Teachers could add other rules as necessary, e.g., a clearer statement of criteria to include the quality of the poem and, especially for our purposes, the quality of the performance. Also, it might make sense for the teacher to serve as the guest judge. However the slam is organized, the whole affair could provide a lively last day for a poetry unit or perhaps a great way to celebrate National Poetry Day in the fall. Who knows?—it could even serve as the first step in sending competitors to the official annual High School Performance Poetry Slam, first held on April 18, 1998, at the Charter Oak Cultural Center in Hartford, Connecticut.

Chants and Choral Reading

A chant is defined by Ron Padgett as "a poem of no fixed form, but in which one or more lines are repeated over and over" (1987, 147). Chants can be fun to read because they are so steady and compelling. As examples, Padgett includes excerpts from "War God's Horse Song II" by Frank Mitchell, who is Navajo; "Raining," a more modern chant by Allan Kaprow; and an unattributed poem entitled "Skin Meat BONES (chant)," which is followed by directions for reading it aloud: "This piece is intended to be read aloud, singing the words 'skin,' 'Meat,' 'BONES,' as notes: 'skin,' high soprano; 'Meat,' tenor; 'BONES,' basso profundo. The 3 notes may vary, but the different registers should be markedly distinguishable" (1987, 147). Native American chants are available in *Songs of the Dream People: Chants and Images from the Indians and Eskimos of North America* by James Houston and *Four Corners of the Sky: Poems, Chants, and Oratory*, compiled by Theodore Clymer.

Occasionally contemporary chant-like poems are found elsewhere, like the rhythmic "The Swimmer's Chant" by Carol D. Spelius and the following work by a high school student from *Mad, Sad & Glad: Poems from Scholastic Creative Writing Awards*:

Chant at Sundown

Patience Merriman

breath of incense
legs of stone
eyes of topaz
every bone
of him is mine

I take my time.

Like so many other performance approaches to teaching, choral reading seems to go in and out of favor. Popular in the 1930s, it faded during the '60s and then enjoyed a revival in the student-centered movement of the '70s before waning again in the vanguard of back-to-the-basics. Still, choral reading has always been around and comes in different formats, from simple to complex. In some places, it becomes almost an art form with large groups presenting programs of polish and sophistication. Since the idea in this chapter is to get all students involved in poetry, I've omitted some of the more demanding forms, like cumulative reading and unison reading.

Line Reading

This simplest pattern allows an entire class to take part in the reading of a poem, with each student taking a line. Obviously the best poems for this kind of reading are those where each line is almost a separate entity. Catalog or list poems work especially well, such as "Swift Things Are Beautiful" by Elizabeth Coatsworth, "Crows" by David McCord, and "These I Have Loved" by Rupert Brooke. Another excellent poem for line reading is "Reply" by Lucille Clifton (p. 60). In this simple but moving poem, a different student could read each of the first fourteen lines and then join in unison for the last three.

Two-Part Reading

In another simple approach, students read alternate lines or couplets. The format works especially well with conversation poems like "Two Friends" by David Ignatow, "Saying Yes" by Diana Chang, "When in Rome" by Mari Evans, "Mutterings over the Crib of a Deaf Child" by James Wright, "HE: Age doesn't matter when you're both in love!" by Julia Alvarez, and the "poems for two voices" by Paul Fleischman. Few poets in recent years have done as much to promote choral reading as Fleischman, whose *Joyful Noise: Poems for Two Voices* won the Newbery Medal for 1989.[1] Fleischman's books—he also wrote the similar *I Am Phoenix* in 1985—feature poems about insects and birds, respectively. Each poem—"The Walking Stick," "Praying Mantis," "Blue Jay," and so on—is formatted for two readers or groups of readers, one taking the left side of a given poem, the other the right (with both reading lines they have in common). In "The Passenger Pigeon," written from the point of view of the bird whose numbers in early America reached into the billions, Fleischman conveys the awful descent into extinction from

> [a] world
> inconceivable   inconceivable
>   without us.

Several of Robert Frost's long, dramatic poems can be read effectively by two voices, especially "The Death of the Hired Man," "Blueberries," "The Witch of Coos" (a ghost story), "The Fear," and "Snow."

In a variation of this approach, some of the poems in *Cool Salsa: Bilingual Poems on Growing Up Latino in the United States* could be effectively read in a bilingual class, one reader taking the English, the other the Spanish lines. This works especially well with "Good Hot Dogs" by Sandra Cisneros and "An Unexpected Conversion" by Carolina Hospital. In "Learning English" by Luis Alberto Ambroggio, a poem about the regrets of having to learn a new language, the lines could be read alternately—with the last line ("the same person"/"la misma persona") spoken by the two readers simultaneously.

Multiple-Part Reading

In this format, individuals, pairs, and groups read lines or sections of poems. Low (often referred to as "dark") and high ("light") voices are assigned as appropriate. Because it requires precision, this approach can be more demanding, but the effects are often impressive. Sometimes it's best to begin small. Among the many works that lend themselves to this treatment is the following brief poem we read earlier:

Vacation

William Stafford

One scene as I bow to pour her coffee:—	*solo low voice*
Three Indians in the scouring drouth huddle at a grave scooped in the gravel, lean to the wind as our train goes by.	*group of mixed voices*
Someone is gone.	*solo high voice*
There is dust on everything in Nevada.	*group of mixed voices*
I pour the cream.	*solo low voice*

And just think what a class could do in a darkened room with Keith Gunderson's wonderful "Do-It-Yourself Night" using pairs for most of the lines, but individuals equipped with flashlights for the "dots" and the deepest voice in the class for the "thomp" of a moon:

```
    Just
take a
big space
growing
dark
and use       dot dot
mainly        and need
stars:        even dot
dot dot       more
dot           dot dot
that's        to make
```

enough	dot dot
dot	the night
for dusk	dot
but we	complete
can't dot	dot dot
wait	dot dot
dot dot	dot dot
too long	well dot
dot dot	that dot
	does it
	except
	thomp
	for a
	moon.

Does this sound childish? Are tenth graders "above and beyond" it? It all depends on how the teacher approaches it. What it can be is fun—making poetry playful.

"Swift Things Are Beautiful" is also effectively read by a variety of voices: in her book *The Speech Choir*, Marjorie Gullan suggests that "all the chorus should give the first line of each stanza, and the rest should be divided either among individuals or small groups of two or three speakers each" (1937, 178). Other useful poems for multiple-part reading are "My Mother Is a God Fearing Woman" by Cornelius Eady, "Good Times" by Lucille Clifton, and "Sence You Went Away" by James Weldon Johnson, all to be found in *In Search of Color Everywhere: A Collection of African-American Poetry*.

Antiphonal Reading

Similar to the responsive reading in many churches, antiphonal reading involves a performance where groups "reply" to each other. As such, it is an extension of two-part reading. Useful poems for this approach often have a question-and-answer pattern. Two excellent examples are James Wright's "Mutterings over the Crib of a Deaf Child" (which, as we've seen, can be used in a variety of ways) and "Ballad of Birmingham" by Dudley Randall. Other poems with two "voices" are those with refrains, like "Jesse James" by William Rose Benét and "Two Red Roses across the Moon" by William Morris.

Readers Theater

Perhaps less well known but even more dramatic is readers theater, an interpretive reading activity that involves everyone in a class, performers as well as the audience. In their very useful *Readers Theatre Handbook: A*

Dramatic Approach to Literature, Leslie Irene Coger and Melvin R. White define the approach as "a medium in which two or more oral interpreters employ vivid vocal and physical clues to cause an audience to see and hear characters expressing their attitudes toward an action so vitally that the literature becomes a living experience—both for the readers and for their audience" (1982, 5–6).

In readers theater, a group of students selects a poem and creates (or follows) a method of presenting it that conveys a particular interpretation. They plan the reading carefully. In *Readers Theatre: Story Dramatization in the Classroom*, Shirlee Sloyer (1982, 35) offers several examples of the planning process with poems like "Inside a Poem" by Eve Merriam and the famous and often anthologized "Mother to Son" by Langston Hughes. In the latter poem of twenty lines, one student in the role of Mother is responsible for the opening two lines:

> Well, son, I'll tell you:
> Life for me ain't been no crystal stair.

The remaining eighteen lines are assigned to individual students in the roles of Shadows or to the entire group—as follows:

Shadow I:	line 3
Shadow II:	line 4
Shadow III:	line 5
Shadow IV:	line 6
All:	line 7
Mother:	lines 8–9
Shadow I:	line 10
Shadow II:	line 11
Shadow III:	line 12
Shadow IV:	line 13
Mother:	line 14
Shadow I:	lines 15–16
All:	line 17
Mother:	lines 18–20

With or without props or costumes, seated (often on stools) or standing at specific locations on the "stage," the students read their assigned parts of the poem. The technique is similar to multiple-part choral reading, but the performers in readers theater always face the audience from the front of the class. Also—and this is especially important—*they imagine a mirror along the back wall that reflects all the readers, with each reader focusing on a particular spot*, as in the figure below. The dramatic effect is one in which any given reader seems to be talking to another (the person "reflected").

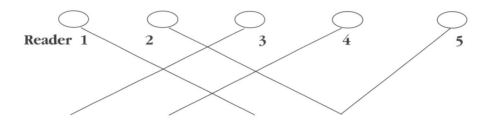

In the Spring 1981 issue of *The English Quarterly*, Peter J. Spencer provides an example of readers theater in a high school class using the poem "David" by Earl Birney (available in *Some Haystacks Don't Even Have Any Needle*). The poem, a dramatic monologue, tells the story of two young mountain climbers, one of whom must make a terrible decision when the other is injured. Events are narrated by Bob, but there are passages of dialogue by both him and David as well as descriptions of alpine scenery. Spencer designs the reading so that two students assume the major roles with other solo readers given "alter ego" lines and two small choruses responsible for the description (29–39).

Coger and White mention several other poems suitable for adaptation for readers theater, such as Peter Bowman's long poem "Beach Red" and shorter works like Amy Lowell's "The Day That Was the Day," Roy Helton's "Old Christmas Morning," Robert Graves's "Not at Home," and Robert Frost's "Home Burial" (1982, 50). Some of the poems mentioned above under two-part choral reading could also be used.

Dance, Mime, and Creative Dramatics

Denys Thompson writes that "the earliest language may have been a verbal supplement to dancing. . . . The whole expressive side of man was engaged in an activity that combined music and movement and poetry" (1978, 20).

> It is reasonably clear that poetry came before prose and was linked with ritual dancing; this is fully consistent with our knowledge that in many countries poetry used to accompany dancing and that traces of the connection are well marked in old poems, and in some of the terms, such as rondeau and rondel (reminding us of round dances), used to describe verse forms (20).

Despite this early connection between the two, comparatively little has been done in schools to link dance with poetry, but the potential is clearly there. A memorable poem that strongly suggests such a blending of the two is "The Dance" by William Carlos Williams (available in Perrine and

Arp's eighth edition of *Sound and Sense* among other sources). Based on a famous sixteenth century painting of a peasant dance by Peter Breughel, "The Elder," the poem—like the dance—is circular, repetitive, and liltingly rhythmic. With an image of the painting projected on a screen (and fiddles and bagpipes "tweedling" from a recording), one or two groups of students could "go round and around" while a leader reads the twelve-line poem two or three times. Coger and White contend that "an integration of the spoken word with stylized dance movement adds not only a spatial dimension but also evokes an active involvement of the audience through kinesthetic empathic responses" (1982, 50). As poems with potential for a reader and dancer working together, they cite Gerard Manley Hopkins's "The Windhover" as well as a possible program called "anyone lived in a pretty how town" based on excerpts from thirty-five poems by e. e. cummings.[2] Finally, the first section of Lillian Morrison's *Rhythm Road: Poems to Move To* includes twelve "poems to dance to," like "Boogie Chant and Dance," "Attic Dance" by Joan Drew Ritchings, and "Dance Poem" by Nikki Giovanni.

Mime is even richer with opportunities. Given a chance, many high school students will enjoy acting out the physical movements described in such sports poems as "The Foul Shot" by Edwin A. Hoey, "Patrick Ewing Takes a Foul Shot" by Diane Ackerman, "The Base Stealer" by Robert Francis (p. 93), "Slam, Dunk, & Hook" by Yusef Komunyakaa, "Shooting Baskets at Dusk" by Michael McFee (p. 43), and "Makin' Jump Shots" by Michael S. Harper. With a poem like "Cardinal Ideograms" by May Swenson, students can mime the numbers. In Emmett Williams's concrete poem "Like Attracts Like," two students could move closer and closer together while repeating the "likes" individually (and "attract" chorally) with increasing speed. *Rhythm Road* also includes numerous poems for miming—like "Ten Tom-Toms," "Jenny the Juvenile Juggler" by Dennis Lee, "In the Pocket" by James Dickey, and "Crystal Rowe (Track Star)" by Mel Glenn.

In a way, creative dramatics—more specifically, role playing and improvisation—is even more feasibly connected to poetry because activities can draw upon poetry as a source but then move away from it. Here are examples from poems we've already seen:

- "Conversation with a Fireman from Brooklyn" (excerpt on p. 41)— Have four or five students take the following parts: a sexist firefighter; a more liberal firefighter who has three daughters, one of whom says she wants to be a firefighter; a feminist; and a more traditional woman. Their task is to improvise a conversation similar to the one in the poem.

- "The Whipping" (p. 39)—One student takes the role of not the old woman in the poem but someone like her; another, that of the poem's speaker; another, someone who opposes corporal punishment altogether; and another, someone who advocates it. They are all part of a breakout group meeting after they've heard a speaker talk about parent-child relations.

- "Mutterings over the Crib of a Deaf Child" by James Wright—Over an imaginary crib, two students alternate the reading of the stanzas. They assume the roles of two parents *or* a parent and another child *or* a parent and his or her other voice—whatever they choose. After the final stanza is read, the two students could continue with improvised dialogue.

- "The Fish"(p. 7) and "Lullabye for 17"(p. 58)—After reading and discussing the two poems, have four students role play a version of *The Oprah Winfrey Show* in which the speakers in the two poems, the mother in "The Fish," and Oprah herself discuss the topic How to Be a Good Mother to Daughters in the Twenty-First Century.

As I think we've seen, linking poetry to performance is really not that hard. What can be hard for some of us is daring ourselves to try it, taking poetry into a realm as remote as the one imagined earlier for our alien Minister of Culture. Imagine her once more, this time visiting, in whatever form, a classroom, perhaps your own, where poetry and performance go hand in hand. Here is what she might see, an improvised version of *The Oprah Winfrey Show* based on the last bulleted activity above.

Scenario

Oprah [Student A]: Ladies and gentlemen, our guests today are two mothers from suburban Chicago, Mrs. Day and Mrs. Jones, and also Mrs. Barr here, who is the daughter of Mrs. Jones and herself the mother of a six-year-old girl. And you all know, of course, that our topic is "How to Be a Good Mother to Daughters in the Twenty-First Century." Now all three of you have experience, but you represent two different generations, so I'm sure we'll have an interesting discussion. I think we'll begin with you, Mrs. Jones. What initial advice do you have for our viewers out there who may be young mothers?

Mrs. Jones, mother in "The Fish" [Student B]: Well, I would just like to say that I think you have to be firm. You have to control. I think my own daughter will agree that I knew from the outset what I wanted her to be and I worked hard to make sure she would be the kind of person I thought she could be and needed to be. And I think she will tell you that she benefited from that. I think she—

Mrs. Barr, daughter in "The Fish" [Student C]: Well, actually, Mother, I—

Mrs. Jones: Please, dear, don't interrupt. What I'm saying is, I think too many mothers these days have no idea of how to mold a child, a daughter. They dilly-dally around and let their girls get away with murder and . . . well, they just flounder. They give them no direction.

Daughter: But, Mother, I think you overdid it. You—

Mrs. Jones: Nonsense!

Oprah: Well, maybe it would be good for us to hear your daughter's point of view.

Daughter: Well, I don't mean to criticize, *Motherrr,* but there were times when I wish you had just laid off me a little. Honestly, you treated me like those stupid fish you had in the bathtub. And by the way, I never could figure out why you had those fish in there anyway.

Mrs. Day, mother in "Lullabye for 17" [Student D]: If I may, I would just like to say that there were times when I, like Mrs. Jones here, felt the need to be a little controlling, to interfere. There was a time, I remember, when my daughter was going with this just awful young man who I absolutely detested. I wanted to wring his neck. But she couldn't see it. That's the way it is with daughters sometimes. They don't have the experience we mothers have and they just don't understand.

Daughter: But we shouldn't be treated like creatures, like pets or whatever. I think my mother here confined me too much. Like she just said, she had this idea of how she wanted me to be and I—

Mrs. Jones: You needed confining. In this day and age, there's far too much parental . . . what do you call it . . . parental laxity. Parents just let their children do anything they want. They go out when they want, they come in when they want, they wear what they want, they smoke, they drink, they do anything.

Daughter: But you wanted me to be like you!

Mrs. Jones: You bet your sweet bippy.

Daughter: But I wanted to be me!

And so on. All of this would be great fun for a class, and the other students could be involved later in the "program" when Oprah takes questions from the audience and call-ins from hither and yon. It would also be productive: the students would extend their understanding of not only the two poems, but the overall issue by imagining how the three "characters" would address it and each other. They might even understand something more about themselves.

After seeing such a class as this, our Minister of Culture from "Southbound on the Freeway" would surely write a different report, claiming that poetry is active and alive in the classrooms of this new and wondrous world, a world where perhaps "performance . . . holds the key to poetry's future" (Gioia 1992, 23).

Notes

1. A helpful article about using Fleischman's poetry in the classroom is Carol Peck's "Joyful Noise Resounds: The New Look of an Old Form" in the September–October 1992 issue of *Teachers & Writers Magazine*.

2. One of the best is *Oral Interpretation* by Charlotte I. Lee and Timothy Gura (Houghton Mifflin, 1996), now in its 9th edition.

8 Poetry and Writing

Despite its origin in song and dance, poetry in the western world is largely a written form. And in the schools, poetry is the jumping-off place for different kinds of writing.

In classrooms, we often have students write, in effect, *from* a poem, with a poem as the stimulus: a student reads "The Fish" (p. 7) and writes in her journal an appreciation of her own mother, who takes her as she is.

> If mom were like this, I'd freak!! Like J's, always wanting her to go with guys from Christ Church and all that crap. I like "sever my head just below the gills." That's Jennifer's mom—not letting her breathe—not giving her *any* slack. Mom won't let me do anything I want but at least she gives me space . . . .

A boy reads "Deer Hunter" by Judson Jerome and writes, almost angrily, an assigned essay in opposition to people who routinely condemn hunting as sport.

Often we have students write *about* a poem: A tenth grader explains the speaker in Cynthia McDonald's "Accomplishments." A junior examines the verbs in Lucille Clifton's "Reply" (p. 60). Or a senior critiques James Merrill's "Laboratory Poem."

Perhaps more than anything else, we engage our students in the writing of poems—a haiku that emerges as a girl observes a sparrow on a wire, or a sweet-and-sour list poem about school written as a class collaboration.

> School is passing a note that Mr. Bellows doesn't see.
>
> School is holding hands in the hall for just a minute before class.
>
> School is cardboard pizza.
>
> School is sweaty palms when you see the teacher at the front of the row, licking her fingers before passing out tests from a stack . . . .

Unlike the idea of poetry as performance, none of this is new to the high school classroom. We've all done it for decades, had students writing from poetry, about poetry, writing poems themselves. In fact, in the last ten or fifteen years especially, the writing of poetry has attracted more notice and seen the publication of more books than all the other aspects of poetry instruction combined.

Writing from Poetry

Teachers have always used poems as springboards, especially for the writing of personal reflections and even papers. Example: a teacher has her students keep a journal for jotting reactions—a word, a phrase, a sentence—to many of the poems they read, like these written about *American Sports Poems* (edited by Knudson and Swenson):

> "The Rabbit-Hunter" by R. Frost—I liked the title. The poem stinks.
>
> "Uneven Parallel Bars" by Patricia Gary—It's neat how the writer makes the words look like the movement on the bar, like at the end.
>
> "The Origin of Baseball" by Kenneth Patchen—not for me.
>
> "Clothespins" by Stuart Dybek—don't like it.
>
> "Motorcycle Racer Thinks of Quitting" by Grace Butcher—I like how the poem doesn't rhyme at first and then rhymes a little in the second stanza and ends with a pair of lines that rhyme. *Easily* my favorite so far.

Later the teacher asks the students to look back over all their entries for a topic that might lead to a paper, an essay.[1]

Another teacher prefers to give more direction with assignments like these:

- On the basis of "The Sacred" (p. 30): Write a paragraph about your sacred place (not your car). Tell what makes it sacred. Try to be specific, including the details of the place that make it so special.

- From "Makin' Jump Shots" by Michael S. Harper or "Shooting Baskets at Dusk" by Michael McFee (p. 43): Write about a physical activity you really enjoy—dancing, swimming, shooting pool, skateboarding, etc. Try to convey to the reader exactly why the activity is so appealing. Mention the senses—the sounds, sights, the touch and feel of the activity.

- From "Deer Hunt" by Judson Jerome: Write about a time when you were forced or persuaded to do something that you really didn't want to do and that you later regretted. *Or*—write about a time when you were afraid of something, but even more afraid to show you were afraid. Tell what happened.

- From "Traveling through the Dark" by William Stafford and "The Road Not Taken" by Robert Frost: Write about a dilemma you have faced. Include why you considered the decision so difficult (the pros and cons), the decision you made, and the results.

Other kinds of writing *from* poetry, of course, are less personal:

- From "Names of Horses" by Donald Hall (a poem about the speaker's affinity for farm horses ending with a simple line consisting only of seven names): Using a book like *The Jockey Club's Illustrated History of Thoroughbred Racing in America* or perhaps an Internet source, write a paragraph about your favorite names of great racehorses. Explain why you like each one. For example, a name I would choose is "Whirlaway" because it suggests overcoming one's opponents with a burst of speed.

■ From "Passenger Pigeon" by Paul Fleischman: Write a one- to two-page paper on the demise of the passenger pigeon in America during the nineteenth century. Be sure to include the numbers and, most important, the causes of the bird's extinction.

■ From "To the Field Goal Kicker in a Slump" (p. 58): You're the author of an advice column for young writers. Write a paragraph offering four or five ways of dealing with writer's block.

Teachers should exercise caution when getting students to write *from* poetry. We don't want an assignment to dwarf or trivialize a poem. For example, it would be inappropriate to have students write a research paper comparing Buicks and Oldsmobiles on the basis of their having read "The Sacred."

Writing about Poetry

We may have overdone this kind of writing, however we view it:

■ As *explication*, with its focus on meaning and interpretation: "Write a paper in which you explain the idea of responsibility in Robert Hayden's 'Those Winter Sundays.'"

■ As *critique*, the analysis of form and meaning: "Write an explanation of the starling as a metaphor in Richard Wilbur's 'The Writer.'"

■ As *research writing*: "Using at least three sources, write a paper on the critical view of Whitman's use of apostrophe in 'Song of Myself.'"

For teachers who hope to make poetry live in the classroom, writing *about* poetry is often the genre's guillotine. Still, there is a placc for it. Shouldn't most students be expected to say something thoughtful in writing about a poem before they're allowed to graduate from high school? I think so. The question is how to make it less painful and fraught with failure. More on this in Chapter 9 (Teaching Form and Technique).

Writing Poetry

This little poem (Fig. 8.1) is something of a fraud. I wrote it several years ago as a model for a clippings poem, a type of poetry that is wonderfully accessible to aspiring (or even unaspiring) young poets. Here is how it works.

Figure 8.1

Clippings poems—known by some as headline poems—are unique in the sense that students are given (actually they select) the words to work with. Each student is handed a magazine or two. Any will work, but slick, sophisticated magazines like *The New Yorker* and *Vogue* are especially good. The instructions are simple: page slowly through the issue, noting ads, captions, and headlines in particular. Clip or tear out any words or phrases that, for whatever reason, appeal to you. Here are some that struck my fancy in the first few pages of a recent issue of *The New Yorker*: "before dinosaurs roamed," "no, this isn't a misprint," "partners in power," "gamblers," "sh-sh-sh-sh!," and "like getting married." The idea is to accumulate a huge number of clippings—a hundred or more—and spread them out on a desk or tabletop. Then look them over and try to find connections. Somehow they appear: a word relates to a phrase and both link up with another, and soon you have a poetic line or two and the germ of an idea. The only requirement is that everything make some sort of sense. Before

Figure 8.2

long a poem in everything but form emerges, and the only thing left to do is shape it. Here's another clippings poem, this one written by a student (Fig. 8.2).

Clippings poems are popular with students because the raw material (especially the clever language of ads) is so accessible and the act of assembling it so creative. The process is really a shortcut for what poets do, more or less: they develop an idea from a storehouse of words (their own vocabulary) from which they select, assemble, and arrange. In fact, some "real" poets compose poems using a modified version of this approach.

All of this raises a question: if students allegedly dislike poetry (hopefully we've assaulted this myth by now) and allegedly hate to write anything, why is it so many of them like to write poetry? The answer, I think, is simple: writing poetry is expressive, much of it is easily based on models and patterns, and the process can be quick and painless and even fun. Let's face it: writing poems is not like writing essays.

HIGHLIGHT 8.1

Poems with Magnetism

Teachers who like the idea of clippings poems, especially the process of having students move ready-made words around to create poetry, might take advantage of one of the most popular marketing ideas for poetry in recent years—the Magnetic Poetry Kit. Available in many bookstores and elsewhere, the kit consists of hundreds of magnetized word tabs available for manipulating.

At home the resulting poems seem to end up mostly on refrigerators, but in the classroom they could go on filing cabinets, metal doors, or even on cookie trays attached to bulletin boards. If you can't find the kit in a store, it is available from Electronic Marketplace, Inc., 5550 Druid Lane, Dallas, TX 75209 or through the company's Web site at http://www.magpo.com/index.html. The latter also features an anthology and suggestions for teachers.

Several variants on the basic kit are available—and even a book: *The Magnetic Poetry Book of Poetry* by Dave Kapell and Sally Steenland from Workman Publishing.

Still, few high school students write poetry on their own. Most of them have to be nudged and directed, and most good teachers use some variation of the following approach:

1. Model the process. Show and discuss several examples of the kind of poetry you're asking students to write. If I were teaching haiku, for example, I'd begin with examples by Bashô, Buson, and Shiki, then show a few by modern poets, and finally some written by former students.

2. Provide what Kenneth Koch (1980) calls "poetry ideas," practical suggestions for helping students jump start their own poems . These could be a single sentence, a brainstorming activity, or a series of exercises:

For a list poem: Brainstorm the things you do as a spectator at a baseball game during the lulls between pitches, plays, and innings. Possibilities:

> watch the kid in front of me eat cotton candy
>
> count the number of times the first baseman spits
>
> try to figure out a coach's signs
>
> time the seconds between pitches
>
> compare the styles of beer vendors
>
> check out the guys/check out the girls

For a diamante: Look back through several diary or journal entries and look for contrasting words or ideas stated or implied. (A student might come up with "Mom and Dad," "my algebra teacher and my piano teacher," "soccer vs. football," "Taco Bell and Red Lobster," "rage and bliss," "hip-hop and hymns.")

For a haiku: Write a list of images from nature that you associate with a particular season. For winter, one student jots down the following lines:

> a snowman with a plaid scarf
>
> dripping icicles
>
> the sound of skis shushing
>
> the screams of jays
>
> feet tromping on the porch to get rid of snow
>
> tires spinning in snow
>
> iced-over windshields
>
> dirty slush piled up in driveways and gutters
>
> whoops when people slip and fall
>
> scratchy wool caps and scarves

3. From the results of brainstorming or exploring, of generating raw material (or in the case of the clippings poem, assembling the scraps of print), ask students to *select* the items they feel have the most potential to work with. (From the jottings above, a student chooses the ones about skis and windshields, then settles on the latter.)

4. As needed, help them phrase and rephrase, arrange, polish, and shape.

Haiku   *first draft*

Early morning ice,
windshield cold and blurry
inside my Escort.

Winter Haiku   *second draft*

  January view:
Inside my Escort icebox
  a windshield white and frosted.

5. If you like, have the class compose a collaboration to show how easy it is. This works better with some forms—like list poems—than others.

6. Always with the students' permission, display as many poems as possible. Let them see each other's work.

These five or six steps are simple and sensible, and they work with almost every kind of poetry.

List Poems

This is a great starting place for writing poetry because list poems are so easy and there are so many good poems to use as models:

- Perhaps the most famous list poem ever written is "These I Have Loved" by Rupert Brooke excerpted from his long poem *The Great Lover:*

    These I have loved:
        White plates and cups, clean-gleaming,
    Ringed with blue lines; and feathery, faëry dust;
    Wet roofs, beneath the lamp-light; the strong crust
    Of friendly bread; and many-tasting food;
    Rainbows; and the blue bitter smoke of wood; . . .

- "Swift Things Are Beautiful" by Elizabeth Coatsworth
- "Daily" by Naomi Shihab Nye (p. 56)
- "Things That Go Away and Come Back" by Anne Waldman
- "If Death . . ." by Miguel Huezo Mixco
- "Common Things" by Ivor Gurney

- "My Favorite Things," the song from *The Sound of Music* by Rodgers and Hammerstein
- Billy Joel's song, "We Didn't Start the Fire"

Even the famous Peanuts book by Charles Schulz, *Happiness Is a Warm Puppy*, is a kind of list poem.

Any of these could serve as springboards: Write a poem called "Dark Things [or Round Things or Soft Things] Are Beautiful." Or, on the basis of Nye's poem, write a poem that catalogs some of the daily things you do to "worship the world." Some of the best list poems are about colors, for which the little collection *Hailstones and Halibut Bones* by Mary O'Neill is helpful even though it is more often used in lower grades. The best resource on the subject is *The List Poem: A Guide to Teaching & Writing Catalog Verse* (1991) by Larry Fagin.

Haiku

Everyone knows this traditional Japanese three-line poem. Dozens of books have been written on haiku, which teachers present in almost every grade. Although the form has few of the qualities of poetry that students like (rhythm, rhyme, humor, etc.), many enjoy writing haiku. Besides the three lines, the standard features include seventeen syllables (5-7-5: allow lots of leeway, please), nature as a topic, observation as a habit, and a sense of immediacy conveyed by the present tense. Haiku has an ancient history. The poem below was written by the Japanese poet Moritake (1452–1540).

Fallen petals rise
back to the branch—I watch:
oh . . . butterflies!

HIGHLIGHT 8.3

Haiku Resources for Teachers

Few forms have been written about as often as haiku. Among the many books useful to teachers are *The Haiku Handbook: How to Write, Share, and Teach Haiku* (discussed on p. 141). *Haiku in English* by Harold G. Henderson; *Haiku Moment: An Anthology of Contemporary North American Haiku* by Bruce Ross; *The Essential Haiku: Versions of Bashô, Buson, and Issa* by Robert Hass; *The Classic Tradition of Haiku: An Anthology* by Faubion Bowers; and *The Haiku Anthology: Haiku and Senryu in English* by Cor Van den Heuvel.

Picture books with haiku include *Black Swan, White Crow* by J. Patrick Lewis and Christopher Manson and *In a Spring Garden* by Richard Lewis and Ezra Jack Keats.

The Haiku Society of America (c/o Japan Society, 333 East 47th Street, New York, NY 10017) publishes a journal, *frogpond*, featuring original work as well as reviews and articles.

Among several Internet Web sites devoted to the form is *The Shiki Internet Haiku Salon* (p. 188). *Dogwood Blossoms* is an electronic journal for haiku (http://glwarner.narrowgate.net/haiku/hkuframe.html).

Cinquain

Pronounced "cin-*kain*," this five-line form was invented by Adelaide Crapsey, who used a wavelike syllable count of two-four-six-eight-two. Following is perhaps her most famous example as well as a cinquain by a student:

November Night

Adelaide Crapsey

Listen . . .
With faint dry sound,
Like steps of passing ghosts
The leaves, frost-crisped, break from the trees
And fall.

Engagement

Vivian Riner

Promise
of heart and hand
ring of stone and gold band.
Days of sweet anticipation
Waiting.

An easier pattern may make the form more manageable for some students: a one-word title, two adjectives describing the title, three *-ing* participles, a related phrase, and a synonym for the title:

Sheepdog
Gentle, shaggy
ambling, rambling, shambling
a rollicking hayrick of unruly hair
Sadie

Diamante

Students may tell you that a Diamante is a style of car by Mitsubishi, but before it was ever an automobile, it was a seven-line, diamond-shaped poem based on contrasting words:

Winter
white and silver
fading, sleeping, slowing down
March exchanges vows with April
nodding, rising, waking up
green and goldburst
Spring

The pattern is clear: lines two and six are two adjectives describing the beginning and ending nouns; lines three and five, three participles (*-ing* or *-ed* words) also describing the nouns; and line four, the pivotal turning point, which may be four words or a phrase. As noted earlier, it's easy to get students started with diamantes: offer a few polarities with potential: *good/evil, sunlight/shadow, dream/nightmare, Beauty/Beast.* The trick is the fourth line—making the transition smooth.

Acrostic Poems

These are easy and often surprisingly effective. Acrostic poems are written down the page with each line beginning with the succeeding letters in a word. Most of them are based on names, like this example written by a high school student:

Beer-drinking guy
In a bar singing
Loud
Lingering songs.

Rough
On
Girls' hearts.
Even
Rough is
Smooth.

Besides their own names, some students base acrostic poems on qualities (love, jealousy, pain, etc.), sports, food, hobbies, even book titles.

Concrete Poems

Again, fun and easy. With concrete poems, the shape dramatically reinforces the meaning, in fact, often *is* the meaning. Some of the best to use as models are these:

"Easter Wings" by George Herbert, an English poet who wrote in the 17th century

"Siesta of a Hungarian Snake" by Edwin Morgan

"Seal" by William Jay Smith

"Forsythia" by Mary Ellen Solt

"Poem" by Philip Tannenbaum

"Letter Slot" by John Updike

"Concrete Cat" by Dorthi Charles

"like attracts like" and "She Loves Me" by Emmett Williams

"Love" by B. P. Nichol

"Apfel" by Reinhard Döhl

"400-Meter Freestyle" by Maxine Kumin

"Art" by Malcolm Glass

One of the best concrete poems is this one by Roger McGough:

40——Love

middle	aged
couple	playing
ten	nis
when	the
game	ends
and	they
go	home
the	net
will	still
be	be
tween	them

One way to get students started with these is to have them play around with the shapes of words:

l o o s e   **tight**

From there, it isn't too difficult to shape a poem around its subject, as Reinhard Döhl does with "Apfel" (with the *wurm* hidden in the middle) and Maxine Kumin with "400-Meter Freestyle," where the lines of the poem turn at the ends like a swimmer moving back and forth across the pool.

Here is another concrete poem about sports:

$\boxed{\text{2nd}}$
base is where
a darting double sends the
speedy batter, unless a fielder errs, then
$\boxed{\text{3rd}}$. But say the runner forgot to touch $\boxed{\text{1st:}}$
If another fielder tells the ump, he'll yell,
"Out!," keeping the hapless hitter
from ever getting
$\boxed{\text{Home.}}$

Sonnets

Sonnets are anything but easy. For most young adults, wrestling with the structural demands of eight-plus-six iambic pentameter is like stuffing a python into a sack. (Just think of Millay's title, "I Will Put Chaos into Fourteen Lines.") A few verbally gifted students may be up to the challenge, but most are not. I'd offer other models, like the following reed-thin sonnet-of-sorts by an anonymous poet, which appears in *Patterns of Poetry: An Encyclopedia of Forms* (1986, 161) by Miller Williams.

An Aeronaut to His Love

I
Through
Blue
Sky
Fly
To
You.
Why?
Sweet
Love,
Feet
Move
So
Slow.

I'd let students try their hand at writing variants of sonnets like this one, which follows a *abba/abba/cdcdee* rhyme scheme. I might even give them a beginning or two:

Ashley's
simple
dimple

flashes.
Sherry's
smile is
guileless,
merry.
Girlish
charms
set off
alarms,
————
————.

Obviously, the teacher could blank out the last four or six (or even ten) lines, depending on the degree of challenge she wished to impose.

Found Poetry

Found poems are just that: they are found, discovered. A student finds a passage she considers poetic in a novel, a newspaper, or even an ad. To create a found poem, she transforms the piece, reworking it here and there, omitting a word or two, and shaping the revision to fit the meaning. Here is a found poem created from a passage in Zibby Oneal's young adult novel, *In Summer Light* (1985, 117):

Love (a found poem)

Once she had asked her mother
How a person knew when she loved someone.

You'll know.

And it was true: she knew.

She would say the word to herself—
For the pure pleasure of saying it:

Listening to the lovely, liquid opening
  of the vowel,
    and the *v*
      that closes
      and contains it.

Some modern poets have written found poems. Two examples are "Found Poem" by Howard Nemerov (based on an article in *The St. Louis Post Dispatch*) and "Genuine Poem, Found on a Blackboard in a Bowling Alley in Story City, Iowa" by Ted Kooser. An excellent article on how to introduce found poetry to a class is "Let Found Poetry Help Your Students Find Poetry" by Nancy Gorrell in the February, 1989 issue of the *English Journal*.

Parodies

Parodies can be wonderfully fun to read, like the following opening lines of "Jack and Jill," a Whitman spoof by Charles Battell Loomis from the book *The Brand-X Anthology of Poetry* by William Zaranka (1981, 207):

> I celebrate the personality of Jack!
>
> I love his dirty hands, his tangled hair, his locomotion blundering.
>
> Each wart upon his hands I sing,
>
> Paeans I chant to his hulking shoulder blades. . . .

Like sonnets, parodies can be demanding, but for students with a sense of humor and an ear for style, they're great fun. Have them work with poets whose manner is highly idiosyncratic and therefore more easily imitated, like Emily Dickinson, Frost, Sandburg, cummings, or William Carlos Williams. Give them starters. Parodies of Williams's famous "This Is Just to Say" might begin

I have eaten	I dissected
the gorp	the cat
You left in the garbage.	in biology lab.
My sheepdog	Mrs. Gundersack
Ignored it:	said it's
Too grey	required
and forlorn. . . .	for an A. . . .

Models

Speaking of starters—or models—one of the best ways a teacher can inspire his students to write poetry is to write poems himself and share them. Young adults love to see a teacher grapple with the same challenges he has issued, and they love to see the results. Here are two poems written and shared by a teacher now working in the same high school where I once taught. The second could especially be used as a pattern for students.

Nancy

Mike Kaplan

Comes to school
Dressed in no one cared clothes,
Her hands and face
Are dirty before the day begins.

Always alone
But not by choice,
With her around
No one else fears being teased or ridiculed.

We sit across
From one another at lunch,
Sometimes I think
I'm all she's got.

And I'm not nearly enough.

Don

Mike Kaplan

He's from Mississippi,
I'm from Brooklyn.
He's a Christian,
I'm a Jew.
He uses herbicides,
I'm organic.
He's blue collar,
I'm white.
He chews tobacco,
I jog.
He drives a truck,
I've got a Volvo.

So very different
Yet so much alike.

Poems like these offer an invitation from teacher to students: "Hey, I can come up with something like this. So can you! Give it a shot!"

Obviously there are many other forms and types of poetry to teach besides the ones I've mentioned—couplets, odes, raps, tanka, senryu, pantoums, limericks, skeletonic poems, ballads, blues poems, sestinas, terza rimas, rondeaus, even triolets and villanelles.[2] Almost all of them, and others, have been explained in the dozens of books written in the last twenty years about the writing of poetry. These are six of the best:

- *Getting from Here to There: Writing and Reading Poetry* (1982) by Florence Grossman. This book has ten chapters on ten types of poems, some of them unconventional: lists, things, signs, people, clothes, sound/silence, dreams and fantasies, etc. In the chapter on signs, Grossman has students writing poems about punctuation marks, numbers, and geometric figures. The book offers numerous models by published poets and unpublished students and numerous exercises. In Grossman's own words,

    Each exercise leads you to a source for your own poem, a place to collect your material, a way to trigger your imagination. The sources will always go back to your own experience, real or imagined. Concrete suggestions will help you begin, and poems by other students will show you how they responded to a particular poetry idea. . . . You must write almost the way you speak, not in the flowery words that are sometimes mistaken for poetry, but in what poets call your own voice (n.p.).

■ *Getting the Knack: 20 Poetry Writing Exercises 20* by Stephen Dunning and William Stafford. This is the best of two worlds—a collaboration between acclaimed poetry teacher and acclaimed poet. Using a chatty, encouraging style, step-by-step instructions, and many student examples, the authors provide elaborate, helpful guides for writing twenty kinds of poetry, including found poems, pantoums, recipe poems, memory maps, and monologue poems. A typical exercise—for memory mapping—asks students "to draw a map (or floor plan) of the room you slept in at age four or five. Whether you slept alone, with someone else, or with a slew of people, for this exercise think of it as *your* room." From there, "you" are asked to label items, share your map with someone, show where books and games and toys are kept, what you see from the window, how you feel when you are sent to your room, and so on. All of this leads through eight steps to the writing of a poem based on the "thread" of a memory (1992, 96).

■ *The Haiku Handbook: How to Write, Share, and Teach Haiku* (1992) by William J. Higginson with Penny Harter. An indispensable book for teachers of the form. It offers a history of haiku, chapters on form and craft as well as the haiku seasons, lists of publishers and magazines, a glossary of terms, a bibliography, and lesson plans. The book features not only the four great Japanese masters of the form (Bashô, Buson, Issa, and Shiki), but important Western authors as well.

■ *The Practice of Poetry: Writing Exercises from Poets Who Teach*, edited by Robin Behn and Chase Twichell. As the subtitle suggests, this book is unique. Molly Peacock teaches how to write a villanelle, Garrett Hongo how to base a poem on a secret about yourself, and Lynne McMahon how "to jump-start the dead poem." Rita Dove has us

> write a ten-line poem. The poem must include a proverb, adage, or familiar phrase (examples: she's a brick house, between the devil and the deep blue sea, one foot in the grave, a stitch in time saves nine, don't count your chickens before they hatch, someday my prince will come, the whole nine yards, a needle in a haystack) *that you have changed in some way*, as well as five of the following words: *cliff, blackberry, needle, cloud, voice, mother, whirl, lick.* You have ten minutes (1992, 13).

There are over ninety exercises organized around getting ideas, using the self as a source, writing images and metaphors, shape and structure, sound and rhythm, and writer's block.

- *Wishes, Lies, and Dreams: Teaching Children to Write Poetry* by Kenneth Koch. A classic. The book was generated by the author's experiences with students in elementary and middle schools, but the ideas apply to high school as well. The title is instructive: Koch asks students to write about wishes, lies, dreams, noises, colors, etc.; he asks for comparisons, sestinas, and metaphors, for collaborations and contrasts (e.g., I Used To/But Now; I Seem To Be/But Really I Am). Koch believes that "a poetry idea should be easy to understand, it should be immediately interesting, and it should bring something new into the children's poems." (1980, 8)[3]

- *Poemcrazy: Freeing Your Life with Words* (1996) by Susan Goldsmith Wooldridge. The spirit of this lively, accessible book is conveyed by the title and the cover—a picture of a young woman leaping joyously down an urban street. Written by a California Poet in the Schools, *Poemcrazy* offers sixty brief chapters, sixty techniques for getting people to play with words in fresh, imaginative ways. Wooldridge has us collecting words, borrowing words, coloring words, juxtaposing words, comparing, exaggerating, venturing into the absurd. The book almost takes us back to kindergarten when every experience was a new one waiting to be made meaningful by language.

HIGHLIGHT 8.4

Markets

Teachers who engage their students in writing sometimes send works of particular promise to publishers, mostly magazines aimed at young adults. Most of the following suggest reading one or more issues before submitting work; they will send guidelines if you include a self-addressed envelope.

- *The Acorn* (1530 Seventh St., Rock Island, IL 61201). A newsletter established in 1989 aimed at students K–12. Published four times a year, twenty poems per issue.

- *The Apprentice Writer* (c/o Gary Fincke, Editor, Susquehanna University, Selinsgrove, PA 17870-1001.) Annual magazine accepting prose and poetry by high school students; deadline May 15.

- *Merlyn's Pen: The National Magazine of Student Writing* (Dept. PM, Box 1058, East Greenwich, RI 02818). Perhaps the most established national magazine of writing from students in grades 9–12; published alternate months during the school year. Manuscripts must be accompanied by a completed official cover sheet available upon request.

▶

- *Skipping Stones* (P. O. Box 3939, Eugene, OR 97403). A multicultural magazine. Publishes five issues a year, fifteen to twenty poems per issue. For children eighteen and under. Celebrates "cultural and environmental richness."

- *Southern Voices* (Cedar Creek School, 2400 Cedar Creek Drive, Ruston, LA 71270). A journal of award-winning prose and poetry from young writers across the southeastern United States.

- *Writes of Passage* (817 Broadway, 6th Floor, New York, NY 10003. A literary journal for teenagers published by the nonprofit organization of the same name. Published twice a year; accepts poetry and short stories from young people ages twelve to nineteen.

For teachers wishing to submit students' work to competitions, the best known is probably the *Scholastic Writing Awards* (Dept. PM, Scholastic Inc., 730 Broadway, New York, NY 10003). For students in grades 7–12; teachers should write for entry information in September.

For the names of other magazines and other competitions, the best reference resources are *Poet's Market* by Chantelle Bentley and *1999 Children's, Writer's, and Illustrator's Market,* by Alice Pope (the section on Young Writer's & Illustrator's Markets); and *Market Guide for Young Writers* by Kathy Henderson.

These six books and all the many others written to help teachers help students write poetry have changed the landscape of poetry teaching. Since the early 1980s, they have broadened student involvement in the genre by responding, in effect, to suggestions by poets like Tess Gallagher and Sandra McPherson. First, Gallagher: "I think the best way for anybody to understand poetry is to write some." And McPherson: "You can teach [students] about poetry by making them write it. It might be that that's the approach of the future, to make them write it first" (Cooke and Thompson 1980, 135, 137–38).

For Gallagher and McPherson, then, understanding is key. Understanding the language of poetry—what poems mean. Understanding the connections between meaning and form—how poems mean (the imposing topic we explore in the next chapter). And surely understanding ourselves and others. If writing poems, and writing from and about them, will lead to these kinds of understanding, we can hardly ask for more.

Notes

1. For an extended example of this kind of writing, see High School Vignette #4 in *Standards for the English Language Arts* (1996, 64–65). The example shows an eleventh grader developing an essay based on reading log entries to "Traveling through the Dark" by William Stafford.

2. Two of the best sources on forms are *Patterns of Poetry: An Encyclopedia of Forms* by Miller Williams and *The Teachers & Writers Handbook of Poetic Forms* by Ron Padgett.

3. Another useful book by Koch is *Rose, Where Did You Get That Red?: Teaching Great Poetry to Children* (1990) which employs poems by traditional poets as models. One of the most interesting and useful is Wallace Stevens's famous poem "Thirteen Ways of Looking at a Blackbird."

9 Teaching Form and Technique

As noted briefly in Chapter 8, this business of structure seems to be the poetry teacher's greatest bugaboo. We often seem torn: on the one hand, we hear the great misgivings routinely voiced about "analyzing poetry to death." Even many poets themselves argue for easing up: Robert Kendall confirms our awareness that students are "bored by talk about technique or theory." Mark Hillringhouse argues against teaching such matters as scansion, "filling the blackboard with dashes and accents" (Lockward 1994, 66). And Dana Gioia contends that "poetry teachers especially at the high school and undergraduate levels should spend less time on analysis. . ." (1992, 23).

But there are other voices—those of the "cultural literacists" like E. D. Hirsch, Harold Bloom and William Bennett, the voices of colleges and universities heavy with "expectations," our great bureaucracies of testing like The College Board, and the poets and critics who have written such classics on poetics as *Understanding Poetry* (Cleanth Brooks and Robert Penn Warren) and *Sound and Sense* (Laurence Perrine). These voices clamor for the teaching of culture and art and the way art—including poetry—works.

Reduced to its barest essentials, the question is simple: should we expect students to learn anything *about* poetry? And if so, what? To me the answer to the basic question is "Yes." I believe more than anything else in making poetry accessible and meaningful to students, in teaching serious poetry so that we create more future readers of it. But I also believe in teaching some appreciation of poetry as a craft, as an art form.[1] And even though the professional advocacy for teaching poetics has waned somewhat since its heyday in the 1960s, form and technique are still routinely taught. I dare say every high school literature textbook (not to mention every standardized achievement test) pays due homage. Even the *Standards for the English Language Arts* acknowledges the importance of poetics: "As students learn to read and respond to literary texts, they discover the special features of these texts, and they develop the special skills and vocabulary needed to experience and appreciate literature fully, in all its forms. They learn, for example, that literary language is rich with metaphor, imagery, rhyme, and other figures and devices" (1996, 29).

The "figures and devices" most English teachers teach include most, if not all, of the following, listed roughly in descending order of frequency:

- simile
- metaphor
- onomatopoeia
- alliteration
- imagery
- tone
- metrics (iambic pentameter, blank verse, and the like)
- stanza
- forms (haiku, sonnet, cinquain, etc.)
- symbol
- irony
- paradox
- consonance and assonance

The most prevailing approach is deductive: define the terms, give examples, and have the students find them in poems. In some ways, the method is logical and efficient. Yet year after year, most of our students barely tolerate our efforts. Few recall it with affection, and fewer reflect upon it later as a source of insight and inspiration. It is hard to imagine a student looking back to the tenth grade some years later and thinking, "I really loved the way Ms. Steinbrenner taught metrics."

It would seem the question is not what to teach, but *how*. How might we teach this knowledge we deem so important more productively and more creatively? Here are some solid, if not sure-fire suggestions:

GUIDELINE ONE

Instead of definitions, begin with generalizations. Actually, begin with specifics (poems) that lead to generalizations—inductive teaching. Here's an example: well into a unit on poetry (perhaps week two), we might dip our toes into form and structure by looking at the following poem, one we saw in the preceding chapter:

40——Love

Roger McGough

middle	aged
couple	playing
ten	nis

when	the
game	ends
and	they
go	home
the	net
will	still
be	be
tween	them

This is a clever poem, easy to "get" and fun to talk about. It lacks any measure of intimidation at all, and so it provides a harmless entrance into the world of structure and design. Some of the questions I might ask are these.

- This poem is obviously about tennis. How does McGough show that?
- Why does the poet draw a vertical line down the middle?
- Why do you think he split the word *tennis* into two parts in line 3?
- Why do you think he chose to divide the word *between* between the last two lines?
- Why did he choose the title, "40-Love"?

Without picking the poem apart, without referring to terms themselves, we are getting at structure; we are talking about technique. What we are really talking about—what we should always talk about at the beginning—is the concept of *choice*. We are also working our way toward a broad generalization, the most important generalization of all to teach students about form and technique (trumpet fanfare, please): *Poets make choices.* (We could elaborate a little if we chose—poets make informed choices; they make choices for reasons; etc.—but most important, they choose.)

So begin here: poets make choices about everything. They choose words. They choose rhythms. They choose where to change the rhythm. They choose sounds. They choose rhymes—or they choose not to rhyme. They choose shapes. They choose to make comparisons. They choose a particular image; they choose to use a word as a symbol (a rose, a claw, a white dress). They choose line lengths and line breaks.

Jump Cabling

Linda Pastan

When our cars	touched
When you lifted the hood	of mine
To see the intimate workings	underneath,
When we were bound	together
By a pulse of pure	energy,
When my car like the	princess

In the tale woke with a   start,
I thought why not ride the rest of the way together?

I'd read this wonderful little multi-layered poem aloud a time or two, pausing significantly, dramatically, at the gaps. Then I'd ask, "Why did the poet choose to break up each of the first seven lines the way she did? *And then*—why did she change the last line? Students would see this clearly. The interruptions, and then the smooth unbroken flow of words in line 8, didn't just happen. Linda Pastan *chose* to do them that way. She wanted the first seven lines to lurch and hesitate like a balky engine, and then she smoothed out line 8 to convey the motor waking "with a start" and purring sweetly. These were choices having to do with form and technique (in this case, sound and rhythm), and meaning.

So here we've shown a class two poems, and we've talked harmlessly about what poets do: they tinker with technique. But so far, no mention of *technique* by name. No reference to *form*. No terms, no definitions. We are concerned with the larger picture.

Some of you are surely saying, "Of course" or "Big deal; we do this"—and maybe some of us do. But most of us, I am convinced, overlook it. We teach the trees—"Define metaphor." "Find the similes." "Explain consonance."—while overlooking the much more important forest: *Poets choose—words, rhythms, sounds, images, everything.*

GUIDELINE TWO

Approach form and technique from an angle. Use sleight-of-hand. Have fun. Most students couldn't care less about The Great Revelation that "Poets Choose." We have to pull a fast one, trick them, seduce them. We have to approach this (for them) dreadful business of form and technique through a side door.

Scenario

Ms. Simms at the start: Before we look at poems today, I want to show you something. Eyes up here at the screen, please *[The teacher shows a transparency of two automobiles—a Jaguar XK8 and a Mercedes Benz SL500.[2] The cars are both convertibles and although they are remarkably similar, even an untrained eye can detect differences.]* OK, as you can see, these are two models of cars. If you could have one—just on the basis of looks, which one would you choose?

Sammy: Ooooh, I like the Vette.

Philippe: They ain't no Vette, man.

Sammy: You crazy. What is it then, the red one?

Philippe: It's a Jag XK8.

Ms. Simms: It is a Jaguar XK8, as Philippe says. Why do you like it, Sammy?

Sammy: Cause it's sleek.

Caroline: Streamlined.

Ms. Simms: But isn't the other one streamlined too?

Sammy: Yeah, but the XK8 is bootleggy.

Ms. Simms: Bootleggy?

Sammy: Yeah, you know . . . bootleggy . . . cool.

Ms. Simms: Be more specific.

Sammy: I like the way the headlights slant back. Like cats' eyes.

Tessa: I like the other one's headlights better. What is it?

Philippe: Merc SL500.

Ms. Simms: OK, let's think about just the headlight design on the two cars for a moment. Why do you think they're different?

Randy: That's just the way they wanted 'em.

Ms. Simms: I know, but why? Or who? Who wanted them . . . who made them different?

Randy: Well, . . . the people who made the cars.

Ms. Simms: All right, but with cars, who decides what they will look like?

Caroline: I dunno. I guess the people in design.

Ms. Simms: Right. And for a minute now, just think about how that might happen. Imagine some man or woman working in the automobile design section of the Jaguar Motor Works or whatever. Why do you think this guy decided the XK8 should have this swept-back headlight?

Tessa: Because she liked it, liked the way it looks . . . maybe she thought it ought to look like a cat since it's a Jaguar.

Ms. Simms: So she decided on this design [*points to the XK8*] instead of the other, right?

Tessa: Right.

Ms. Simms: So what are we talking about here?

Robert: We talking about style.

Ms. Simms: Exactly! And what is style?

Beneatha: Style is fashion.

Troy: Style is what makes something special.

Tessa: Style is what gives your clothes . . . oh, I don't know. It's what turns heads.

Ms. Simms: OK, now look at these passages from two poems. You knew I was getting at something, didn't you?

> (1) Insects fly around the room,
>   Always near the ceiling.
>   My daughter lies asleep in the breeze
>   unaware of the danger or the wind,
>   and unaware of life's larger disturbances
>   that await her in a future unforeseen.

> (2) Wasps or hornets rattle on the sills
>   and fill the vestibule with danger;
>   my daughter, rocked by lullabies
>   of wind, naps inside mosquito netting
>   like a bride before the veil is lifted
>   for the rough world to injure with its kiss.

[The second is from a poem called "Her Sleep" by Jill Hoffman.]

Ms. Simms: Which do you like better?

Freddie: Tell you the truth, I'm not wild about either one.

Sallie: Makes me squirm.

Robert: I like the second one better.

Ms. Simms: Why?

Robert: I like parts of it, like "rocked by lullabies of wind."

Sheila: It's more vivid. Like the part about the bride. I like that.

Joanna: I don't like it; I don't get it. What's it mean "injure with its kiss"?

Sheila: It means you gotta take it easy out there. The world's a rough place.

Ms. Simms: You know what I'm getting at, of course. Are we also talking about style here?

Freddie: I don't see how.

Ms. Simms: Does anyone see?

Sallie: Yeah, I guess. Kinda.

Ms. Simms: OK, we've been talking about what designers do with cars. They take a car and they sweep it back, maybe flatten out the rear, add a new hood ornament. It's all about style. And I'm just trying to say that poets do the same thing. They look for different ways to say the same thing. They choose one word instead of another—or one phrase, like "wasps or hornets rattle on the sills" instead of "insects fly around the room." They *design* a poem. They fashion it, shape it, put an image here, a simile there.

And so the teacher has used cars as the entrée into talking about style, about technique and form. She has approached a difficult subject by using an appealing analogy.

Corollary: Go to extremes. Look for ways to give your teaching flavor and pizzazz. For example, when teaching alliteration, bring in Margaret Atwood's hilarious *Princess Prunella and the Purple Peanut.* Even though it's a picture book, many high school students will like the zany humor conveyed by the fact that every word begins with the letter *p* (or so it seems). If you teach euphony (the notion of pleasant sounds), have a contest for the most beautiful word in the English language. I once read an article that argued for *dawn, lullaby, hush, golden,* and *murmuring,* among others, and the French allegedly love the sound of our *cellar door,* but my choice would be *Shenandoah.*

GUIDELINE THREE

As we've just seen, have students compare poems—or pieces of poems—with versions that you find or versions of your own devising. Here is another example involving three treatments of an old nursery rhyme[3]:

(1) Humpty Dumpty sat on a wall,
Humpty Dumpty had a great fall.
All the king's horses and all the
king's men
Couldn't put Humpty together again.

(2) Humpty Dumpty
Sat on a wall,
Humpty Dumpty
Had a great fall.
All the king's horses
And all the king's men
Couldn't put Humpty
Together again.

(3) H
(umpty)   sat
D   on a wall
H
(umpty) had a grEAT f
D   a
                          l
                          l
                horses
Alltheking's   and
                men
Couldn't pu (tHump)ty
tgthr(oee)   aGAIN

We would talk about which version they liked best and why, always coming back to choices and reasons for choices. Sometimes I might show three versions of a single line:

(1) the woods are lovely, dark and deep

(2) the woods are pretty, quiet and deep

(3) the woods are wonderful and deep.

Or three versions of a simile: In David Huddle's poem, "Icicle" (in the collection *Strings: A Gathering of Family Poems*), which shows the speaker's regret years later of a childhood act when he bloodied his brother's nose with an icicle, there is this comparison: "cold as Russia." Why not, I would ask, "cold as Norway" or "cold as Greenland," both of which suffice in terms of meaning and rhythm? Why did the poet *choose* Russia?

I would show "40-Love" again, this time alongside a modified sentence version ("There's a middle-aged couple playing tennis. When the game ends, . . .") and a poem version without the "net." By now, we would be more than ready for another generalization—*Poets shape their poems to fit their meaning*—and another guideline:

GUIDELINE FOUR

Whenever there is an opportunity, emphasize the connection between form and meaning. We've already seen this at work with concepts like line breaks ("Jump Cabling"), imagery ("Her Sleep"), and shape or form ("40-Love"). It can also be done with others, like meter. I might begin, typically, with another set of lines:

(1) Old Paint, sweaty and alarmed, ran through the field.

(2) The pastured horse conveyed concern by running.

(3) The galloping hooves in the meadow elicited danger.

Just in terms of the *sounds* of these three sentences (or, if you will, lines of poetry), which one do you like the best? In which one does the rhythm of the sentence best convey the action, the sense of what is happening? We would talk about this; I might drum my fingers on a desktop to imitate horses running. Sooner or later I might tell the class which I prefer, or I might leave the class guessing. It isn't important. What is important is that we talk, again, about poets choosing—in this case, sound and rhythm to fit their ideas.

From here, I might show the class some of the useful exercises in Chapter 13 of *Sound and Sense* by Laurence Perrine and Thomas R. Arp (1992). The authors present several paired lines of poetry, one of which in each case is the original:

(1) The curfew tolls the knell of parting day,
     The lowing cattle slowly cross the lea,
     The plowman goes wearily plodding his homeward way,
     Leaving the world to the darkening night and me.

(2) The curfew tolls the knell of parting day,
     The lowing herd wind slowly o'er the lea,

> The plowman homeward plods his weary way,
> And leaves the world to darkness and to me.
>
> *(Thomas Gray)*

Again, the idea is to talk about which piece has the better match of sound and meaning. Of the two, which one is actually from Gray's *Elegy in a Country Churchyard?* (1992, 205–6).

What happens when we fail to talk about form and meaning is this: we isolate concepts and terms as though they function apart from any other consideration in a poem.

GUIDELINE FIVE

Gradually work downward toward definitions. From the broadest possible generalization (poets choose) through ever more specific levels (poets match their rhythms to their meanings), I'd make my way toward terms. So far we've avoided them: through all of the discussion of sound and rhythm above, there has been no mention of the word *meter* itself or the notion of *metric feet.* And certainly none to *iambic pentameter.* We haven't had to. Sooner or later, though, a teacher would probably write a term and a definition on the board: *meter—the steady rhythm in a line of poetry.* She might even teach the different kinds of metric feet. Still, always in the background is the poet and the idea of poets choosing forms and techniques.

GUIDELINE SIX

Whether you use a deductive approach or the inductive one I've suggested, give your students lots of "looks" at any given concept; have them work with it in different ways. Take *imagery.* Have students create a video commercial for it. Or a concrete poem about it. Or an acrostic poem. Have them defend it in a court of law. Challenge someone to write a rap around it.

GUIDELINE SEVEN

Show poets at work. Show drafts of poems written by poets, but also some written by former students and some you've done yourself (save them). The point here is to reinforce again—it can never be said too many times— that poets choose, and that sometimes their choices don't work. They scribble poems on the backs of grocery lists and postcards. They write and rewrite, then wad up the paper, trash it, and start all over again. They write anew. They let the poem sit awhile. They come back to it a month or even a year later and madly cross out words, draw arrows hither and yon, reword and rephrase. Finally they like a little of what they've written and begin to build on what they like—etc., etc., etc. It's important for students to see all this.

There are several wonderful resources for showing students the process of poets in action, poets revising. One of the best is *Fifty Contemporary Poets: The Creative Process* by Alberta T. Turner. True to the title, the book leads the reader through the revision process of poets like Robert Francis, Philip Booth, Donald Hall, Linda Pastan, Donald Justice, and Denise Levertov. Each presents a poem and addresses the following questions, among others, posed by Turner: How did the poem start? What changes did it go through from start to finish? What principles of technique did you consciously use? The discussions by Richard Wilbur ("The Eye"), James Tate ("A Box for Tom"), and William Stafford ("Ask Me") are particularly useful because each shares the final poem as well as earlier marked-over drafts.

An equally useful book is *The Hand of the Poet: Poems and Papers in Manuscript* by Rodney Phillips et al. Based on an exhibition at the New York Public Library, this book (in the words of the front flap) "draws the reader into the real world of the poet—ink spots, tobacco stains, and all— by presenting a wide range of working drafts, letters, diary entries, photographs, and memorabilia." *The Hand of the Poet* includes the work of a broad historical range: from Donne and Pope through Keats and Whitman and Dickinson to such moderns as Frost, Millay, Wilbur, Plath, Levertov, and James Wright.

A superb Internet Web page that reveals a poet at work over a long period of time is *Drafts of Donald Hall's "Ox-Cart Man"* (http://www sc.library.unh.edu/specoll/exhibits/drafts.htm). The site takes us through several years and nineteen drafts of the poem from longhand to a first published version in *The New Yorker* in 1977 and modifications in three of Hall's books. The last is the text for a children's picture book (the illustrations for which won the 1980 Caldecott Medal for Barbara Cooney). Any student perusing these remarkable stages of a poem, with words crossed out and added hither and yon, cannot help but gain insight into poetic decision-making.

An excellent article along these lines is "A Poet Re-Views Her Work" by Nick Otten and Marjorie Stelmach, which appears in the January, 1988 issue of the *English Journal*. Otten and Stelmach show three evolving versions of the following poem by Judith Peraino:

Thoughts

My hair makes a fool of me.
It mocks my face, clinging
in some affection
I do not feel.

It hangs in temperamental curls
of brown—
and like the brooding thoughts it
surrounds, must be wrestled
back into a fashionable form:
unnatural

Some like my hair, but do not
know its price. Mornings bring
a fierce fight, tearing
knotted strands.

Yet I let it grow now,
like many things,
on the edge of my control.

This original version was written when Peraino was a junior in high school; the second, which she retitled "Unnatural," shortly thereafter; and the third, "Quarreling," six years later. What we see is an ongoing exercise in compression: the first poem of seventeen lines is revised to a poem of eight lines (which Peraino was never satisfied with), which is subsequently compressed to only four. Peraino explains the process at length: "In my first attempt at rewriting the poem, I pulled from each stanza those phrases which I felt were the most poetical, emotionally powerful, and pertinent to my intentions. I deleted those phrases which were conceptually redundant and awkward" (93). Clearly here is a poet making choices.

As a teacher, I would show all three versions as well as Peraino's comments. High school students would enjoy knowing that a young adult had written the original; some, of course, might prefer it to either revision. The important thing would be talking about the changes that she made.

Although manuscript revisions are not shown, two other extremely useful books for showing how poets get ideas for poems and develop them are Paul Janeczko's *Poetspeak: In Their Words, about Their Work* and *The Place My Words Are Looking For: What Poets Say about and through Their Work*. In both, poets like Gregory Corso, Marge Piercy, X. J. Kennedy, and Paul Zimmer discuss the origins and evolution of their work. In doing so, they show young readers a great deal about the process of writing poetry. They help us all to focus on the poet.

One of the payoffs of showing revisions and of teaching the poet's process of choosing, of making decisions concerning form and technique —is that we never lose sight of the poet at work.

GUIDELINE EIGHT

Have students try their own hand at using the techniques themselves. As I suggested in Chapter 8, getting students to write poems is easy and often fun, and sometimes they surprise us with a figure of speech, perhaps without even knowing what it is. Look again at this acrostic poem we saw in Chapter 8:

> **B**eer-drinking guy
> **I**n a bar singing
> **L**oud
> **L**ingering songs.
>
> **R**ough
> **O**n
> **G**irls' hearts.
> **E**ven
> **R**ough is
> **S**mooth.

The last three lines offer a fine example of paradox. Even though a student example like this may be uncommon, and even though teachers should exercise caution in forcing figures of speech into the poetry of young writers—even with these caveats, students can be nudged into trying certain techniques.

Imagine, for example, that Ms. Simms has spent a day or two on metaphor. She has shown poems like "The Fish" (p. 7), "To the Field Goal Kicker in a Slump"(p. 58), and perhaps Sylvia Plath's riddle poem, "Metaphors." She has taught generalizations: "a metaphor is a comparison ('to my mother, I was just another fish')"; "metaphors are often surprising"; and "metaphors often illuminate a poem." At some point, she presents a sequenced exercise for writing a haiku variant:

1. She brings to class several fruits and vegetables, especially those with interesting shapes: crookneck squash, jalapeño peppers, okra, an ear of white corn, bananas, onions, pears, acorn squash, assorted mushrooms, a coconut. She writes the names of them in a column on the board.

2. In another column to the left, she writes the following: endless keyboard, umbrellas, a sumo wrestler, telephones, head of an ape, fat green arrow, Christmas lights.

Ms. Simms has the students draw arrows connecting items on the two lists.

3. Finally she has students match items in the original list with some of the following less obvious possibilities in a column to the right: pearly enigma, middle age, death forest, optimistic commas, earth in the year 9000, Picasso nudes, meltdown.

4. Finally, the teacher shows some examples of resulting haiku before having students try their hand:

Translucent onion: Jalapeño peppers
You are a pearly enigma   are the green Christmas lights
   To all my inquiries.   around the border of my door.

This is a painless little exercise that's productive, fun, and maybe even memorable. Perhaps one student in thirty might indeed recall years later how Ms. Simms taught metaphor with squash and peppers.

GUIDELINE NINE

A final guideline: Be selective. It's better to teach a few concepts and techniques well than to hurriedly rush through a dozen or more. To most people who devote their lives to poetics, the sine qua nons are the first seven or eight in the list on p. 146. Some of these are revisited in units on fiction, and surely none of them need to be retaught year after year in poetry. A sensible approach might be for a high school's English department to allot one batch of the concepts to 9th and 11th grades and another to 10th and 12th.

Once more—I'd be careful with all of this teaching of form and technique. Teachers cannot ignore reality: we still live in a world where we're expected to teach some things about poetry, some knowledge about the genre and how it works. Teachers and schools are still held accountable. Until the profession reaches consensus that knowledge about poetry is no longer expected or required, we will continue to teach imagery, metaphor, and metrics. Still, I'd be careful. I'd keep in mind what I was up against. I'd try awfully hard to be creative and resourceful. If I couldn't have some fun with poetics, I don't think I could bear to teach it. Clearly I think we can.

Notes

1. Obviously knowledge "about poetry" can include knowledge about poets, about poetry movements or periods, and about poetics. This book, this chapter, deals entirely with poetics. This is not to say I would ignore the biographical and historical trappings of poetry. It is to say I would keep them to a minimum.

2. Photographs of cars like these can be found in almost any issue of a magazine like *Car & Driver, Motor Trends,* or *Road & Track.*

3. The idea itself is borrowed from three similar variations of "Mary Had a Little Lamb" by Judson Jerome in his *The Poet and the Poem,* 1974, p. 104.

10 Assessing the Teaching and Learning of Poetry

P ass/Fail" is a poem by Linda Pastan about the dream that often disturbs the sleep of former college students (I've had it many times). In the dream as well as the poem, the student is scheduled for a test in a course he has never taken. The test looms ahead just out of reach, imposing and inescapable, "waiting to be failed." It is the classic Catch-22, and the only way out is waking up.

"Pass/Fail" is one of the few poems written about tests and examinations. *The Columbia Granger's Index to Poetry* doesn't even assign the subject a heading. Is assessment, one wonders, unworthy of consideration by poets? Are future poets permanently traumatized in school by true-false items and essay questions? Are poetry and testing mutually exclusive realms?

Whatever the concerns, poetry *is* an element of the English language arts curriculum, and is, as such, like spelling, reading for inference, and vocabulary, subject to assessment. At least, it is subject to be considered for assessment.

Some would say our work with poetry should not be evaluated at all. In her article, "Poets on Teaching Poetry," Diane Lockward quotes Lois Harrod on the subject: "the worst thing a teacher could do with one of [my] poems would be to put it on a multiple choice test." Of a similar misgiving by another poet, Marie Howe, Lockward says, "When I reminded [Howe] that English teachers have to produce grades, she suggested that we ask students to bring in poems they like and write about one of them. This could be a poem already discussed in class, a different one by a poet whose other works have been studied, or one by a poet not covered in class" (1994, 65–66).

So, we entertain another question: How much about the teaching and learning of poetry should we try to evaluate and what forms should such evaluation take?

Traditional Assessment

Just for fun, go back and read the poem "The Whipping" on p. 39. Read it two or three times and then return. Now complete the following test:

Example Test 1

1. "The Whipping" was written by _____.
2. True or False: "The Whipping" is about a boy who shoplifts.
3. The speaker in the poem is

   a. the old woman

   b. the boy who was whipped

   c. an observer of the whipping

   d. the principal of the boy's school
4. True or False: The speaker in the poem was himself once whipped.
5. True or False: The old woman in the poem has herself been a victim.

If necessary, go back and check your answers against the poem. You probably did pretty well. On the other hand, what does a score of, say, 80 percent on a test like this prove? Is this what we want our students to be able to demonstrate at the end of a poetry unit? I would hope not—for at least three reasons: (1) the test assesses facts alone; (2) in its focus on facts, it depends on recall of literal information; and (3) it requires no thoughtful development of an extended response.

As an alternative, consider another test. A teacher spends three weeks on poetry, follows all the guidelines and suggestions offered in earlier chapters of this book (she is indeed exemplary), and presents the following written assessment on day 15:

Example Test 2

Directions: We have spent the last three weeks reading and discussing and studying numerous poems, many of your own selection. We have talked at length about some of the ideas that poets write about and some of the techniques that they use. On this test, choose *one* of the following three new poems *[they would be attached]* and complete *each* of the following exercises:

1. Write five questions that would encourage students to think about one of the poem's themes, to consider the meaning, the "point."
2. Explain how the poet has used one of the concepts we have studied. Explain in particular how the concept is used to reinforce the poem's meaning.

By almost any measure, this is better than *Example Test 1*. For one thing, it offers students choices—not only one of the three poems, but their choice of questions to formulate and a concept in the poem to write about.

Also, this test operates on a higher level than the first: it asks students to apply what they have learned to a poem they have not discussed in class.

In my view, this second test is a justifiable kind of assessment of the knowledge students learn about poetry—*as long as a few critical requirements are met*:

1. The students have been thoroughly prepared to take the test. In this case, it would mean a good deal of previous class discussion of several poems in which idea and theme are revealed and much attention given to selected poetic concepts. Moreover, students would have had previous opportunities to develop sets of questions around a variety of poems, perhaps in small groups for the members of other groups or the entire class to respond to.

2. The "materials" the students are to work with—the three new poems—are selected with utmost care, particularly in terms of accessibility and relevance.

3. The students are intellectually prepared for the kinds of mental operations required by the test, in this case for the most part, application.

Several efforts have been made by psychologists over the years to describe the various levels of learning or intellectual functioning, perhaps none more widely known and used than Bloom's taxonomy. As most teachers know, the levels or stages of Bloom's hierarchy in order of complexity are *knowledge (recall)*, *comprehension, application, analysis, synthesis*, and *evaluation*. Applied to "The Whipping," a teacher's use of the taxonomy to generate test items might yield the following questions (which are similar to those presented on the same poem in Chapter 6):

Knowledge: Where does the poem take place? Is the old woman angry? *(The student recalls the answers from the text of the poem.)*

Comprehension: Explain who you think the speaker is. *(The student expresses an inferred answer in her own words.)*

Application: Do you think the situation would have been different if the old woman had been well educated (assuming for a moment that she wasn't)? *(In responding, the student applies what he knows to a new situation.)*

Analysis: Explain the varied use of punctuation marks by the poet. *(The student responds after examining how commas, a colon, an ellipsis, and dash function in the poem.)*

Synthesis: If you had to predict, what kind of parent do you think "the boy" will become, especially considering line 19? *(The student projects—in effect, creates—a hypothetical outcome.)*

Evaluation: Do you think the shift in point of view in lines 13–18 is clear—or confusing? Is this a good poem? *(The student makes judgments based on established criteria.)*

It could be argued, of course, that the latter questions in the set are more demanding and thus more worthy of placing on a test, but this determination would depend on the teacher's response to the first and third conditions. Even when we acknowledge the superiority of *Example Test 2*, any teacher knows that a major problem remains: the test will take a lot of time to grade. The only way to address the challenge of testing on higher levels of thought while cutting down on grading time is to include on any test, along with an essay question or two, a section of objective questions that demand more than recall.

Imagine, for example, a teacher who has just taught a three-week unit in which she placed a good deal of emphasis on the concepts of speaker, figurative language, sound, and theme. She wants in some way to evaluate the extent to which the students have a grasp on those concepts. To do this, the teacher could include a poem the students haven't read (like the following, which *we* first saw in Chapter 4) along with the accompanying questions:

Example Test 3

Flying at Night

Ted Kooser

Above us, stars. Beneath us, constellations.
Five billion miles away, a galaxy dies
like a snowflake falling on water. Below us,
some farmer, feeling the chill of that distant death,
snaps on his yard light, drawing his sheds and barn
back into the little system of his care.
All night, the cities, like shimmering novas,
tug with bright streets at lonely lights like his.

Directions: Complete the following five questions in response to the above poem:

1. The speaker in this poem is most likely (1) a farmer; (2) a pilot; (3) an alien; or (4) an astronomer.

2. The phrase "like a snowflake" is a (1) metaphor; (2) paradox; (3) simile; or (4) symbol.

3. Of the following lines, which one has an example of alliteration? (1) line 2; (2) line 3; (3) line 5; or (4) line 8.

4. Of the following, which one is the best reason for placing the alliteration in that line?

   a. to make the line sound lighter

   b. to make the line sound heavier

   c. to emphasize the line

5. Of the following, which one do you think best expresses the theme of the poem?

   a. Even though we may seem alone, we are drawn together by mutual caring.

   b. Rural life is better than city life.

   c. The sky at night is beautiful, but it reminds us of how insignificant we are.

By having students apply their knowledge to this new poem, the teacher has tested well above the level of recall. Yet this part of the test would take, for each student, no more than fifteen seconds to grade. I would complete the test by adding an essay question like this:

> From your folder of poems that you like, choose one to illustrate your response to *one* of the following statements:
>
> (1) Imagery in a poem helps the reader vividly see, hear, and feel the speaker's experience.
>
> (2) The speaker in a poem is not necessarily the poet.
>
> (3) Metaphor in a poem often helps us to understand the poet's intended point or meaning.

With traditional testing, then, my approach would be to design a test that counts between 15 and 25 percent of the unit grade. On the test, I would develop several higher-level questions around a new poem and at least one essay question. Such a test achieves several ends: (1) in part, it tests above the knowledge level; (2) it requires the writing of one essay response; and (3) it reduces to some degree the time required for grading.

Even with an assessment like *Example Test 3*, the teaching of poetry will often call for other kinds of evaluation besides tests to account for the unit's additional 75–85 percent. At times, rating scales, checklists, and other devices can be created and used. Here are two examples:

Rating Scale for Original Poems

Originality

/_____/_____/_____/_____/_____/

  poor   *fair*   *good*   *excellent*

Clarity

/_____/_____/_____/_____/_____/

Use of imagery

/_____/_____/_____/_____/_____/

Use of figurative language

/_____ /_____ /_____ /_____ /_____ /

Compression of expression

/_____ /_____ /_____ /_____ /_____ /

Mechanics

/_____ /_____ /_____ /_____ /_____ /

The teacher would present the scale well in advance of the writing of poems and make certain that students understood the six criteria. If she wished (I wouldn't), she could assign numbers across the scale (1 to 6) and thus achieve a numerical rating, perhaps with ranges of resulting grades (e.g., 34–36 = A, 31–33 = B, etc.). She could even double the numbers for criteria she wanted to weigh more heavily, e.g., assigning Originality a range of 2 through 12 instead of 1 through 6.

Checklist for Small Group Multimedia Presentation of a Poem

( ) 1. At least three pieces of equipment were used in the presentation.

( ) 2. Each piece of equipment was used effectively.

( ) 3. The poem was presented both aurally and visually.

( ) 4. Each member of the group was involved in the presentation.

( ) 5. *Other relevant points.*

Here the teacher simply indicates with a check (✓) whether or not each criterion is met.

Authentic Assessment

Even acknowledging the effectiveness of *Example Test 3*, there remain many poets and teachers among us who would prefer that assessment of the teaching and learning of poetry include no tests at all. Instead, if there must be evaluation, they would argue for some version that falls under the umbrella of *authentic assessment.*

Authentic assessment, of course, represents an effort to evaluate students' ability to *use* knowledge or skills in real or simulated settings that more closely mirror the demands of "real life" (hence the word *authentic*).[1] As such, the approach is ongoing and individualized. It informs students at the outset of the standards and of how their performance will be judged. Thus, it involves students in the evaluation process. Authentic assessment often makes use of products, projects, or performances. For any given student, the organizational system is often a *portfolio*, a collection of work developed and maintained by the student and presented for consideration at various stages during a unit or some other period of time. When the student and his teacher decide that the portfolio is ready for assessment, the process often involves several people, certainly the two of them, but possibly other teachers, an administrator, even a parent or a person from the community (maybe a poet!).

In a poetry unit, a portfolio of work might include some of the following items (each followed here with examples of criteria to be used):

(1) *a folder of poems the student likes, some with written reasons for her preferences*

> Criteria: total number of poems, evidence of breadth of search, evidence of maturity in appreciation (e.g., poems that do not rhyme in addition to some that do), evidence of enthusiasm for particular favorites

> Criteria for written explanations: clarity, detail, conciseness, absence of errors

(2) *a collection of original poems as well as the draft versions of those poems; the student might select two or three for final evaluation*

> Criteria: originality, clarity, compression of thought, vividness of language, use of selected forms and techniques, absence of errors in mechanics

(3) *a set of critiques of selected poems, with one or two highlighted*

> Criteria: quality of thought, reference to (use of) concepts studied, variety of poems critiqued, quality of writing

(4) *an annotated collection of Internet sites on poetry that the student has found interesting or useful either to himself or to a given audience (e.g., a poetry teacher)*

> Criteria: variety of sites, quality of sites, evidence of effort, accuracy of URLs (Web site addresses), quality of writing in the annotations

(5) *drawings or paintings to accompany one or more favorite poems accompanied by explanations of choices and purposes*

> Criteria: quality of the art work (to be judged by an art teacher), quality of writing in the explanations

(6) *the oral reading of a number of selected poems*

> Criteria: quality of performance in terms of appropriateness of intonation, volume, pronunciation, and pace; number and variety of poems selected

(7) *the performance of a poem (perhaps involving other students): choral reading, mime, dance, readers theater, etc.*

> Criteria: originality of performance, quality of performance, depth of interpretation

(8) *a multimedia presentation of a selected poem*

> Criteria: variety of media used, quality of presentation (continuity, clarity, etc.)

(9) *a bibliography of works on a selected favorite poet*

> Criteria: length of bibliography, variety of sources consulted, accuracy of citations

(10) *a research study of a selected poet or poem*

> Criteria: number and quality of sources consulted, effectiveness in use of resources (integration of more than one into a single paragraph, etc.), quality of writing, accuracy of citations

The student would work with his teacher in advance to select those projects he prefers as well as a schedule of stages and deadlines. The two would work together, meeting at regular intervals so the student could receive adequate ongoing feedback. Ideally, authentic assessment promotes not only ongoing assessment, but also the development of the student's ability to evaluate his or her own performance. The use of grades is discouraged, although they can be accommodated.

As a poetry teacher, I would use authentic assessment. I like its emphasis on gradual improvement, on the student having a voice, on the development of a close working relationship between teacher and student, and on the student's growth in evaluating his or her own work. It all makes a lot of sense. Still, I'm not sure I'm ready to assign traditional testing to the ashheap. There would be times, I think, when I'd like to see what my students could do with poetry on a pencil-and-paper test.

So I would use both approaches. Just as I would choose both Orchestrator and Facilitator as classroom personas (Chapter 5), here with assessment I would be both innovative and conventional. I'd be "authentic," but occasionally, I think, I'd toss in a test, one that was fair and reliable, that encouraged my students to think, that required them to defend their ideas and opinions in writing—and that led to the demise of the intimidating "Pass/Fail" dream in Linda Pastan's poem.

Note

1. Synonymous terms include *performance-based assessment, alternative assessment,* and *portfolio assessment.*

11 Teaching Poetry across the Curriculum

Good poetry is all about connections. In Richard Wilbur's poem "The Writer" (a wonderful poem for any English teacher or parent), the speaker oversees his daughter in her room struggling with a paper, banging away at her typewriter. Suddenly he remembers an earlier struggle, an incident when a trapped starling tried to escape that very room. The speaker makes an apt comparison (the poet, a metaphor) —a connection. Similarly, Linda Pastan makes a connection between a writer and a field-goal kicker in a slump (p. 58). In a different way, in "Vacation" (p. 49) William Stafford connects, ironically, the sight of a desert burial from a train window to the precise formality of privilege in a dining car.

In its wide affiliation with the world, poetry connects with *everything*.

"Patrick Ewing Takes a Foul Shot" by Diane Ackerman

"At Every Gas Station There Are Mechanics" by Stephen Dunn

"The Belly Dancer in the Nursing Home" by Ronald Wallace

"Gettysburg, July 1, 1863" by Jane Kenyon

"Arithmetic" by Carl Sandburg

"Conjugation of the Verb, 'To Hope'" by Lou Lipsitz

"The Microscope" by Maxine Kumin

"Monet's Waterlilies" by Robert Hayden

"I Live in Music" by Ntozake Shange

Some of these titles—the last six anyway—suggest a possible connection with schools and school subjects: history, mathematics, grammar, science, art, music. They bring to mind a phrase we have heard in American schools for many years—teaching across the curriculum, the sensible idea of interweaving more of what we do. All areas of the school curriculum are often touched by poets and poems, none of them, it seems, more than music.

Poetry and Music

At least since the late 1960s, when paperback anthologies of rock lyrics were published routinely,[1] teachers of poetry have used popular songs as a come-on to students, an almost sure-fire way to engage them in the genre. The standard approach is to play a song or two at the beginning of a unit, look at the lyrics, and talk about some of their poetic qualities. Then, students are encouraged to bring in their own favorite songs. The only criterion: the song must have some citable poetic quality the student can defend (if not define), e.g., a steady beat, an apt simile or metaphor, vivid images, whatever. Over the years, here are some songs I have used, several of which were first shown to me by students:

1. "The Rose" by Bette Midler (lyrics by Amanda McBroom): "Some say love, it is a river that drowns the tender reed. . . ."

2. "Eleanor Rigby" by John Lennon and Paul McCartney (The Beatles): "Waits at the window/Wearing the face that she keeps in a jar by the door. . . ."

3. "Only a Dream" by Mary Chapin Carpenter: "A big truck was parked in the drive one day/They wrapped us in paper and moved us away. . . ."

4. "Amelia" by Joni Mitchell: "A ghost of aviation/she was swallowed by the sky/or by the sea, like me she had a dream to fly. . . ."

5. "At Seventeen" by Janis Ian: "Their small-town eyes will gape at you in dull surprise when payment due/Exceeds accounts received at seventeen. . . ."

6. "Ballet for a Rainy Day" by XTC: "I push my paintbrush/To conjure a new world/While this one is slowly washed away. . . ."

7. "We Didn't Start the Fire" by Billy Joel: "'Wheel of Fortune,' Sally Ride, heavy metal, suicide/Foreign debts, homeless vets, AIDS, crack, Bernie Goetz/Hypodermics on the shores, China's under martial law/Rock and roller cola wars, I can't take it any more."

8. "Russians" by Sting: "How can I save my little boy from Oppenheimer's deadly toy/There is no monopoly of common sense. . . ."

9. "Southland in the Springtime" by Emily Saliers (The Indigo Girls): "In Georgia nights are softer than a whisper/ beneath a quilt somebody's mother made by hand. . . ."

(lyrics.ch 1998)

Classes can also discuss the lyrics, of course, as they would a poem. For "We Didn't Start the Fire," a teacher might ask "Why did Billy Joel choose these items? Who is Sally Ride? Bernie Goetz? Why were they included? Why 'Wheel of Fortune'? Why heavy metal? If the song were written today, what similar images would be good to include? What is 'the fire'?"

Lyrics to songs can be found in several places. The best published source is *Find That Tune: An Index to Rock, Folk-Rock, Disco & Soul* (see

Appendix B), which is available in many libraries. In addition, libraries and bookstores have numerous anthologies of lyrics like *Big Book of Latin American Songs,* (Hal Leonard Publishing Corporation, 1992), *The Blues Fake Book* by Woody Mann (Oak Publications, 1995), *The Bob Dylan Anthology* (Amsco Publications, 1990), *Rock 'n' Roll: The Famous Lyrics* by Scott Buchanan (Harper Perennial, 1994), *Songs of Protests and Civil Rights* by Jerry Silverman (Chelsea House Publishers, 1992), and *Songs of the Eighties: The Decade Series* (Hal Leonard Publishing Corporation). The last title is part of a series, each featuring over forty top songs of a decade beginning with the 1890s. The Eighties volume includes "Ebony and Ivory," "Every Breath You Take," and "Somewhere Out There."

The Internet now has several song sites (e.g., *The International Lyrics Server* (p. 190) that allow the user to access lyrics by simply typing in the title of a song. And of course the printed lyrics are often included in the notes that accompany cassettes and CDs.

Occasionally rock lyrics are based on a work of literature. In her article "Rock Poetry: The Literature Our Students Listen To," Moi cites "Wuthering Heights" by Kate Bush, "1984" by Rick Wakeman, "The Rime of the Ancient Mariner" by Iron Maiden, and "Extraordinary Narrations" by Alan Parson's Project, which is based on the stories of Poe. The idea of a lyricist basing a song on a novel or story might be interesting to some students.

Once a class is intrigued by the lyrics it finds, a teacher might segue to poems *about* music. At least three sources are helpful:

- *Mixed Voices: Contemporary Poems about Music* (1991), a broad collection edited by Emilie Buchwald and Ruth Roston and organized into sections with names like Keyboard, Instruction to the Players, Voices, Composers (Mostly Mozart), and a miscellany called Blues, Bebop, Rock, Funk, and All That Jazz. The represented poets include Linda Pastan, Sylvia Plath, Anne Sexton, David Wagoner, Ray Gonzalez, David Huddle, Denise Levertov, and Philip Dacey, whose poem "The Drummer" (66) describes a fifteen-year-old boy absorbed in his room

  hunched over snares, cymbals, and bass
  like someone hunched over

  a fresh kill. . . .

Other titles of note in this anthology are "Playing the Flute for the TMR Class" by Jan Epton Seale, "Reasons for Loving the Harmonica" by Julie Kane, "Scott Joplin" by Bill Holm, and "Why Your Grandfather Stopped Playing the Viola" by Alice Worth Gray.

- *Sweet Nothings: An Anthology of Rock and Roll in American Poetry*, edited by Jim Elledge, which includes over 120 poems. With titles like "The Supremes," "Cruising with the Beach Boys," and "The Death of Janis Joplin," this collection may strike more chords with teachers than with students. Still, poems like Joyce Carol Oates's "Waiting on Elvis, 1956" and Rachel Loden's "'Tumbling Dice'" will appeal to any age.

- *The Jazz Poetry Anthology*, compiled by Sascha Feinstein and Yusef Komunyakaa. This collection includes Jack Kerouac's well-known "239th Chorus," Ted Joans's "Jazz Is My Religion," Steve Jonas's "One of Three Musicians" (based on Picasso's painting *Three Musicians*) and twelve poems about the legendary saxophonist John Coltrane. Few young adults are jazz aficionados, but a teacher might profitably play a recording of Coltrane to see if a class could infer his appeal to so many poets.(A second jazz volume by the same authors is titled *The Second Set.*)

And speaking of jazz, Hutchinson and Suhor (1996) advocate a connection between jazz and poetry that highlights performance. Jazz enthusiasts themselves, they encourage teachers to have students write poems and set them to jazz accompaniments, creating collaborative "jazz poems." Among the problems they address is the question of sequence, i.e., how to have the music and poetry interact. The authors offer several possibilities:

- Music begins, then poetry enters;
- Poetry first, music entering at appropriate point;
- Alternation of short poems and short musical vignettes;
- Short sections within a longer poem—whether stanzas or other useful grouping of content—with interspersed musical vignettes or phrases;
- Musical backdrop of one or more tunes for a string of short poems on a common theme. (80–81)

Hutchinson and Suhor also consider the variety of musical accompaniment, the effective blending of poetry and music to create a whole impression, and questions concerning mood, program, and allusion. This whole approach depends, of course, on the presence of a jazz performer or two in the classroom. If they are unavailable, however, a teacher could still engage students in a modified kind of collaboration by having them write poems in response to recorded jazz pieces, like Dave Brubeck's *Take Five*, Duke Ellington's *Black, Brown, and Beige*, and Louis Armstrong's *Hotter Than That*, among many others.

Rap Music

No teacher should overlook rap. Since the late 1970s, rap music, or hip-hop, has been an important offshoot of rock, especially among young African Americans. Rap is defined as a style of music that features rhythmic talking, instead of singing, to a rudimentary musical accompaniment. Rap lyrics typically rhyme, and while the music pulses with a strong beat, it pays little attention to metric consistency. Rap is often funny, outrageous, obscene, didactic, and provocative; and while some rap cannot be used in a classroom, a lot of it has great potential. One example, advocating the teaching of African American history, is "You Must Learn" by Boogie Down Productions.

Edward Anderson suggests that teachers play and discuss the content of raps (and rap videos) with a positive message and have students write and present raps on a variety of subjects in the curriculum (1993, 12). Rap has already been appropriated for all sorts of educational purposes—to teach the multiplication tables, cardiopulmonary resuscitation, even *Romeo and Juliet.* "The CPR Rap", written by Dr. William G. Cutts Jr., to promote the teaching of the life-saving technique to young people, includes sixteen stanzas of critical information:

> Feel the neck, so you can tell
> If the carotid pulse is full or frail.
>
> If it's not throbbing, now you know what to do.
> Continue CPR, through and through.
> Give 2 ventilations for oxygenation,
> Then, 15 chest compressions for the circulation. . . .

The Romeo and Juliet *RAP* (1991) by Frank Jacobs, available on cassette from Teacher's Discovery, presents Shakespeare in a whole new light. The lengthy production (over 100 lines) ends with the narrator describing the final gloomy scene:

> There's just one problem that lies ahead—Poor Romeo hears that Juliet's dead!
>
> He opens the tomb for a final look, and you gotta know that he's really shook;
>
> When he sees the bod of his beautiful chick, he swallows some poison that kills him quick.
>
> He's lyin' there cold, no longer alive, When Juliet begins to revive;
>
> She looks around, and what does she see, But Romeo—as dead as can be!
>
> With him not around, what good is life? So she stabs herself with a suicide knife.

> With both of 'em dead, it's not good news for the Capulets and
> the Montagues;
>
> There's sobbin' and weepin' and they're all unglued, when they
> see the result of their family feud;
>
> They know in their hearts they've all been wrong, so they prom-
> ise each other they'll get along;
>
> Though they'll have to do it, they all regret, without Romeo or
> Juliet.

Related activities for raps like these are obvious: students could write hip-hop versions of other procedures (baking a cake, washing a dog, braiding hair) and other literary works, Shakespearean or otherwise. Imagine rap treatments of *Macbeth* and *Of Mice and Men*. Or hip-hop accounts of historical events and scientific discoveries.

For teachers, there are several useful resources. *Say It Loud!: The Story of Rap Music* by K. Maurice Jones offers a history of the form. *Rap: The Lyrics* by Lawrence A. Stanley includes the words to 150 rap songs by performers like Beastie Boys, Jazzy Jeff & the Fresh Prince, M. C. Hammer, and Run-D.M.C. Lyrics are also available on several Web sites on the Internet. As with most contemporary music, of course, the *best* source of current information is students themselves, whose knowledge of the rap scene will almost always exceed the teacher's.

Poetry and Art

For many of us who remember the 1970s, few songs were as affecting in lyrics, melody, and theme as "Vincent" by Don McLean. The song portrayed the tortured life of Van Gogh, drawing some of its images from his painting, *The Starry Night*:

> Starry, starry night
> Flaming flowers that brightly blaze
> Swirling clouds in violet haze
> Reflecting Vincent's eyes of china blue
> Colors changing hue. . . .
>
> (lyrics.ch 1998)

"Vincent" was one of the first rock songs to concern itself with an artist, but poetry and art have a long and strong connection. The bond is most evident in the inspiration numerous poets have drawn from paintings and other works of art:

> "Musée des Beaux Arts" by W. H. Auden (based on *Landscape with the Fall of Icarus* by Pieter Brueghel the Elder)

"Monet's Waterlilies" by Robert Hayden

"Edward Hopper's *Nighthawks*" by Joyce Carol Oates

"Nude Descending a Staircase" by X. J. Kennedy (based on the painting by Marcel Duchamp)

"Max Schmitt in a Single Scull" by Richmond Lattimore (based on the painting of the same name by Thomas Eakins)

"Wormwood: The Penitents" by Ellen Bryant Voigt (based on *Black Cross, New Mexico* by Georgia O'Keeffe)

"Seurat's Sunday Afternoon Along the Seine" by Delmore Schwartz (based on Georges Seurat's *A Sunday on La Grande Jatte—1884*)

Teachers could show these poems and many others with slides of the paintings that inspired them. Some, like the Hayden poem, are largely emotional responses to the work ("the serene great picture that I love"); others—the Schwartz poem, the poem by Oates (1989, 40)—describe the painting in great detail:

> . . . the woman is wearing
> a short-sleeved red dress cut to expose her arms,
> a curve of her creamy chest; she's contemplating
> a cigarette in her right hand, thinking that
> her companion has finally left his wife but
> can she trust him? . . .

The class could discuss not only the accuracy of the poet's depiction, but the apparent, or possible, reasons why the painting triggered a poem in the first place. What did Oates see in this famous work of three late-night patrons of a dimly lit urban diner? In viewing the Seurat painting, one of the icons of French Impressionism, what does Schwartz (1992) mean by his opening lines?

> What are they looking at? Is it the river?
> The sunlight on the river, the summer, leisure,
> Or the luxury and nothingness of consciousness?
>   . . .
> Everyone holds his heart within his hands:
>
> A prayer, a pledge of grace or gratitude
> A devout offering to the god of summer, Sunday, and
> plentitude.
> The Sunday people are looking at hope itself.

Also, teachers could show other poems for comparison, like Ira Sadoff's prose poem "Hopper's 'Nighthawks'" and Frank O'Hara's "On

Looking at *La Grand Jatte*, the Czar Wept Anew." Sources of painting-and-poem comparisons are readily available. Among other books, teachers could consult *The Gazer's Spirit: Poems Speaking to Silent Works of Art* by John Hollander (University of Chicago, 1995), *The Poetry of Solitude: A Tribute to Edward Hopper* by Gail Levin (Universe Publishing, 1995), *Transforming Vision: Writers on Art* by Edward Hirsch (The Art Institute of Chicago/Bullfinch Press, 1994), *Voices in the Gallery* by Dannie and Joan Abse (Tate Gallery, 1986), and *With a Poet's Eye: A Tate Gallery Anthology* by Pat Adams (Tate Gallery, 1993).

In addition to engaging classes in discussing artistic connections like these, some teachers try the same kind of stimuli out on their students. In her advocacy of art as a springboard for student poems, Marilyn Bates presents a series of steps, one of which is to keep a journal of the feelings evoked by a painting: "Whatever [students] write, it should be specific, including as many of the concrete details of the painting as possible. This attention to details increases their awareness of the various elements of the work, such as line, color, texture and shape, and these early responses may then be crafted into finished poems later, using the language captured in their journals (1993, 42). Among other works she has used, Bates mentions Mark Rothko's *Red on Maroon*, John Singer Sargent's *Portrait of a Boy*, Magritte's *Menaced Assassin*, and Edvard Munch's provocative *The Scream*. For the most part, modern art provides the best stimuli for students—works by artists like Picasso, Matisse, Dali, Braque, Miro, Klee, Gris, Chagall, Mondrian, and Francis Bacon. Here is a brief poem written as a model by a teacher in response to Klee's "The Twittering Machine":

> on the tv antenna,
>   a bird swallows
>   an exclamation mark
>   another's throat constricts
> within   is   silence

In reverse, teachers can use poems to motivate art—drawings, fingerpaintings, chalk sketches, even calligraphy. With their little snapshots of moments in nature, haiku are especially good for this. Or teachers can have students design poem mobiles. The works of several poets are often adaptable, especially poems that range across or tumble down the page. I'd try works by cummings, Lawrence Ferlinghetti, and William Carlos Williams, whose famous "Poem," about a cat stepping down into a flowerpot, would be perfect.

HIGHLIGHT 11.1

Poems as Picture Books

More and more often, poems show up as the text for beautifully illustrated picture books—another kind of connection between art and poetry. And while the genre has long been associated with young children, picture books are increasingly appropriate for young adults as well. Here are just a few:

Arithmetic by Carl Sandburg. Illustrated by Ted Rand.

Birches by Robert Frost. Illustrated by Ed Young.

Casey at the Bat by Ernest Thayer. Illustrated by Barry Moser.

Casey at the Bat by Ernest Thayer. Illustrated by Wallace Tripp.

The Cremation of Sam McGee by Robert W. Service. Illustrated by Ted Harrison.

The Highwayman by Alfred Noyes. Illustrated by Charles Mikolaycak.

The Highwayman by Alfred Noyes. Illustrated by Neil Waldman.

I Live in Music by Ntozake Shange. Illustrated by Romare Bearden.

In a Spring Garden by Richard Lewis. Illustrated by Ezra Jack Keats. A collection of haiku.

Ox-Cart Man by Donald Hall. Illustrated by Barbara Cooney.

Paul Revere's Ride by Henry Wadsworth Longfellow. Illustrated by Ted Rand.

Stopping by Woods on a Snowy Evening by Robert Frost. Illustrated by Susan Jeffers.

Poetry and Other Subjects in the Curriculum

One might expect poetry to bond with music and art, but poetry relates to other subjects almost as well.

History, Geography, and Government

English teachers with colleagues in history, for example, can find many opportunities to recommend poems to be read at "teachable moments"—or they can teach them themselves, supplying their own historical context:

"Adolph Hitler Meditates on the Jewish Problem" by Oscar Hahn

"Carentan O Carentan" by Louis Simpson (World War II)

Works by the World War I poets Rupert Brooke, Wilfred Owen, and
Siegfried Sassoon

"Dakota: October, 1822: Hunkpapa Warrior" by Rod Taylor

"I Am Accused of Tending to the Past" by Lucille Clifton

"Frederick Douglass" by Robert Hayden

"A Break from the Bush" by Yusef Komunyakaa (Vietnam War)

"The Times They Are A-Changin'" by Bob Dylan

Sourcebooks of poetry with history connections often seem limited
to war poems, like *The Columbia Book of Civil War Poetry* and *Poetry of the
World Wars*, but there are also collections about the Holocaust, like *Art
from the Ashes: A Holocaust Anthology* by Lawrence L. Langer (Oxford
University Press, 1995) and *I Never Saw Another Butterfly, Children's
Drawings and Poems from Terezin Concentration Camp, 1942–1944* by
Hana Volavkova (Schocken Books, 1993). A more general collection is
America in Poetry by Charles Sullivan (Abrams, 1988), which includes
"The Gift Outright" by Robert Frost and "I Am Waiting" by Lawrence
Ferlinghetti among many others.

For teachers who agree with Carlyle that history is biography, there
are many poems about historical figures. Besides the obvious ("O Captain!
My Captain!," Whitman's tribute to the slain Lincoln), I might use poems
like "Lindbergh" by Diane Ackerman, "Report to Crazy Horse" by William
Stafford, "Martin Luther King, Jr." by Gwendolyn Brooks, and "Columbus"
by Louis Simpson. A history teacher could also engage a class in a
discussion of what makes a person historically significant after reading
Stephen Spender's "I Continually Think of Those Who Were Truly Great."

Some history (or English) teachers engage their students in the
writing of odes to famous figures; in a lighter mode, students might write
clerihews or double dactyls. While the former are undemanding, double
dactyls are something else again:

Clerihew (a quatrain of comical couplets about a famous person).

Alexander Graham Bell
Spilled some acid, truth to tell,
So he rang up Mr. Watson on his brand-new contraption:
"Come here, my able assistant, I need you to take some action."

Double dactyls (also known as higgledy-piggledies)

Higgledy-piggledy	*nonsense double dactyl introduction*
Susan B. Anthony,	*double dactylic name of a famous person*
feminist advocate	*double dactyl*
extraordinaire,	*/ UU - /*

argued her points with such	*double dactyl*
impetuosity	*one word double dactyl*
all her disciples sang	*double dactyl*
praises to spare.	*/ UU - /*

Ten-zero-sixty-six
William the Conqueror
sailed o'er the Channel
cheeky and tall,

hawking French culture. An
implausibility?
Angles and Saxons said,
"Boy, he had Gaul!"

A teacher of geography might have her students read and discuss "The Mapmaker on His Art" by Howard Nemerov or any of the dozens of poems that evoke different parts of the country or the world, like "Summer: West Side" by John Updike and poems in the collections *Poetry of the American West: A Columbia Anthology, America Is Not All Traffic Lights: Poems of the Midwest,* and *The Made Thing: An Anthology of Contemporary Southern Poetry.*

A teacher of government could draw upon an anthology like *The Faber Book of Political Poetry* or *Poetry Like Bread: Poets of the Political Imagination.* It might be fun to have students read the poems of writers like Robert Bly, Carolyn Forché, Martin Espada, and Claribel Alegria, whose work is often spurred by political indignation—and then write their own political poems (especially raps) against Big Business or Big Government. A good poem to start with is "They Are Planning to Cancel the School Milk Program to Fund a Tax Cut for the Middle Class" by Liz Rosenberg.

HIGHLIGHT 11.2

Poetry in School-to-Work Programs

One of the recent curricular innovations in schools across the country has been School-to-Work programs. Their general purpose is to increase connections between schools and businesses and to ease the transitions students make from one to the other.

▶

In general, the literature programs for these students do not differ dramatically from those in the mainstream curriculum. Still, there are opportunities for interested teachers to make connections between the worlds of work and poetry (arenas that may seem to some quite unrelated).

A useful collection in the school-to-work context is *For a Living: The Poetry of Work* by Nicholas Coles and Peter Oresick, which includes poems (and a useful index) about bosses, clerks, cooks, janitors, waitresses, doctors and nurses, and many other jobs. Among the poems students might like are "For People Who Can't Open Their Hoods" by Jim Daniels, "Jorge the Church Janitor Finally Quits" by Martin Espada, "A Waitress's Instructions on Tipping or Get the Cash Up and Don't Waste My Time" by Jan Beatty, and "A Song of Survival" (excerpt, 26–27) by Jimmy Santiago Baca, a list poem about blue-collar jobs:

> . . . I worked as a woodchopper in the mountains,
> the snow was marvelous,
> glittering in the morning with the smell of wood
> everywhere, fresh wet bark, speckled with dew,
> and broken sticks oozing sap, tree boughs
> shaking with squirrels, deer on their pointing toes
> watched me from a distance eyes brimming with sparks.
> And I worked as a dishwasher,
> two big stainless steel sinks filled with tumultuous
> heaps of pans and skillets and chef-spoons,
> big-bellied pots with burned black bottoms, with
> sleeves rolled up and rubber apron on, I'd bend over,
> scrubbing as fast as I could, . . .

Science

Poets often question science (see Whitman's "When I Heard the Learn'd Astronomer," John Updike's "V. B. Nimble, V. B. Quick," and Ogden Nash's "The Purist," for example), but science teachers can also find poems where the treatment is more objective, like "Laboratory Poem" by James Merrill, "The Microscope" by Maxine Kumin, "The Scientist" by Jonathan Holden, and "Studying Physics with My Daughter" by Jeanne Murray Walker. From another direction, biology teachers can take advantage of haiku's emphasis on the close observation of nature. Here is a haiku written as a model for a unit on vertebrates. After showing it, a teacher could have her students write a poem of their own about a concept they had studied—like, in this case, migration.

The Arctic Tern

Ted Jamison

Pole-to-pole flyer—
each equinox your leap to flight
leaves us in earthbound awe.

Science and poetry may reach their ultimate intermingling in the poem "West-Running Brook" by Robert Frost, which has been recommended for teaching the Second Law of Thermodynamics in physics (Romer 1993). For other possibilities, teachers might consider *Imagination's Other Place: Poems of Science and Mathematics* by Helen Plotz (Crowell 1955), although the book has long been out of print.

Mathematics

Poetry and mathematics may seem like the odd couple of the curriculum, but there are surprising connections between them. Several poems can serve as stimuli for writing. For example, teachers can have students write their own versions of May Swenson's "Cardinal Ideograms" (1978, 172), which offers imaginative looks at figures:

3   Shallow mitten for two-fingered hand.

. . .

7   A step

detached from its stair.

Similarly, some teachers have their students write concrete poems about mathematical concepts of their choice, like the following:

The Parallelogram

Anonymous

The parallelogram shoulders its weight
into the wind like an oceanic ship, a
rectangle gone wrong, an architectur-
al slab gone Wright, like Tennessee.

Other poems are best discussed: "Barbie Says Math Is Hard" by Kyoko Mori, "Geometry" by Rita Dove, "Prudent Triangle" by Vasco Popa, "Arithmetic" by Carl Sandburg, "Algebra" by Linda Pastan, and "In Place of Zigzags" by Jane O. Wayne.

As some poets take harmless pot shots at science, others make light of mathematics. A long, amusing poem on the folly of applying formulas to affection is the following verse first published in 1874 (Richards and Gibbons 1993, 16–17). A teacher might assign the poem toward the end of the year and have students, as an option, write a paragraph or two on where the mathematician went wrong in his calculations. Or she could use the poem as part of a review: "Be ready tomorrow to explain each mathematical term used in the poem."

The Mathematician in Love

W. J. M. Rankine

1

A MATHEMATICIAN fell madly in love
    With a lady, young, handsome, and charming:
By angles and ratios harmonic he strove
Her curves and proportions all faultless to prove.
    As he scrawled hieroglyphics alarming.

2

He measured with care, from the ends of a base,
    The arcs which her features subtended;
Then he framed transcendental equations, to trace
The flowing outlines of her figure and face,
    And thought the result very splendid.

3

He studied (since music has charms for the fair)
    The theory of fiddles and whistles,
Then composed, by acoustic equations, an air,
Which, when 'twas performed, made the lady's long hair
    Stand on end, like a porcupine's bristles.

4

The lady loved dancing—he therefore applied,
    To the polka and waltz, an equation;
But when to rotate on his axis he tried,
His centre of gravity swayed to one side,
    And he fell, by the earth's gravitation.

5

No doubts of the fate of his suit made him pause,
    For he proved, to his own satisfaction,
That the fair one returned his affection;—because,
As everyone knows, by mechanical laws,
    "Reaction is equal to action."

6

"Let x denote beauty,—y, manners well-bred,
    z, Fortune,—(this last is essential),—
"Let L stand for love"—our philosopher said,
"Then L is a function of x, y, and z,
    "Of the kind which is known as potential."

7

"Now integrate L with respect to $d\,t$,"
    (t Standing for time and persuasion).

"Then, between proper limits, 'tis easy to see,
"The definite integral *Marriage* must be:
    "(A very concise demonstration)."

                    8
Said he—"If the wandering course of the moon
    "By Algebra can be predicted,
"The female affections must yield to it soon"
—But the lady ran off with a dashing dragoon,
    And left him amazed and afflicted.

Grammar, Writing, and Literature

For the English teacher, poems don't have to be confined to the poetry unit. Besides "Nouns" by Charles Wright (p. 91) there are many poems that could be tucked into a unit on grammar, like "Conjugation of the Verb 'To Hope'" by Lou Lipsitz, "Permanently" by Kenneth Koch, "Grammar Lesson" by Linda Pastan, and "The Possessive Case" by Lisel Mueller. And of course, as we saw in Chapter 8, the writing of certain pattern poems, especially cinquain and diamante (pp. 134–35), is grounded in grammatical terms. Eve Merriam has written several poems about punctuation marks—"Markings, the Comma," "Markings, the Exclamation," "Markings, the Period," "Markings, the Question," and "Markings, the Semicolon"—all of which appear in her book *A Sky Full of Poems*. And there are occasional poems about writing—Richard Wilbur's "The Writer" and Linda Pastan's "To the Field Goal Kicker in a Slump" prominent among them—as well as poems about poetry itself (see Highlight 11.3).

And there are poems about authors and their works. Perhaps unsurprisingly, poets often write about other poets—as in "Emily Dickinson's To-Do List" by Andrea Carlisle and "Visiting Emily Dickinson's Grave with Robert Francis" by Robert Bly; "On Whitman's Birthday" by Anne Waldman; and "For Robert Frost" by Galway Kinnell, among many more. And they write about other authors too: "Hemingway Thinks about Suicide" by Michael Anderson and "Herman Melville" by W. H. Auden are but two examples. They even write about literary works themselves: a teacher of *Romeo and Juliet* could share Maxine Kumin's amusing "Purgatory," a sonnet speculating on the all-too-realistic fate of the lovers had they survived ("And suppose the darlings get to Mantua. . .").

We have come full circle, then—from an English teacher and his students sharing the poetic lyrics of songs like "Eleanor Rigby" to an English teacher offering poems about poetry. "Circle" is the right word because it suggests the endless, ultimate connection. And "connection"

HIGHLIGHT 11.3

Poems about Poetry

"About Motion Pictures" by Ann Darr

"Ars Poetica" by Archibald MacLeish

"Because You Asked about the Line between Prose and Poetry" by Howard Nemerov

"Beware, Do Not Read This Poem" by Ishmael Reed

"Constantly Risking Absurdity" by Lawrence Ferlinghetti

"Eating Poetry" by Mark Strand

"For Poets" by Al Young

"Glass" by Robert Francis

"Gone Forever" by Barriss Mills

"How Poetry Comes to Me" by Gary Snyder

"How to Eat a Poem" by Eve Merriam

"Kidnap Poem" by Nikki Giovanni

"The Poem You Asked For" by Larry Levis

"Reply to the Question: *'How Can You Become a Poet?'*" by Eve Merriam

"Ten Definitions of Poetry" by Carl Sandburg

"Terrorist Poem" by Frank Finale

"To Build a Poem" by Christine E. Hemp

"Unfolding Bud" by Naoshi Koriyama

"Uses of Poetry" by Winfield Townley Scott

"Wild Horse" by Elder Olson

"Your Poem, Man . . ." by Edward Lueders

is right because it implies that all of us are in this together. If poetry (not to mention countless other subjects in the curriculum) is to enjoy its fullest success in American classrooms, we need to find ways to broaden its scope. Sharing some of the poems and approaches we've seen, as well as others, will only help.

Note

1. Two of them were *Richard Goldstein's The Poetry of Rock* (Bantam, 1969) and *Favorite Pop/Rock Lyrics* (Scholastic, 1971).

12 Poetry and the Internet

Any effort to describe the presence of poetry or any other topic on the sprawling Internet is rife with risk. The moment the ink dries—or the cursor blinks off—the news is old. Still, with almost every American school already online a book like this can hardly keep its head in the sand.

By now there's no need to explain what the Internet is. Even those who haven't jumped on board are well aware of its presence. We've all seen the cover stories in *Time* and *Newsweek* and the shelves of books in every library and bookstore (*The Internet for Dummies*, et al.). The yellow pages of even midsize city phone directories now have multiple listings under "Internet Services" (mine has twenty-nine). Web site addresses abound, and "www dot whatever dot com" has become one of the mantras of our age.

But surely poetry, some might wanly hope—this purest and gentlest of genres with its flashes of imagination and subtle layers of meaning—surely poetry has remained impervious to cyberspace. Not so. The Internet offers students and teachers of poetry a wealth of resources, among them files of information about poetry and poets, texts of poems (for the most part the classics, whose copyrights long ago expired, or the poems of "Wordsworth wannabes" anxious to offer their work online), and discussion groups of poets, teachers, and sometimes just readers and admirers of poetry. Even lesson plans for teaching poetry are available.

Also consider this: when I first began looking for Internet homepages on poetry in the spring of 1995, I found a few hundred. As of this writing (spring 1999), they number in the thousands, with many more to come.

For teachers there are many possible avenues of access. Some enter specific homepage addresses (URLs). Without them, the best device is a "search engine" like Yahoo, Lycos, or Infoseek. Search engines allow the user to type in a word or phrase, like "haiku" or "Robert Frost." In a matter of seconds, the engine riffles through its thousands of Web sites in search of the word and generates a list of matching items. When I entered the all-encompassing *poetry*, I was given a hierarchy of subheadings:

Anthologies   Magazines
Awards   Organizations
Beat Generation   Performance
Children's   Poem of the Day

Commercial Books	Poem of the Week
Countries and Cultures	Poets
Events	Publishers
Haiku	Science Fiction, Fantasy, Horror
Humorous	Web published poetry
Journals	Writing

Clicking on one of the items (e.g., Events) led to an annotated list of homepages (e.g., The Asheville Poetry Festival). In this way, search engines guide the user down through the hierarchy until he finds something interesting.

The above columns of headings represent to some degree the kinds of Web sites devoted to poetry. Among the best of them are general, all-purpose sites that embrace almost every aspect of the genre.[1]

General Poetry Sites

Perhaps the best of these sites is *The Academy of American Poets* home-page (http://www.poets.org/). This is a handsome, well-designed production. It includes a listening booth where you can hear over ninety contemporary poets reading their work, a calendar of online poetry events (e.g., Seamus Heaney reading at the 92nd Street Y in New York City on September 28, 1998), and a variety of exhibits useful to teachers (like thematic collections on Daughters, Poems of Grief, Poems of Love, and Poems of Ancestry). There is also a Find-a-Poet database and a clickable list of almost a hundred links to other sites. This is a tremendous resource.

Another general site well worth exploring is *Poetry Society of America* (http://www.poetrysociety.org/). This page includes sections on a Calendar of Events, Awards, an Online Peer Workshop (where poets can post poems and have them discussed), Resources, and Poetry in Motion, the program that places placards of poems on buses and subways in New York City, Atlanta, Portland, and other cities. Poetry in Motion has a feature enabling users to send a friend a beautifully illustrated e-mail Poetry Postcard.

Web sites on Poets

Like all other categories, Web sites devoted to acclaimed poets are growing in number. Most of them are developed and maintained by individuals with university connections who have a particular fondness for a poet; some are not unlike fan clubs.

It is hard to imagine a more comprehensive and beautiful home-page on modern poets than *Twentieth-century Poetry in English* (http://www.lit.kobe-u.ac.jp/~hishika/20c_poet.htm). This is a Japanese Web site created and maintained by Michael Eiichi Kishikawa. It includes not only handsome pages on Auden, Eliot, Frost, Stevens, Williams, and several other modern giants, but hundreds of links to others.

More contemporary in its focus is *The Internet Poetry Archive* (http://metalab.unc. edu/dykki/poetry/), a joint venture of the University of North Carolina and the North Carolina Arts Council. This site currently presents biographical information, poems (including audio files), a bibliography, and photographs of six poets—Seamus Heaney, Czeslaw Milosz, Philip Levine, Robert Pinsky, Margaret Walker, and Yusef Komunyakaa.

Even more restricted is *Cowboy Poets on the Internet* (http://www.westfolk.org/), a handsome homepage sponsored by the Western Folk-life Center in Elko, Nevada. Sections include poems and songs, a brief history of cowboy poetry, an exhibit gallery, audio clips, and lists of recordings and books.

Increasingly, there are homepages on particular poets:

Emily Dickinson (http://www.planet.net/pkrisxle/emily/dickinson.html) includes links to 460 of her poems, a biography, pictures, access to a discussion list on the poet, even her recipe for Black Cake. There is also a list of FAQs (Frequently Asked Questions) about her.

Maya Angelou Pages (http://members.aol.com/bonvibre/mangelou.html) and the *Maya Angelou Home Page* (http://www.cwrl.utexas.edu/~mmaynard/Maya/maya5.html) are both sites with pictures, a biography, and poems. The first is linked to sites on other poets.

Life at Eagle Pond: The Poetry of Jane Kenyon and Donald Hall (http://wwwsc.library.unh.edu/specoll/exhibits/kenhall.htm) is a beauti-ful Web site that includes selected poems, twenty drafts of Hall's poem "Ox-Cart Man," and a tribute to Kenyon, who died of leukemia in 1995.

Web sites sponsored by acclaimed poets themselves are less com-mon, but Marge Piercy has her own, the *Marge Piercy Homepage* (http://www.capecod.net/~tmpiercy/), which includes sections on resumé and biography, new projects, bibliography, interviews, and criticism, as well as several poems. Carolyn Forché also has her own site—*Carolyn Forché* (http://osf1.gmu.edu/~cforchem/index.html).

Much of the Internet's magic, of course, is serendipitous. Often I've lucked into interesting collections of poems by virtually unknown poets. One worth perusing is *In the Pockets of the Night*, a small group of poems by Elizabeth Herron on exhibit at the Sonoma State University Web site in California (http://libweb.sonoma.edu/exhibits/EH/). Many high school students would like her "Lake Trout," "Song," "When I Kiss You," and "Migration."

Migration

If my words can be
as honest as desire
they will go to you

like a flow of caribou over ice.
They will lick the air
like a migration

of wild geese, spill
like salmon up
stream. Words of a primal

instinct, pulling us
into an urgent journey
knowing though we know not

where, we're going
home.

Another lucky find for me was *Karen Tellefsen* (http://www. interactive.net/~kat/karen.html). Tellefsen is a chemist who writes mostly poems that rhyme. She has posted some fifty of them on her own homepage, including this one:

Galatea

Her face is like a feather, but her skull is more a stone.
Her hair is coiled in dreadlocks that resist the sculptor's comb.
Stalagtite stoicism is bred deeper than the bone.
She rises very early, and she always sleeps alone.

Her skin is thin as plaster milk; her fragrance is of chalk
that scratches on a dusty slate. Her every morning walk
is briskly clipped and measured so she never stops to talk
of alabaster fountains rising in a fleshy stalk.

She models flesh of perfect form while posing on her block,
so stiff, she never winces while cosmetic chisels knock
her less than lovely bits away. A stone may only mock
the breath that shatters life, and she is marble, solid rock.

Unlike these, most of the Web sites of obscure poets are the creations of beginners whose work is anything but polished. For them, the Internet has become an enormous vanity press. There are hundreds of them, and while all of them deserve respect, most are quite forgettable and best left unexplored.

Collections of Poetry

The Internet is fast becoming an enormous collection of poetry written mostly by dead poets whose copyright privileges have also long since expired. Check out *Project Bartleby Archive* (http://www.columbia.edu/acis/bartleby), where you will find hundreds of poems by the likes of Dickinson, Eliot, Frost (over a hundred poems), Hardy, Hopkins, Housman, Millay, Sandburg, Sassoon, Whitman, and Yeats.

The CMU Poetry Index of Canonical Verse (http://eng.hss.cmu.edu/poetry/) sounds impressive and is. Like *Project Bartleby*, it has complete texts of many poems by mostly deceased poets (Browning, Byron, Marvell, Spenser, Whitman, etc.), but also a few by moderns like Angelou, Auden, cummings, Housman, Millay, and Pound.

Even better is *Poetry Daily* (http://www.poems.com/), which features a new poem every day by a contemporary poet—it was "Aurelia Aurita" by Regina O'Melveny the last day I looked—as well as a huge archive of all the poems shown in the past, over four hundred as of May 1999. *Poetry Daily* also has a wonderful News and Features section.

The Writer's Almanac (http://almanac.mpr.org) is the Web site for Garrison Keillor's daily five-minute radio program of the same name featured on many public stations. Keillor ends each program with a poem, many of which are included in the Web site's Archives. The site also links to numerous others about poets and poetry.

Poetry Magazines and Journals

Established magazines are devoting Web sites to poetry. Among the best is the online version of *Poets & Writers Magazine* (http://www.pw.org), a cornucopia of goodies, including access to *P & W*'s catalog, a directory of addresses of poets and writers, suggestions on publishing, access to online conversations about poetry, and "News from the Writing World." Also worth a look is *Atlantic Unbound: Poetry Pages* (http://www.theatlantic.com/poetry/poetry.htm), a Web site of *The Atlantic Monthly* with articles, poems published in the magazine, and an "Audible Anthology" of dozens of contemporary poets reading their own work.

Just as there are dozens of "little magazines" throughout the country devoted to poetry, there are many online journals ("webzines") embracing the same cause. Many have gaudy names—*Breakfast Surreal, Green Bison Quarterly, Headless Buddha*, and *Angel Exhaust*. A few are as conventional as their printed counterparts, but many push the envelope: *Forklift, Ohio* describes itself as a journal "of poetry, cooking, and light industrial safety." The quality of the poetry in most of these Web sites is spotty at best, but some of them may surprise. Four worth exploring are *Switched-on Gutenberg* (http://weber.u.washington.edu/~jnh/), *web del sol* (http://www.webdelsol.com/), *CrossConnect* (http://tech1.dccs.upenn.edu/~xconnect/) and the *Quarterly Review of Literature Poetry Series* (http://www.princeton.edu/~qrl/poetryseries.html).

In the future, established literary magazines will surely develop their own Web sites, following the lead of *Ploughshares* (http://www.emerson.edu/ploughshares/Ploughshares.html), the esteemed little magazine that has been publishing quality poetry and fiction since 1971. A journal aimed at young adults with its own Web site is *Writes of Passage* (http://www.writes.org/).

Web Sites on Writing Poetry

A classic homepage on writing poetry is *The Shiki Internet Haiku Salon* (http://mikan.cc.matsuyama-u.ac.jp:80/~shiki/). *Shiki* is a fascinating Japan-based site that introduces the familiar three-line poem. It includes a wonderful lesson plan for teaching the form and opportunities for users to add their own haiku to the collection in the database. A related site is *The Bi-weekly Kukai Report* (http://mikan.cc.matsuyama-u.ac.jp:80/~shiki/kukai.html), which offers a judged competition. Participants are invited to submit haiku on an identified "season word" (e.g., *beach* or *autumn wind*) and await the results.

On the other end of the continuum, perhaps, is *Poetry [a click and drag diversion]* (http://www.prominence.com/java/poetry/). Using Java technology and inspired by the Magnetic Poetry Kit available in bookstores, this clever Web site gives users dozens of word tabs for dragging around the screen to create a poem. It's great fun!

The Albany Poetry Workshop (http://www.sonic.net/poetry/albany/) offers "an interactive forum for poets and writers." Opportunities include on-going group poems, writing exercises, and feedback sessions for submitted poems.

Lesson Plans and Class Projects

Cyberspace is loaded with lesson plans although most seem to be written for elementary school math and science teachers. Still, there are sites with plans for teaching high school poetry as well, like *The Poetry Page* (http://www3.sympatico.ca/ray.saitz/poetry.htm) and *Virtual Seminars for Teaching Literature* (http://info.ox.ac.uk/jtap/), a British production which features a polished tutorial on the poetry of World War I.

Occasional projects that sponsor the sharing of poetry written by students are offered on the *Global Schoolhouse* Web site (http://www.gsn.org). Users should explore the search feature and the Hilites archive, which contains hundreds of collaborative projects sent in by teachers in schools throughout the world. One of the more interesting efforts I found was The Peace Poem, a United Nations-sponsored project that invited schools around the world to reflect upon the idea of peace by writing a collaborative electronic global poem. Others from the past were Found Poetry and Poetry Writing Activity. In the latter, "the high school English Department at the International School of Stavanger [Norway] invites year 9 and 10 students to participate in a poetry writing activity on the WWW. The aim of the activity is to create genuine opportunities for students to publish their writing and have other students read it."

Discussion Groups

Discussion groups (newsgroups, usenets) and listservs on poetry are also available. These are ongoing talk sessions of sorts organized around a topic of interest. Subscribers can observe (as "lurkers") or participate in "discussions" on anything concerning the topic. Probably the most popular is *rec.arts.poems*, where most participants submit original verse ("Are there any others out there who enjoy sonnets? Here are a few of mine.") for review and commentary. The talk is unfettered, uncensored, and unpredictable. Often announcements are made about meetings, readings, journals starting up, and the like ("We meet every Wednesday evening at the Three Johns Public House. . . ."). There are frequent requests:

> "I need a piece of poetry that would convey to my girlfriend that even though we are 700 miles apart, she is still in my heart."

> "I am interested in different analyses of this poem [Frost's 'Design']."

> "*Highbeams*, an online journal on the Beloit College gopher, seeks innovative poetry, fiction, and nonfiction. . . ."

> "Can anyone tell me who wrote the following lines from a poem I remember as a child?"

There are other poetry discussion groups besides rec.arts.poems. Possibly more appropriate ones for young adults, at least at this writing, are alt.teens.poetry.and.stuff and ucd.rec.poetry. Do realize, however, that discussion groups are totally democratic and free-wheeling. Don't be surprised or shocked at what shows up.

Mailing lists are similar but they require subscribing, usually by sending an e-mail to the server address. Among the poetry lists I found in a recent directory are CAP-L, a discussion of contemporary American poetry accessible by e-mailing cap-l@virginia.edu; POETRY-W, a poetry writing workshop at listserv@lists.psu.edu; and HUMOR&POETRY at requests@lists.expand.com. Young adults especially might be interested in TEEN-POETS (majordomo@cyber.citilink.com) and TEENWRITE (listserv@psuvm.psu.edu), which is a creative writing workshop for young people. Also of interest to English language arts teachers is NCTE-TALK (majordomo@serv1.ncte.org), an electronic discussion group of the National Council of Teachers of English, where issues having to do with the teaching of poetry are among the many topics of conversation.

For an updated list of newsgroups and mailing lists, access *Liszt of Newsgroups* (http://www.liszt.com/news/). Some listings include links that provide direct access.

Miscellaneous Sites

For the teacher who can't quite think of a poem but recalls a line or two, huge computerized databases are ready to help. One is the search function for *Project Bartleby Archive* cited earlier (http://www.columbia.edu/acis/bartleby/). This service will comb through the complete works of Keats, Shelley, Wordsworth, Dickinson, and Oscar Wilde plus Whitman's *Leaves of Grass*, Bartlett's *Familiar Quotations*, and other works. I typed in the word *coffee* and found eighty-four matches in thirty-four files, including Eliot's "I have measured out my life with coffee spoons" from *The Love Song of J. Alfred Prufrock*.

Poem Finder (http://www.poemfinder.com/) is another, even larger database which catalogs over 550,000 poems, 40,000 of them in full text. Available by subscription and continually updated, *Poem Finder* locates works by title, first line, last line, book title, author, and thousands of subjects. Another search site more restricted in its focus is *The Database of African-American Poetry, 1760–1900* (http://etext.lib.virginia.edu/aapd.html), a collection of over 2,500 poems.

Lyrics.ch: The International Lyrics Server (http://www.lyrics.ch/) is one of several homepages aimed at helping users find the lyrics to popular songs. The service has a file of almost 100,000 titles and searches authors, titles, and cassettes/CDs. When I entered "Desperado" by The Eagles, I received the song in a flash.[2]

The Geraldine R. Dodge Poetry Festival (http://www.grdodge.org/poetry/index.html) is the Web site for the largest poetry event in North America, a biennial four-day festival of readings, discussions, and workshops in historic Waterloo Village, New Jersey. Some events are aimed at high school students and teachers.

Glossary of Poetic Terms (http://shoga.wwa.com/~rgs/glossary.html) is exactly what it says, a dictionary of hundreds of terms defined, "pronounced," and cross-referenced.

The Semantic Rhyming Dictionary (http://bobo.link.cs.cmu.edu/dougb). Type in a word—and presto!

National Slam Poetry Championships (http://www.machine1.com/97nationals/) is one of the best homepages on slams. Another is *The International Organization of Performing Poets* (http://www.slamnews.com/iopp.htm).

Dimocopo (http://student.uq.edu.au/~s271502/animgif.html) is a lively Australian Web site featuring electronic poetry, animated "poems" that dance and flicker on the screen. It's like concrete poetry come to life. This is a site to explore: take a look at "she left," "roller coaster," and "easter." But beware: one or two of these cyberpoems are R-rated.

––––––––––

For many critics of the Internet, this final homepage has ominous overtones. *Dimocopo* suggests a kind of far-out poetry-on-the-fringe consisting of words that gleam and vibrate on a screen. In fact for skeptics, the Internet as a whole is little more than a slick, pulsating dog-and-pony show, shallow and compelling. For others (one is reminded of the claims of many politicians), it is the beckoning answer to all our classroom problems.

Of course it is neither. For teachers of poetry, the Internet has clear limitations. It cannot write a poem, not a good one anyway. It will not teach students how to invest their work with imagination. It will not convey a love of Dickinson or Frost or Jane Kenyon. What it will do is offer information galore about poets and poetry. For poets and teachers, it will provide feedback and conversation and certain kinds of help. If it will not write poems, it will at least offer them—thousands. Here in its infancy, despite a wealth of Web sites that are worthless and beyond consideration, the Internet is a wonderful tool awaiting the imagination and resourcefulness of creative teachers who will make it even better.

Notes

1. All of the Web sites mentioned in this chapter and elsewhere in the book were accessed as recently as May 15, 1999.

2. In January 1999, the International Lyrics Server was shut down until further notice by actions taken by the National Music Publishers Association, an

organization concerned with copyright infringement. Pascal De Vries, the Swiss owner of the Web site, has predicted that the conflict will be resolved in his favor. Meanwhile, teachers and others can try links to similar sites posted at <lyrics.ch>, which remains accessible sans lyrics.

IV Resources

Appendix A: Anthologies of Poetry

As noted in the text, books that are out of print often remain available in school, college, and public libraries. For more selected anthologies see Chapter 3 and Chapter 11.

After Aztlan: Latino Poets of the Nineties. 1992. Edited by Ray Gonzalez. Boston, MA: D. R. Godine.

Against Forgetting: Twentieth-Century Poets of Witness. 1993. Edited by Carolyn Forché. New York: Norton.

Ain't I a Woman! A Book of Women's Poetry from around the World. 1993. Edited by Illona Linthwaite. New York and Avenel, NJ: Wings Books.

America in Poetry. 1988. Edited by Charles Sullivan. New York: Abrams.

America Is Not All Traffic Lights: Poems of the Midwest. 1976. Edited by Alice Fleming. Boston: Little, Brown.

American Sports Poems. 1988. Edited by R. R. Knudson and May Swenson. New York: Orchard Books. A superb collection with over 150 poems on forty sports.

Art from the Ashes: A Holocaust Anthology. 1995. Edited by Lawrence L. Langer. New York: Oxford University Press.

Articulations: The Body and Illness in Poetry. 1993. Edited by Jon Mukand. Iowa City: University of Iowa Press.

Best of the Best American Poetry, The. 1998. Edited by Harold Bloom. New York: Scribner Poetry.

Book of Love Poetry, A. 1986. Edited by Jon Stallworthy. New York: Oxford University Press.

Carrying the Darkness: The Poetry of the Vietnam War. 1989. Edited by W. D. Ehrhart. Lubbock: Texas Tech University Press.

Catch the Fire!!! A Cross-Generational Anthology of Contemporary African-American Poetry. 1998. Edited by Derrick I. M. Gilbert. New York: Riverhead Books.

Columbia Book of Civil War Poetry, The. 1994. Edited by Rochard Marius. New York: Columbia University Press.

Cool Salsa: Bilingual Poems on Growing Up Latino in the United States. 1994. Edited by Lori M. Carlson. New York: Holt. Poems presented bilingually.

Cowboy Poetry: A Gathering. 1985. Edited by Hal Cannon. Salt Lake City, UT: Peregrine Smith Books.

Crazy to Be Alive in Such a Strange World: Poems about People. 1977. Edited by Nancy Larrick. New York: Evans.

Divided Light: Father and Son Poems. 1983. Edited by Jason Shinder. Bronx, NY: Sheep Meadow Press.

Dog Music: Poetry about Dogs. 1993. Edited by Joseph Duemer and Jim Simmerman. New York: St. Martin's Press.

Dont Forget to Fly: A Cycle of Modern Poems. 1981. Selected by Paul B. Janeczko. Scarsdale, NY: Bradbury Press. One of the best; now out-of-print.

Drive, They Said: Poems About Americans and Their Cars. 1994. Edited by Kurt Brown. Minneapolis, MN: Milkweed Editions.

Earth-Shattering Poems. 1997. Edited by Liz Rosenberg. New York: Edge/Holt.

Eternal Light: Grandparent Poems. 1995. Edited by Jason Shinder. San Diego, CA: Harcourt Brace.

Every Shut Eye Ain't Asleep: An Anthology of Poetry by African Americans since 1945. 1994. Edited by Michael S. Harper and Anthony Walton. New York: Little, Brown and Company.

Eye's Delight: Poems of Art and Architecture. 1983. Compiled by Helen Plotz. New York: Greenwillow Books.

Fathers: A Collection of Poems. 1997. Edited by David Ray and Judy Ray. New York: St. Martin's Press.

First Light: Mother and Son Poems. 1992. Edited by Jason Shinder. San Diego, CA: Harcourt Brace.

For a Living: The Poetry of Work. 1995. Edited by Nicholas Coles and Peter Oresick. Urbana: University of Illinois Press.

Gift of Tongues, The: Twenty-five Years of Poetry from Copper Canyon Press. 1996. Edited by Sam Hamill. Port Townsend, WA: Copper Canyon Press.

Gladly Learn and Gladly Teach: Poems of the School Experience. 1981. Edited by Helen Plotz. New York: Greenwillow.

Going Over to Your Place: Poems for Each Other. 1987. Selected by Paul B. Janeczko. New York: Bradbury Press.

Green Place, A: Modern Poems. 1982. Edited by William Jay Smith. New York: Delacorte.

Handspan of Red Earth: An Anthology of American Farm Poems. 1994. Edited by Catherine Lewallen Marconi. Iowa City: University of Iowa Press.

Harper's Anthology of 20th Century Native American Poetry. 1988. Edited by Duane Niatum. San Francisco: Harper.

Harvard Book of Contemporary American Poetry, The. 1985. Edited by Helen Vendler. Cambridge, MA: Belknap Harvard.

Hosannah the Home Run! Poems about Sports. 1972. Edited by Alice Mulcahey Fleming. New York: Little, Brown.

I Am the Darker Brother: An Anthology of Modern Poems by African Americans. 1968, 1997. Edited by Arnold Adoff. New York: Simon & Schuster.

I Feel a Little Jumpy around You: A Book of Her Poems & His Poems Collected in Pairs. 1996. Edited by Naomi Shihab Nye and Paul B. Janeczko. New York: Simon & Schuster. A paperback edition is available from Aladdin.

I Never Saw Another Butterfly, Children's Drawings and Poems from Terezin Concentration Camp, 1942–1944. 1944. Edited by Hana Volavkova. New York: Schocken Books.

I Wouldn't Thank You for a Valentine: Poems for Young Feminists. 1993. Edited by Carol Ann Duffy. New York: Holt.

Imagination's Other Place: Poems of Science and Mathematics. 1955. Edited by Helen Plotz. New York: Crowell.

In Search of Color Everywhere: A Collection of African American Poetry. 1994. Edited by E. Ethelbert Miller. New York: Stewart, Tabori and Chang.

Invisible Ladder, The: An Anthology of Contemporary American Poems for Young Readers. 1996. Edited by Liz Rosenberg. New York: Henry Holt.

Jazz Poetry Anthology, The. 1991. Edited by Sascha Feinstein and Yusef Komunyakaa. Bloomington and Indianapolis: Indiana University Press. A second volume by the same authors is titled *The Second Set.*

Language of Life, The: A Festival of Poets. 1995. Edited by Bill Moyers. New York: Doubleday.

Leaf and Bone: African Praise Poems. 1994. Edited by Judith Gleason. New York: Penguin.

Learning by Heart: Contemporary American Poetry about School. 1999. Edited by Maggie Anderson and David Hassler. Iowa City: University of Iowa Press.

Lifelines: A Poetry Anthology Patterned on the Stages of Life. 1994. Edited by Leonard S. Marcus. New York: Dutton.

Lights, Camera, Poetry!: American Movie Poems, the First Hundred Years. 1996. Edited by Jason Shinder with Ruth Greenstein. San Diego, CA: Harvest Books.

Looking for Your Name: A Collection of Contemporary Poems. 1993. Selected by Paul B. Janeczko. New York: Orchard Books.

Made Thing, The: An Anthology of Contemporary Southern Poetry. 1988. Edited by Leon Stokesbury. Fayetteville: University of Arkansas Press.

Maverick Poets: An Anthology. 1988. Edited by Steve Kowit. Santee, CA: Gorilla Press.

Men of Our Time: An Anthology of Male Poetry in Contemporary America. 1992. Edited by Fred Moramarco and Al Zolynas. Athens: University of Georgia Press.

Mindscapes: Poems for the Real World. 1971. Edited by Richard Peck. New York: Delacorte.

Mixed Voices: Contemporary Poems about Music. 1991. Edited by Emilie Buchwald and Ruth Roston. Minneapolis, MN: Milkweed Editions.

More Light: Father and Daughter Poems. 1993. Edited by Jason Shinder. San Diego, CA: Harcourt Brace.

Morrow Anthology of Younger American Poets, The. 1985. Edited by Dave Smith and David Bottoms. New York: William Morrow.

Music of What Happens, The: Poems That Tell Stories. 1988. Selected by Paul B. Janeczko. New York: Orchard Books.

Night Out: Poems about Hotels, Motels, Restaurants, and Bars. 1997. Edited by Kurt Brown and Laure-Anne Bosselaar. Minneapolis, MN: Milkweek Editions.

99 Poems in Translation: An Anthology. Edited by Harold Pinter et al. New York: Grove Press, 1994.

No More Masks! An Anthology of Twentieth Century American Women Poets. 1993. Edited by Florence Howe. New York: HarperPerennial.

Norton Anthology of Modern Poetry, The. 1988. 3rd ed. Edited by Richard Ellman and Robert O'Clair. New York: Norton.

Norton Anthology of Poetry, The. 1997. The shorter 4th ed. Edited by Margaret Ferguson et al. New York: Norton.

Open Boat, The: Poems from Asian America. 1993. Edited by Garrett Hongo. New York: Anchor Books Doubleday.

Oxford Book of American Light Verse, The. 1979. Edited by William Harmon. New York: Oxford University Press.

Oxford Book of Comic Verse, The. 1994. Edited by John Gross. Oxfordshire and New York: Oxford University Press.

Oxford Book of Short Poems, The. 1985. Edited by P. J. Kavanagh and James Michie. Oxfordshire and New York: Oxford University Press. No poem over thirteen lines.

Oxford Book of War Poetry, The. 1984. Edited by Jon Stallworthy. Oxfordshire and New York: Oxford University Press.

Paper Dance: 55 Latino Poets. 1995. Edited by Victor Hernández Cruz et al. New York: Persea Books.

Peeling the Onion: An Anthology of Poems. 1993. Edited by Ruth Gordon. New York: HarperCollins.

Pictures That Storm Inside My Head: Poems for the Inner You. 1976. Edited by Richard Peck. New York: Avon.

Pierced by a Ray of Sun: Poems about the Times We Feel Alone. 1995. Edited by Ruth Gordon. New York: HarperCollins.

Pittsburgh Book of Contemporary American Poetry, The. 1993. Edited by Ed Ochester and Peter Oresick. Pittsburgh, PA: University of Pittsburgh Press.

Place My Words Are Looking for, The: What Poets Say about and through Their Work. 1990. Selected by Paul B.Janeczko. New York: Bradbury.

Pocket Poems: Selected for a Journey. 1985. Selected by Paul B. Janeczko. New York: Bradbury.

Poems on the Underground. Anniversary Edition. 1996. Edited by Gerard Benson, Judith Chernaik, and Cicely Herbert. London: Cassell Publishers Limited.

Poet Dreaming in the Artist's House, The: Contemporary Poems about the Visual Arts. 1983. Edited by Emilie Buchwald and Ruth Roston. Minneapolis, MN: Milkweed Editions.

Poetical Cat, The: An Anthology. 1995. Edited by Felicity Bast. New York: Farrar, Straus, and Giroux.

"Poetry" Anthology, The: 1912–1977. 1978. Edited by Daryl Hine and Joseph Parisi. Boston, MA: Houghton Mifflin.

Poetry for the Earth. 1991. Edited by Sara Dunn with Alan Scholefield. New York: Fawcett Columbine.

Poetry in Motion: 100 Poems on the Subways and Buses. 1996. Edited by Molly Peacock, Elise Maschen, and Neil Neches. New York: W. W. Norton.

Poetry Like Bread: Poets of the Political Imagination. 1994. Edited by Martin Espada. Willimantic, CT: Curbstone Press.

Poetry of the American West: A Columbia Anthology. 1996. Edited by Alison Hawthorne Deming. New York: Columbia University Press.

Poetry of the World Wars. 1990. Edited by Michael Foss. New York: Peter Bedrick Books.

Poet's Choice: Poems for Everyday Life. 1998. Edited by Robert Hass. Hopewell, NJ: The Ecco Press.

Poetspeak: In Their Words, about Their Work. 1983. Selected by Paul B. Janeczko. Scarsdale, NY: Bradbury.

Postcard Poems: A Collection of Poetry for Sharing. 1979. Selected by Paul B. Janeczko. Scarsdale, NY: Bradbury.

Preposterous: Poems of Youth. 1991. Selected by Paul B. Janeczko. New York: Orchard Books.

Reflections on a Gift of Watermelon Pickle and Other Modern Verse. 1966. Edited by Stephen Dunning et al. New York: Lothrop.

Reflections on a Gift of Watermelon Pickle and Other Modern Verse. 2nd ed. 1995. Edited by Stephen Dunning et al. Glenview, IL: Scott, Foresman A revision of the above with a multicultural emphasis.

Rhythm Road: Poems To Move To. 1988. Edited by Lillian Morrison. New York: Lothrop.

Room for Me and a Mountain Lion: Poetry of Open Spaces. 1974. Edited by Nancy Larrick. New York: Evans.

Second Set, The: The Jazz Poetry Anthology. Volume 2. Edited by Sascha Feinstein and Yusef Komunyakaa. Bloomington: Indiana University Press.

Singing America: Poems That Define a Nation. 1995. Edited by Neil Philip. New York: Viking.

Some Haystacks Don't Even Have Any Needle. 1969. Edited by Stephen Dunning et al. Glenview, IL: Scott, Foresman. One of the best ever compiled for high school; now out of print, but still available in many libraries.

Sound and Sense: An Introduction to Poetry. 8th ed. 1992. Edited by Laurence Perrine and Thomas R. Arp. Fort Worth, TX: Harcourt Brace. Perhaps the best introduction ever written; intended for college students, but a superb resource for high school teachers.

Sounds and Silences: Poetry for Now. 1970. Edited by Richard Peck. New York: Delacorte.

Space between Our Footsteps: Poems and Paintings from the Middle East. 1998. Selected by Naomi Shihab Nye. New York: Simon & Schuster.

Strings: A Gathering of Family Poems. 1984. Selected by Paul B. Janeczko. Scarsdale, NY: Bradbury. An excellent thematic anthology.

Strong Measures: An Anthology of Contemporary American Poetry in Traditional Forms. 1986. Edited by Philip Dacey and David Jauss. New York: Harper & Row.

Sweet Nothings: An Anthology of Rock and Roll in American Poetry. 1994. Edited by Jim Elledge. Bloomington: Indiana University Press.

Tangled Vines: A Collection of Mother and Daughter Poems. 1992. Edited by Lyn Lifshin. San Diego, CA: Harcourt Brace.

This Same Sky: A Collection of Poems from around the World. 1992. Edited by Naomi Shihab Nye. New York: Four Winds Press.

Time Is the Longest Distance. 1991. Edited by Ruth Gordon. New York: HarperCollins.

Touchstones: American Poets on a Favorite Poem. 1996. Edited by Robert Pack and Jany Parini. Hanover, NH: Middlebury College Press.

Under All Silences: The Many Shades of Love. 1987. Edited by Ruth Gordon. New York: Harper & Row.

Unsettling America: An Anthology of Contemporary Multicultural Poetry. 1994. Edited by Maria Mazziotti Gillan and Jennifer Gillan. New York: Penguin Books.

Voice That Is Great Within Us, The. 1970. Edited by Hayden Carruth. New York: Bantam. A "best buy": one of the few collections available in mass market format; includes over 130 modern poets.

Voices of the Rainbow: Contemporary Poetry by Native Americans. 1993. Edited by Kenneth Mark Rosen. New York: Arcade.

Walk on the Wild Side: Urban American Poetry Since 1975. 1994. Edited by Nicholas Christopher. New York: Collier Books.

Western Wind: An Introduction to Poetry. 3rd ed. 1992. Edited by John Frederick Nims. New York: McGraw-Hill. Intended for college, but a very useful resource for teachers, with many poems.

What Will Suffice: Contemporary American Poets on the Art of Poetry. 1995. Edited by Christopher Buckley and Christopher Merrill. Salt Lake City, UT: Gibbs Smith.

Wherever Home Begins: 100 Contemporary Poems. 1995. Selected by Paul B. Janeczko. New York: Orchard Books.

Year in Poetry, A: A Treasury of Classic and Modern Verses for Every Date on the Calendar. 1995. Edited by Thomas E. Foster and Elizabeth C. Guthrie. New York: Crown.

Zero Makes Me Hungry: A Collection of Poems for Today. 1976. Edited by Edward Lueders and Primus St. John. New York: Lothrop, Lee & Shepard. An out-of-print collection that anticipated by twenty years today's overdue emphasis on poets of color.

Appendix B:
Reference Works

Many of these works are available in college and public libraries.

Bentley, Chantelle, ed., 1998. *1999 Poet's Market*. Cincinnati: Writer's Digest Books. Published annually.

Blackburn, G. Meredith III, comp. 1994. *Index To Poetry for Children and Young People, 1988–1992*. Bronx, NY: H. W. Wilson. Indexes by author, subject, title and last lines. Earlier editions should also be consulted.

Ferguson, Gary Lynn, comp. 1995. *Song Finder: A Title Index to 32,000 Popular Songs in Collections, 1854–1992*. Westport, CT and London: Greenwood Press.

Frankovich, Nicholas, ed. 1997. *The Columbia Granger's Index to Poetry in Anthologies*. 11th ed. New York: Columbia University Press. An indispensable reference for teachers who are on the lookout for poems. The eleventh edition indexes over 75,000 poems in anthologies published through January 31, 1997. Includes sections by title, first line, author, and subject. Earlier editions should also be consulted.

Gargan, William and Sue Sharma, eds. 1995. *Find That Tune: An Index to Rock, Folk-Rock, Disco, & Soul in Collections*. New York: Neal-Schuman. Three volumes. A guide to over 12,000 songs.

Hazen, Edith P., ed. 1992. *The Columbia Granger's Dictionary of Poetry Quotations*. New York: Columbia University Press. Organized by poet, subject, and keyword.

Johnson, Curt, ed. 1995. *Who's Who in Writers, Editors, and Poets: United States and Canada*. Highland Park, IL: December Press. Teachers who encourage their students to write to poets may find their addresses here.

Katz, William, Linda Sternberg Katz, and Esther Crain, eds. 1994. *The Columbia Granger's Index to Poetry Anthologies*. 2nd enlarged ed. New York: Columbia University Press.

Kline, Victoria, ed. 1991. *Last Lines: An Index to the Last Lines of Poetry*. New York: Facts on File.

Magill, Frank N., ed. 1982. *Critical Survey of Poetry: English Language Series*. Rev. ed. Pasadena, CA and Englewood Cliffs, NJ: Salem Press. Eight volumes.

Preminger, Alex and T. V. F. Brogan, eds. 1993. *New Princeton Encyclopedia of Poetry and Poetics, The*. Princeton, NJ: Princeton University Press. Probably more on any given topic than anyone would want to know— from *abecedarius* to *Zulu poetry*.

Smith, Dorothy B. Frizzell and Eva L. Andrews, comps. 1977. *Subject Index to Poetry for Children and Young People, 1957–77.* Chicago: American Library Association. A supplement to the 1957 edition. Indexes 263 anthologies.

Trivia Quiz on Famous Poetry Quotations

1. "The woods are lovely, dark and deep"

2. "Rage, rage against the dying of the light."

3. "I thought hard for us all—my only swerving—"

4. "To strive, to seek, to find, and not to yield."

5. "I heard a fly buzz—when I died."

6. "Things fall apart; the centre cannot hold;"

7. "The time you won your town the race
   We chaired you through the market-place;"

8. "Shall I part my hair behind? Do I dare to eat a peach?"

9. "Well, son, I'll tell you:
   Life for me ain't been no crystal stair."

10. "if everything happens that can't be done (and anything's righter than books could plan)"

A teacher might give a quiz like this at the beginning of the year and allow students a week to find the sources. (I wouldn't tell them, but they're all in *Columbia Granger's Dictionary of Poetry Quotations.*)

Appendix C: Selected Media Resources

The following resources are surely useful, but their inclusion here does not imply endorsement. Most companies are now accessible through the Internet.

Audio Cassettes and CDs

As one might expect, recordings of poets reading their works are widely available. The following present multiple poets:

Audiotape Archives. The Academy of American Poets. Thirty-two tapes featuring such poets as John Asbery, W. H. Auden, Gwendolyn Brooks, Lucille Clifton, Maxine Kumin, Howard Nemerov, May Swenson, and James Wright.

Caedmon Treasury of Modern Poets Reading Their Own Poetry. Harper Audio. Two cassettes; 1 hour, 35 minutes. Includes T. S. Eliot reading "The Wasteland"; Dylan Thomas, "Fern Hill"; e. e. cummings, "what if a much of a which of a wind"; Robert Frost, "Birches" and "After Apple Picking"; Stephen Spender, "I Think Continually of Those Who Were Truly Great"; Richard Wilbur, "Love Calls Us to the Things of This World"; and many more.

Cowboy Poetry: The Best of the Gathering. Gibbs Smith Publishing. One cassette.

In Their Own Voices: A Century of Recorded Poetry, Rhino Records, 1996. A four-CD (or cassette) set that opens with a rare c. 1890 recording of Whitman and continues through the likes of Langston Hughes, Frost, Ferlinghetti, Millay, cummings, Thomas, and Angelou.

The Language of Life: A Festival of Poets. Bantam Doubleday Dell. Eight-cassette audiotrack of the PBS series featuring Lucille Clifton, Naomi Shihab Nye, Gary Snyder, Robert Hass, Adrienne Rich, and thirteen other poets.

100 Modern American Poets Reading Their Poems. Spoken Arts, 1985.

Poets in Person: An Audio Series on American Poets and Their Art. Modern Poetry Association, 1991. A seven-cassette series featuring fourteen American poets reading and discussing their poems. Includes Ammons, Dove, Brooks, Kumin, Merrill, Shapiro, and Soto. Also features a 300-page listener's guide.

3 Doz. Poems. Highbridge Audio. A cassette (65 minutes) from *The Writer's Almanac*, Garrison Keillor's daily five-minute program on National Public Radio.

Treasury of Great Poetry, A. Sundance. Six cassettes. A collection of classics: 185 poems (from Chaucer to Whitman and Dickinson).

Voices & Visions. Thirteen cassettes featuring Whitman, Crane, Pound, Williams, Dickinson, Moore, Bishop, Plath, Eliot, Frost, Langston Hughes, Lowell, and Stevens.

Recordings of individual poets are even more plentiful. Several companies dominate the market, including the following:

Audio-Forum. Has produced, in the Watershed Tapes of Contemporary Poetry, single cassettes of dozens of contemporary poets, like Joseph Brodsky, May Sarton, Sharon Olds, Galway Kinnell, Lucille Clifton, Marge Piercy, Adrienne Rich, Gary Snyder, William Stafford, Maxine Kumin, Denise Levertov, James Merrill, and Lawrence Ferlinghetti. In the YM-YWHA Poetry Center Series, poets read and comment on their work: Robert Bly, Philip Booth, John Ciardi, Donald Hall, Galway Kinnell, Stanley Kunitz, Denise Levertov, Howard Nemerov, Stephen Spender, May Swenson, and John Updike—among many others. For a catalog, call 1-800-243-1234.

Harper Audio/Caedmon. Markets single cassettes of numerous poets reading their own works, all with variants of the title *Robert Frost Reads.* Besides Frost, poets include Margaret Atwood, Gwendolyn Brooks, e. e. cummings, Langston Hughes, Williams Carlos Williams, and Sylvia Plath. Also available from Harper Audio is *Poems and Letters of Emily Dickinson*, read by Julie Harris. Call 1-212-207-7000 (or e-mail harperaudio@harpercollins.com) for a catalog.

New Letters. Offers an array of single cassettes, all 29 minutes in length, whose titles are the names of poets: *Jimmy Santiago Baca, Robert Bly, Gwendolyn Brooks* (two parts), *Lucille Clifton, Stephen Dunn, Carolyn Forché, Nikki Giovanni, John Updike, Jane Kenyon, Michael S. Harper, Howard Nemerov, Rita Dove*, and *Gary Soto*—among others.

Spoken Arts. Produces and markets the following titles in single cassettes among others: *W. H. Auden, Poems of James Dickey, Poems of Emily Dickinson, Kenneth Koch Reading His Own Poems*, and *Poems of Richard Wilbur.*

For an exhaustive listing of recordings, see the annual *Words on Cassette*, published by Bowker. The 1998 edition has eleven pages (thirty-one columns) of individual collections and four pages (nine columns) of general anthologies. Also, *Poets' Audio Center* (available at http://www.writer.org/poettapes/pac02.htm) lists numerous recordings.

CD-ROMs

Columbia Granger's World of Poetry, The. 1995. New York: Columbia University Press. Windows and Macintosh. An enormous database indexing 700 anthologies of poetry with 135,000 poems by 20,000 poets. Includes full text from over 10,000 noncopyrighted poems and quotations from 7,500 copyrighted poems. Can be searched by author, title, subject, first and last lines, keyword, or category.

Gale Literary Index CD-ROM. Gale Research, IBM and compatibles. Provides a complete index to all 32 volumes in the Gale Research Literary series, including access to 110,000 authors and 120,000 titles. Volumes include *Contemporary Authors* and *Poetry Criticism.*

In My Own Voice: Multicultural Poets on Identity. Sunburst. Macintosh. Poets like Lucille Clifton, Stanley Kunitz, Naomi Shihab Nye, and Li-Young Lee read and discuss their poetry.

Poem Finder 95: The Ultimate Poetry Reference on CD-ROM. Great Neck, NY: Roth Publishing Company, 1995. IBM (or compatible). Accesses information about thousands of works and hundreds of authors. Can be searched by poet, profession, nationality, and religion; any word in a poem's title, first and last lines, keyword, poem date, and subject. Includes glossary of terms.

Poetry in Motion 1. Ron Mann. Voyager, 1994. Mac and Windows. Features energetic performances of poems by such poets as Charles Bukowski, Allen Ginsberg, Gary Snyder, and Ntozake Shange. *Poetry in Motion 2* is also available from Voyager.

World's Best Poetry on CD, The. 2nd ed. Roth Publishing Company. Contains over 20,000 full-text poems, over 700 critical and biographical essays, and pictures of poets. Strong multicultural emphasis. Allows searching by keyword, theme, author, first line, and words in title.

Posters

Poetry in Motion posters are available from New York City Transit, c/o Customer Service, 130 Livingston St., Room 9011c, Brooklyn, NY 11201.

Posters on poetry are also available from Streetfare, POB 880274, San Francisco, CA 94188-0274.

Videos

Again, a few companies dominate the market, among them Films for the Humanities & Sciences, Filmic Archives, and the Roland Collection.

Films for the Humanities & Sciences has numerous titles, including these:

Amiri Baraka. (25 min., color). Baraka is interviewed by Maya Angelou.

Donald Hall and Jane Kenyon: A Life Together (60 min., color).

Dylan Thomas: A Portrait (26 min., color).

e. e. cummings: The Making of a Poet (24 min., color).

Emily Dickinson: An Interpretation with Music (18 min., color). Presents "Because I could not stop for Death" with the music of John Adams.

Fighting Back (26 min., color). Poetry as a way of exercising political power.

I See a Voice (25 min., color). The many varied uses of poetry in our society, from rock lyrics to advertising jingles and epitaphs.

Language of Life, The: A Festival of Poets. Eight parts (58 min. each; color). Features eighteen contemporary American poets. An award-winning series.

Language of Poets, The. 27 min.; color. Explores the relationship between sound and meaning, including concepts such as onomatopoeia and metrical patterns.

Poet Laureate Rita Dove (60 min., color).

Poetry of World War II (26 min., color).

War Poets, The (60 min., color). Features Brooke, Owen, Sassoon—the poets of the First World War.

William Stafford and Robert Bly: A Literary Friendship (24 min., color).

Filmic Archives distributes, among others, the following:

Dylan Thomas: Return Journey (53 min., color), featuring the poet reading and performing his own work during a trip to America in the last year of his life.

Hidden Drama of a Poem: Person, Situation, Tone (13 min., color), which explores the title concepts.

Shapes a Poem Can Take, The: Different Types of Poetry (15 min., color, 1992), which examines the lyric, haiku, sonnet, ballad, limerick, and blank verse.

When Is Poetry? An Introduction to the Nature of Poetry (22 min., color, 1992), contrasting the language of poetry and science.

The Roland Collection features videos about poets, like *Maya Angelou* (31 min., color), *Allen Ginsberg* (50 min., color), and *Stephen Spender* (53 min., color).

In addition, the following videos may also be of interest:

Baxter Black by Himself (62 min., color, 1995), featuring seventeen poems and stories told on location "at the ranch" by the famous cowboy poet himself. Coyote Cowboy Company.

Cowboy Poets Live at Elko, The (75 min., color, 1994). Readings from the Tenth Annual Cowboy Poetry Festival in Elko, Nevada. The Video Catalog.

United States of Poetry, The. A five-part series filmed during a twelve-week bus tour across the country that features the poetry of the famous (e.g., Joseph Brodsky, Derek Walcott, Robert Creeley, former President Jimmy Carter) and the obscure (e.g., the Crow Indian poet Harry Real Bird and the New York City street poet Sparrow). Originally shown on PBS, now available from ITVS, 51 Federal Street, Suite 401, San Francisco, CA 94107.

Voices & Visions. Thirteen-part series on American poetry featuring Whitman, Crane, Pound, and Williams in Volume 1; Dickinson, Moore, Bishop, and Plath in Volume 2; and Eliot, Frost, Langston Hughes, Lowell, and Stevens in Volume 3. Available from The Annenberg/CPB Multimedia Collection, P.O. Box 2345, S. Burlington, VT 05407-2345 (1-800-532-7637) or Mystic Fire Video, P.O. Box 422, New York, NY 10012-0008 (1-800-292-9001).

Where Poems Come From (60 min., color), with fifteen major poets reading and explaining the origins of their poetry. From the Lannau Foundation.

Appendix D:
Selected Journals

American Poetry Review. Published bimonthly by World Poetry, Inc. A tabloid featuring poems, interviews, criticism, and ads. Since 1972. Address: 1721 Walnut St., Philadelphia, PA 19103.

English Journal. Published monthly (September through April) by the National Council of Teachers of English. Includes articles on the teaching of poetry. Recent April issues have featured a Literary Festival of poems (as well as essays, short stories, and photography) written by teachers and judged by a panel.

Poets & Writers Magazine. Published six times a year by Poets & Writers, Inc. Includes articles (e.g., "Where to Find Literature on Disk"), news, poems, advertisements, reviews, announcements of grants and awards, and classifieds. Since 1973. Address: 72 Spring St., New York 10012.

Teachers & Writers Magazine. Published five times a year by Teachers and Writers Collaborative. Features articles on writing of all kinds, including poetry. Sample topics: writing experimental poetry, writing sonnets, evaluating student poetry. Winner of ten Educational Press Awards for excellence.

Appendix E: Selected Awards

Although they gain little notice in the media, numerous awards are given to honor American poets. Teachers aware of these could design a bulletin board based on them, publicize announcements of new winners, sponsor a contest for the best suggestion on how a poet could spend $100,000 (in twenty-five words or less), and so on.

Bollingen Prize

One of the nation's most prestigious literary honors, the Bollingen Prize was established at the Yale University Library in 1949. It is presented every two years and includes an award of $25,000. Previous winners have included Wallace Stevens, Marianne Moore, Archibald MacLeish, Robert Penn Warren, e. e. cummings, William Carlos Williams—and in the 1990s, Laura Ridings Jackson and Donald Hall (1991), Mark Strand (1993), Kenneth Koch (1995), Gary Snyder (1997), and Robert Creeley (1999).

The Lenore Marshall Poetry Prize

This award is presented annually by the Academy of American Poets in conjunction with *The Nation* magazine to honor the most outstanding book of poetry published in the United States in the previous year. Established in 1975, the $10,000 prize honors the memory of Lenore Marshall (1897–1971), a poet, novelist, and essayist. In this decade, winners have been Michael Ryan (*God Hunger*), John Haines (*New Poems, 1980–88*), Adrienne Rich (*An Atlas of the Difficult World*), Thom Gunn (*The Man with Night Sweats*), W. S. Merwin (*Travels*), Marilyn Hacker (*Winter Numbers*), Charles Wright (*Chickamauga*), Robert Pinsky (*The Figured Wheel: New and Collected Poems 1966–1996*), and Mark Jarman (*Questions for Ecclesiastes*).

National Book Award (Poetry)

The National Book Award is a major literary prize given in several categories, one of which is poetry. Since 1991 (when it was resumed after no award was given for several years), the recipients have been Philip Levine (for *What Is Work?*), Mary Oliver (*New and Selected Poems*), A. R. Ammons (*Garbage*), James Tate (*Worshipful Company of Fletchers*), Stanley Kunitz (*Passing Through*), Hayden Carruth (*Scrambled Eggs & Whiskey, Poems 1991–1995*), William Meredith (*Effort at Speech: New and Selected Poems*), and in 1998 Gerald Stern (*This Time: New and Selected Poems*).

National Book Critics Circle Award (Poetry)

Awarded annually, this prestigious prize was presented in 1998 to Marie Ponsot for *The Bird Catcher*. Other recent winners include Charles Wright for *Black Zodiak*, Robert Hass for *Sun under Wood*, William Matthews for *Time and Money: New Poems*, Mark Rudman for *Rider*, Mark Doty for *My Alexandria*, and Hayden Carruth for *Collected Shorter Poems 1946–1991*. The Circle is made up of over 700 reviewers of books.

Pulitzer Prize for Poetry

The best-known American award for artistic merit. Like the last two mentioned above, the Pulitzer is presented annually in several categories, including poetry. In recent years, the winners have been Mona Van Duyn (for *Near Changes*), James Tate (*Selected Poems*), Louise Glück (*The Wild Iris*), Yusef Komunyakaa (*Neon Vernacular*), Philip Levine (*The Simple Truth*), Jorie Graham (*The Dream of the Unified Field*), Lisel Mueller (*Alive Together*), Charles Wright (*Black Zodiak*), and in 1999 Mark Strand for *Blizzard of One*.

Tanning Prize

Given annually by the Academy of American Poets, this $100,000 prize was endowed by the painter Dorothea Tanning to recognize outstanding and proven mastery in the art of poetry. Since its origin in 1994, winners have been W. S. Merwin, James Tate, Adrienne Rich, Anthony Hecht, and A. R. Ammons.

Works Cited

Abse, Dannie, and Joan Abse. 1986. *Voices in the Gallery*. London: Tate Gallery.

Anderson, Edward. 1993. "Positive Use of Rap Music in the Classroom." Washington, D.C.: U.S. Department of Education, Educational Resources Information Center, ED 353588.

Applebee, Arthur. 1993. *Literature in the Secondary School: Studies of Curriculum and Instruction in the United States*. Urbana, IL: National Council of Teachers of English.

Baker, Russell, ed. 1986. *The Norton Book of Light Verse*. New York: W. W. Norton.

Bates, Marilyn. 1993. "Imitating the Greats: Art as a Catalyst in Student Poetry." *Art Education* 46 (July): 41.

Behn, Robin and Chase Twichell. 1992. *The Practice of Poetry: Writing Exercises from Poets Who Teach*. New York: HarperCollins.

Bentley, Chantelle, ed. 1998. *1999 Poet's Market*. Cincinnati, OH: Writer's Digest Books.

"Bouts of Poetry (the Stress Is on Beat)." 1994. *The New York Times* (June 21): A18.

Bowers, Faubion, ed. 1996. *The Classic Tradition of Haiku: An Anthology*. Mineola, NY: Dover Publications.

Briccetti, Lee. 1996. "April Is the Coolest Month." *American Libraries* 27 (March): 63.

Brooke, Rupert. 1932 (1915). *The Collected Poems of Rupert Brooke*. New York: Dodd, Mead.

Buchwald, Emilie and Ruth Roston, eds. 1991. *Mixed Voices: Contemporary Poems About Music*. Minneapolis, MN: Milkweed Editions.

Ciardi, John. 1989. *Ciardi Himself: Fifteen Essays in the Reading, Writing, and Teaching of Poetry*. Fayetteville: University of Arkansas Press.

———. 1960. *How Does a Poem Mean?* Boston, MA: Houghton Mifflin.

Clausen, Christopher. 1981. *The Place of Poetry: Two Centuries of an Art in Crisis*. Lexington: University of Kentucky Press.

Clymer, Theodore, comp. 1975. *Four Corners of the Sky: Poems, Chants, and Oratory*. New York: Little, Brown.

Coger, Leslie Irene and Melvin R. White. 1982. *Readers Theatre Handbook: A Dramatic Approach to Literature*. 3rd ed. Glenview, IL: Scott, Foresman.

Coles, Nicholas and Peter Oresick, ed. 1995. *For a Living: The Poetry of Work*. Urbana, IL: University of Illinois Press.

Conniff, Richard. 1992. "Please, Audience, Do Not Applaud a Mediocre Poem."
    Smithsonian 23.6 (September): 77–86.

Cooke, John and Jeanie Thompson. 1980. "Three Poets on the Teaching of
    Poetry." *College English* 42 (October): 134–39.

Copeland, Jeffrey S. 1993. *Speaking of Poets: Interviews with Poets Who Write
    for Children and Young Adults.* Urbana, IL: National Council of Teachers
    of English.

Copeland, Jeffrey S., and Vicky L. Copeland. 1995. *Speaking of Poets 2: More
    Interviews with Poets Who Write for Children and Young Adults.* Urbana,
    IL: National Council of Teachers of English.

Cutts, William G., Jr. n.d. *The CPR Rap.* Available: http://168.31.216.60/CPR/RAP
    (Accessed March 1, 1999).

Daniels, Harvey. 1994. *Literature Circles: Voice and Choice in the Student-
    Centered Classroom.* York, ME: Stenhouse.

Dictionary of Literary Biography s.v. "American Poets since World War II."
    Volumes 5, 105, 120, 165, and 169.

Dunning, Stephen. 1966. *Teaching Literature to Adolescents: Poetry.* Glenview,
    IL: Scott, Foresman.

———, ed. 1970. *Mad Sad & Glad.* New York: Scholastic Book Services.

Dunning, Stephen, and William Stafford. 1992. *Getting the Knack: 20 Poetry
    Writing Exercises 20.* Urbana, IL: National Council of Teachers of
    English.

Fagin, Larry. 1991. *The List Poem: A Guide to Teaching & Writing Catalog Verse.*
    New York: Teachers & Writers Collaborative.

Fairchild, Arthur H. R. 1914. *The Teaching of Poetry in the High School.* Boston,
    MA: Houghton Mifflin.

Fleischman, Paul, and Ken Nutt (illustrator). 1985. *I Am Phoenix: Poems for Two
    Voices.* New York: Harper & Row.

Fleischman, Paul, and Eric Beddows (illustrator). 1988. *Joyful Noise: Poems for
    Two Voices.* New York: Harper and Row.

Fox, Geoff and Brian Merrick. 1981. "Thirty-Six Things to Do with a Poem." *The
    Times Educational Supplement* 3374 (February 20).

Gioia, Dana. 1992. *Can Poetry Matter? Essays on Poetry and American Culture.*
    St. Paul, MN: Graywolf.

Goldstein, Thomas. 1980. "Paul Zimmer." *Dictionary of Literary Biography* s.v.
    "American Poets Since World War II." Volume 5. Detroit, MI: Gale
    Research.

Gorrell, Nancy. 1989. "Let Found Poetry Help Your Students Find Poetry."
    English Journal 78 (February): 30–34.

Grossman, Florence. 1982. *Getting from Here to There: Writing and Reading
    Poetry.* Montclair, NJ: Boynton/Cook.

Gullan, Marjorie. 1970 (1937). *The Speech Choir.* Freeport, NY: Books for Libraries Press.

"Hacks." 1991. *The New Yorker* 67 (August 19): 22–23.

Hall, Donald. 1994. *Death to the Death of Poetry: Essays, Reviews, Notes, Interviews.* Ann Arbor: University of Michigan Press.

Hass, Robert, ed. 1995. *The Essential Haiku: Versions of Bashô, Busho, and Issa.* Hopewell, NJ: Ecco Press.

Henderson, Harold G. 1967. *Haiku in English.* North Clarendon, VT: Charles E. Tuttle Company.

Henderson, Kathy. 1996. *The Market Guide for Young Writers: Where and How to Sell What You Write.* 5th ed. Cincinnati, OH: Writer's Digest Books.

Higginson, Thomas Wentworth. 1911. *John Greenleaf Whittier.* New York: MacMillan.

Higginson, William J. 1992. *The Haiku Handbook: How to Write, Share, and Teach Haiku.* With Penny Harter. Tokyo: Kodansha International.

Hirsch, Edward, ed. 1994. *Transforming Vision: Writers on Art.* Chicago: The Art Institute of Chicago/Bullfinch Press.

Hollander, John. 1995. *The Gazer's Spirit: Poems Speaking to Silent Works of Art.* Chicago: University of Chicago Press.

———, ed. 1997. *Committed to Memory: 100 Best Poems to Memorize.* New York: Riverhead Books.

Houston, James, ed. 1972. *Songs of the Dream People: Chants and Images from the Indians and Eskimos of North America.* New York: Atheneum.

Hutchinson, Jamie and Charles Suhor. 1996. "The Jazz and Poetry Connection: A Performance Guide for Teachers and Students." *English Journal* 85 (September): 80–85.

Jacobs, Frank. 1991. *The* Romeo and Juliet *Rap.* Teacher's Discovery cassette.

Janeczko, Paul B., sel. 1983. *Poetspeak: In Their Work, about Their Work.* Scarsdale, NY: Bradbury.

———. 1990. *The Place My Words Are Looking for: What Poets Say about and through Their Work.* New York: Bradbury.

Jerome, Judson. 1974. *The Poet and the Poem.* Cincinnati, OH: The Writer's Digest.

———. 1991. "Reflections: After a Tornado." *Dictionary of Literary Biography* s.v. "American Poets since World War II." Volume 105. Detroit, MI: Gale Research.

Jones, K. Maurice. 1994. *Say It Loud! The Story of Rap Music.* Brookfield, CT: Millbrook Press.

Jones, Kirkland C. 1992. "Rita Dove." *Dictionary of Literary Biography* s.v. "American Poets since World War II." Volume 120. Detroit, MI and London, England: Gale Research.

Kakutani, Michiko. 1995. "A Politician's Poetry: From Life, with No Leaps." *The New York Times* (January 24): C17.

Kapell, Dave, and Sally Steenland, eds. 1997. *The Magnetic Poetry Book of Poetry*. New York: Workman.

Koch, Kenneth. 1973. *Rose, Where Did You Get That Red? Teaching Great Poetry to Children*. New York: Random House.

———. 1980. *Wishes, Lies, and Dreams: Teaching Children to Write Poetry*. New York: HarperCollins.

Lee, Charlotte I., and Timothy Gura. 1996. *Oral Interpretation*. 9th ed. Boston: Houghton Mifflin.

Levin, Gail, ed. 1995. *The Poetry of Solitude: A Tribute to Edward Hopper*. Englewood, NJ: Universe Publishing.

Lockward, Diane. 1994. "Poets on Teaching Poetry." *English Journal* 83 (September): 65–70.

lyrics.ch 1998. *lyrics.ch: The International Lyrics Server*. Available: http://www.lyrics.ch/ (accessed May 15, 1999).

Machine 1 Web sites. 1997. *1997 National Poetry Slam Championship*. Available: http://www.machine1.com/97nationals/ (accessed March 1, 1999).

McArthur, Mary Ellen R. 1989. "Poetry Presentations: That's Entertainment!" *English Journal* 78 (April): 69–71.

Moi, Claudia Monica Ferradas. 1994. "Rock Poetry: The Literature Our Students Listen to." Washington, D.C.: U.S. Department of Education, Educational Resources Information Center, ED 372631.

Moyers, Bill D. 1995. *The Language of Life: A Festival of Poets*. New York: Doubleday.

Nye, Naomi Shihab and Paul B. Janeczko, eds. 1996. *I Feel a Little Jumpy around You: A Book of Her Poems & His Poems Collected in Pairs*. New York: Simon & Schuster.

Oates, Joyce Carol. 1989. *The Time Traveler*. New York: E. P. Dutton.

Oneal, Zibby. 1985. *In Summer Light*. New York: Viking Penguin.

Otten, Nick and Marjorie Stelmach. 1988. "A Poet Re-Views Her Work". *English Journal* 77 (January): 92–93.

Packard, William. 1987. *The Poet's Craft: Interviews from* The New York Quarterly. New York: Paragon House.

Padgett, Ron, ed. 1987. *The Teachers & Writers Handbook of Poetic Forms*. New York: Teachers & Writers Collaborative.

Parisi, Joy. 1994. The Poetics of Readings. *Publishers Weekly* 241 (March 14): 18.

Parker, Elinor, ed. 1964. *Poems of William Wordsworth*. New York: Crowell.

Peck, Carol. 1992. "Joyful Noise Resounds: The New Look of an Old Form." *Teacher & Writers Magazine* 24 (September–October).

Perilli, Paul. 1997. "Poetry Book Sales Are Climbing: Is This a Trend or a Temporary Rise?" *Poets & Writers Magazine* 25 (March/April): 38–43.

Perrine, Laurence and Thomas R. Arp. 1992. *Sound and Sense: An Introduction to Poetry.* 8th ed. Fort Worth, TX: Harcourt Brace.

Phillips, Rodney et al. 1997. *The Hand of the Poet: Poems and Papers in Manuscript.* New York: Rizzoli.

"Poetry Underground." 1992–93. *The New Yorker* 68 (December 28–January 4): 57–58.

Pope, Alice, ed. 1999. *1999 Children's, Writer's, and Illustrator's Market: 800+ Editors and Art Directors Who Buy Your Writing and Illustrations.* Cincinnati, OH: Writer's Digest Books.

Quintana, Ricardo, ed. 1947. *Two Hundred Poems.* Freeport, NY: Books for Libraries Press.

Reeve, F. D. 1993. "What's the Matter with Poetry?" *The Nation* 256 (May 24): 709.

Rhodenbaugh, Suzanne. 1992. "One Heart's Canon." *American Scholar* 61 (Summer): 389–98.

Richards, Chris and Ray Gibbons. 1993. "Vain Calculations." *Mathematics Teaching* 145 (December): 16–17.

Romer, Robert H. 1993. "Robert Frost and the Second Law of Thermodynamics." *Physics Teacher* 31 (September): 360.

Ross, Bruce, ed. 1993. *Haiku Moment: An Anthology of Contemporary North American Haiku.* North Clarendon, VT: Charles E. Tuttle Co.

Rubin, Robert Alden, ed. 1993. *Poetry Out Loud.* Chapel Hill, NC: Algonquin Books of Chapel Hill.

Schemo, Diana Jean. 1995. "Poets' Poetry and Reflections, in Their Voices for All Time." *The New York Times*, January 16: C11.

Schwartz, Delmore. 1992. "Seurat's Sunday Afternoon along the Seine" in *Western Wind: An Introduction to Poetry.* 3rd ed. John Frederick Nims. New York: McGraw-Hill.

Scott, Janny. 1994. "Along With the Bible, a Poetry Anthology." *The New York Times.* March 15: B1.

Simpson, Janice C. 1991. "Hey, Let's Do a Few Lines!" *Time* 138 (December 16): 76–77.

Sloyer, Shirlee. 1982. *Readers Theatre: Story Dramatization in the Classroom.* Urbana, IL: National Council of Teachers of English.

Spencer, Peter J. 1981. "A Readers Theatre Approach to 'David'." *The English Quarterly* 14 (Spring): 29–39.

Standards for the English Language Arts. 1996. Newark, DE and Urbana, IL: International Reading Association and National Council of Teachers of English.

Stanley, Lawrence A. 1992. *Rap: The Lyrics*. New York: Penguin USA.

Sturges, Henry C., ed. 1969. *The Poetical Works of William Cullen Bryant*. Roslyn Edition. New York: AMS Press.

Swenson, May. 1978. *New & Selected Things Taking Place*. Boston, MA, and Toronto: Little, Brown.

Thompson, Denys. 1978. *The Uses of Poetry*. Cambridge, England: Cambridge University Press.

Travers, Molly. 1984. "The Poetry Teacher: Behavior and Attitudes." *Research in the Teaching of English* 18 (December): 216–17, 380.

———. 1987. "Responding to Poetry: Create, Comprehend, Criticize." In *Readers, Texts, Teachers*. Bill Cochcoran and Emrys Evans, eds. Montclair, NJ: Boynton/Cook.

Turner, Alberta T. 1977. *Fifty Contemporary Poets: The Creative Process*. New York: Longman.

Van den Heuvel, Cor, ed. 1999. *The Haiku Anthology: Haiku and Senryu in English*. 3rd ed. New York: W.W. Norton.

Van Gelder, Lawrence. 1998. "Poetry, and a Little Madness in Spring." *The New York Times* April 1: E3.

Williams, Miller. 1986. *Patterns of Poetry: An Encyclopedia of Forms*. Baton Rouge, LA and London: Louisiana State University Press.

Wilson, Craig. 1998. "This Johnny Appleseed Sows Seeds of Literacy." *USA Today* April 1: D1–D2.

Woolridge, Susan Goldsmith. 1996. *Poemcrazy: Freeing Your Life with Words*. New York: Three Rivers Press.

Zaranka, William. 1981. *The Brand-X Anthology of Poetry: A Parody Anthology*. Cambridge, MA and Watertown, CT: Apple-Wood Books.

Author

Photograph by Charlie Register

Albert B. Somers is professor emeritus of education at Furman University in Greenville, South Carolina. A native of Wilkesboro, North Carolina, he earned a B.A. in English and an M.A. in Education from the University of North Carolina at Chapel Hill and a Ph.D. in English education from Florida State University. His professional experience includes teaching high school English, working as an English language arts consultant at district and state levels, and teaching English and education in college. Somers is coauthor (with Janet Evans Worthington) of three other books: *Response Guides for Teaching Children's Books* (1978); *Candles and Mirrors: Response Guides for Teaching Novels and Plays in Grades 6–12* (1984), and *Novels and Plays: Thirty Creative Teaching Guides for Grades 6–12* (1997).

This book was typeset in Avant Garde and Garamond by Electronic Imaging.
Typefaces used on the cover were Usherwood Medium and Architectura.
The book was printed by Versa Press on 60-lb. offset opaque.